DANGEROUS BOOKS

"Exactly what's wrong with conservative politics"
New Republic

"polarizing ... counterproductive"
Dartmouth Review

"undignified, cold, and low"
American Thinker

"Doesn't deserve Twitter"
New York Observer

"Idiot"
ABC Nightline

"Transphobia on tour"
Advocate

"Hate-monger"
Complex

"An icon of the fringe internet ... cartoonish ...
astonishingly self-important"
Vox

"flamboyant homosexual with movie-star good looks"
The New American

DANGEROUS

MILO

DANGEROUS BOOKS

To John

CONTENTS

SO, ABOUT THAT
WHOLE DRAMA...

You didn't really think I was going anywhere, did you? I am far too hot, popular, and quick-witted to be disappeared by outraged op-eds appearing in every major news publication in the world. Darlings, it's *Milo* we're talking about. I don't count media coverage by the inches, I measure it with a wooden yardstick. The only thing that can stop me is a well-placed mirror. Social justice warriors, the conservative establishment, and mainstream media have thrown every label in the book at me: sexist, misogynist, self-hating homophobe, self-hating anti-Semite, Islamophobe, transphobe, racist, fascist, "alt-right," white supremacist, Nazi, and, finally, "pedophile advocate." The only thing left is to accuse me of torturing kittens. So, preemptively: I do not torture small animals. I kill them quickly.

It was never my intention to begin my first book by discussing the differences between pedophilia and hebephilia, and how those words relate to my own childhood. And yet, as Father Mike always said, "God won't put anything in front of you that you can't take."

Let me make it abundantly clear: no matter what your news sources have told you, I do not condone, in any way, pedophilia or hebephilia. I believe you know this, otherwise you wouldn't have bought my book, and for that, I thank you. Sincerely. These have been trying times and I have been tested. There were a few days when I almost gave up on my mission. But thousands of fans reached out, my friends and family had my back, and the people of this world I respect the most kept taking my calls. I couldn't let you all down.

My enemies thought I had been vanquished, that I would go into hiding in the hills of Dartmoor with my dick between my legs like some weak ass pussy faggot. They couldn't be more wrong. All they've done is piss me off.

As for the infamous podcast, the one which lost me three jobs, effectively putting a dent in the percentage of employed black men vs white, I will openly admit that I was inarticulate and imprecise with my language. My ego is massive but I am not so far gone that I can't admit when I've said something stupid. I make my living by speaking openly, bluntly, and often. I do not plan out or memorize arguments before appearing on a show, because I think that's boring. I said that a grown man having sex with a thirteen-year-old is not pedophilia. This is a factual statement. Pedophilia is an attraction to children who have not gone through puberty. The men I had sex with when I was thirteen were not pedophiles, at least, not with me. They were hebephiles. It's a silly semantic to discuss, and not one I would generally harp on, except when I'm speaking on a podcast at 2 AM, when a nuanced semantic point is all you need.

After the podcast was "leaked" to the media, I was disinvited by the octogenarians at CPAC and the utter pussies at Simon & Schuster canceled my book deal. I then resigned from Breitbart during a press conference, during which I stated I myself was a victim of sexual abuse, and therefore mistakenly thought it was okay to discuss these issues any way I wanted to. My critics *loved* it. *Huffington Post* even had some unpaid hack gloat about it. I, who have made a living bringing reality to victim culture, calling myself a victim, was too rich for them.

The truth, which they are too simple to understand, is that I never saw myself as a victim. I didn't do anything I didn't want to do. I was thirteen and the internet was a new thing. There weren't other out gay kids in school like there are now, my limp wristed routine was the only show in town. I had few options and a high sex drive. If my abusers had been women, I'd be getting high fives all around, not having to start my first book like this.

Looking back now, I can of course see that what happened to me wasn't right, even if I was literally asking for it. I was a victim of sexual abuse. However, I want to make this perfectly clear. The whole thing takes up less space in my head than the time David Bowie called me out on a shitty Louis Vuitton knockoff. I responded by throwing up in his sink, but I've never bought a knockoff bag again. Having sex with a priest when I was thirteen didn't stop me from having and enjoying sex for the rest of my life.

The only way I can truly be a victim is to wallow in what happened and let it define me. If you're reading this, and you have been abused, and you are wallowing, I will give you the most important piece of advice I have: get over it. Move on. Even though it seems like victim status is the best way to earn a living right now (hi Shaun King how's Twitter been), I assure you, it's not. You are far too fabulous and smart for all that. It's easier said than done, I know, but that's my advice. Get the fuck over it. No matter how bad your experiences, victimhood and self-pity are for the people who *won't* buy this book. It is their prison. We must challenge the forces of oppression in society, and we can't do so from a therapy session.

DANGEROUS

Sometimes tragedy can produce greatness. It can make you stronger. Madonna got raped in New York and made *Erotica*, and she never griped about being a victim until the 2010s, when it became in vogue. Tori Amos made a whole career out of being raped, and I should know, I've plagiarized freely from her in this book. Getting over it doesn't mean forgetting it ever happened. It means not being stuck in place by it.

That's not to say I never did any wallowing. My twenties were spent partying, drinking and fucking my way through Western Europe. During this time, I developed my love for all things anti-establishment. Lenny Bruce, Bret Easton Ellis, Marilyn Manson: these were my heroes. If you told me not to swallow a pill I'd mash it up and snort it. If you told me not to have sex with your boyfriend I'd sleep with your brother and send you a recording.

And then one day, while attending Manchester, I was told I could not read *Atlas Shrugged*. I thought, this is poppycock, fuck anyone who tells me what I can and cannot read. I finished it three days later. Everything became clear to me then: my need to rebel against the establishment hadn't changed, but the establishment itself had morphed, right before my eyes. If Capitalists are to be hated then I will champion their causes. If being anti-drug is the new anti-culture, I'll never smoke or snort anything ever again. And if everyone else is kissing Amy Schumer's lazy, untalented ass, I'll write an article called "Feminism is Cancer."

Only the mainstream media, with the collusion of dishonest anti-Trump conservatives, could have the gall to portray me as a pedophilia apologist. It's true, I made light of my personal experiences, and used (and will continue to use) flippant language when discussing them, but that's just one way I deal with the darkness in my youth. The other way is by taking ruthless vengeance on the people who actually harm children.

The media is not interested in fighting pedophilia. If you think CNN's Jake Tapper was angrily tweeting about me on behalf of his anonymous victim prone friend, and not on behalf of his own inclination for grandstanding, then you haven't been paying attention. How did Tapper, who calls himself a journalist, spend so much time talking about me and pedophilia, without once mentioning my role in outing Nicholas Nyberg (aka Sarah Nyberg, aka Sarah Butts), a male-to-female tranny, self-confessed pedophile, and white nationalist apologist?[1] In the thousands of op-eds written about me, was there a single mention of Luke Bozier, a former business associate of the rabidly anti-Trump Louise Mensch, who was arrested on suspicion of viewing indecent images of children after I reported on him?[2] And did any news site that accused me of pandering to pedophiles acknowledge my reporting on Chris Leydon, a London tech journalist who was found guilty of making indecent images of children,[3] and is now facing a rape trial?[4] They ignored all of this, every single one of them did, which proves that they were never really interested in combating pedophilia, just in bringing me down – and they failed at that too.

Dozens of big-name progressives, including former NFL punter Chris Kluwe, *Daily Beast* columnist Arthur Chu, and British comedian Graham Linehan ignored or openly supported the self-confessed pedophile Nicholas/Sarah Nyberg after I outted him.[5]

Right around the same time, *Salon* published the writings of Todd Nickerson, a so-called "virtuous pedophile," who alleges he has never harmed children and never will, yet also said, behind the cover of an internet pseudonym, that his goal was to "protect children from harm, not sex."[6] *Salon* later deleted his articles out of shame, yet *VICE*, another leftist rag, still carries a glowing profile of Nickerson.[7]

While leftist journalists attack me as a "pedophile advocate" for rationalizing my own childhood experience of abuse, they're also trying to normalize attitudes that would lead to more children being abused. For God's sake, I wrote an article on *Breitbart* in 2015 called "Here's Why The Progressive Left Keeps Sticking Up For Pedophiles."[8] These people deserve to be consigned to the gutter of history.

The most surprising publication to defend Nickerson was *National Review*, home of anti-Trump establishment conservativism, where one of the publication's top writers called on society to "think twice" before condemning Nickerson.[9] This is the very same publication whose writers and editors were at the forefront of efforts to disinvite me from CPAC.

I'm no hypocrite. I tell the truth, always. That's my whole fucking problem. For the fake news to imply otherwise, when the facts were right in front of their face, is exactly why President Trump has (correctly) labeled them "the enemy of the people."

But that's the mainstream media's entire game. They have no problem telling the public that black is white, up is down, two plus two equals five. Trying to paint a bitter opponent of pedophilia as an advocate for the crime is just another day at the office for them. Malcolm X said, "If you're not careful, the newspapers will have you hating the people who are being oppressed, and loving the people who are doing the oppressing." He was right then and he's right now. Only the prevailing narratives have changed. Every single thing President Trump has said about the press is 100% accurate. I know, I experienced it firsthand.

MILO

To the victims of child abuse: we will fight against *Salon, VICE, National Review*, and anyone else who seeks to normalize pedophiles – "virtuous" or otherwise. To the real victims of rape: we will restore due process, call out the liars, and end the feminist hysteria that makes you less likely to be believed. To the *real* marginalized voices on college campuses: the Dangerous Faggot is on his way, and, like him, you need to get out of the closet and be fabulous. To the victims of homophobia, patriarchy, street harassment and intolerance: don't worry, we'll put a lid on Muslim immigration.

There are real victims out there, and together, you and I are going to fight for them. We're going to do so without self-pity, without a cult of victimhood, and certainly without safe spaces. As self-centered as I am, this really isn't about me. It's about you. They can call me any name they want, as they have, and as they will continue to do. But they won't stop me from fighting for your right to speak freely, honestly, and rudely, no matter who doesn't like it.

America isn't about where you're from. It's about how grateful you are to be in the greatest country on earth. I love America, and I love what it stands for. For most of 2016 I traveled across America on my Dangerous Faggot college speaking tour. My college tour was the most talked about of the year. I was also the most disinvited speaker of the year. And maybe of all time.

I wasn't just speaking on my tour, however, I was listening. I'm like the raptors in *Jurassic Park*, testing their electrified fences to find weaknesses. I saw some weaknesses, and they were strikingly similar to what I saw in England, right before we opened our borders to the world. But in England, we don't have that wonderful First Amendment that America does.

DANGEROUS

I'm here in America with a warning from England. I know I push buttons. I don't fucking care. If you don't understand what I'm talking about…well, consider this book your red pill.

Let's get started.

ON FREEDOM OF SPEECH AND POLITICAL CORRECTNESS

"If Muslims are primarily the people that are blowing up planes, then I would like them to be searching Muslims before I get on a plane."
—Chelsea Handler

"I used to date Hispanic guys, but now I prefer consensual."
—Amy Schumer

"Behind every successful Rap Billionaire is a double as rich Jewish man."
—Trevor Noah

"The Nazis did have flaws, but they did look fucking fantastic while they were killing people on the basis of their religion and sexuality."
—Russell Brand

"What kind of world do we live in where a totally cute white girl can't say chink on network television?"
—Sarah Silverman

"The Left is filled with hypocrites who choose their targets of outrage based solely on their politics." *—Milo*

Dangerous

M y name is Milo, and this book will tell you how I became what America now knows as "the most fabulous supervillain on the internet," and, "the dangerous faggot."

If Mariah Carey had sex with Patrick Bateman and their progeny picked up a copy of *On Liberty* and developed a taste for gutting sacred cows, that would be very close to me.

I'm a fire-starter and troublemaker who started out as an obscure British tech blogger and rose to infamy as one of America's most in demand speakers on college campuses. The appearance of my expensive shoes and frosted tips and the sound of my laughter ringing across university quads has forced professors, journalists, directors, activists and musicians to realize something no liberal in America has understood for a long time: *emotions do not trump facts.*

My critics hate me because they can't beat me. They say I am responsible for the actions of others. When some anonymous reprobate goes after a celebrity on Twitter, I get the blame.

My supporters see me for what I am: a critical voice in the pushback against political correctness, and a free-speech fundamentalist defending the public's right to express themselves however they please. Young conservatives and libertarians respond to me because I say the things they wish they could.

Mischief-makers love me, but often only in private, because they fear reprisals. I'm down with the DL so I get it. The names in my inbox, which include Hollywood A-listers, rappers, reality TV stars, authors, producers and investors, would make your head explode. Here's a neat trick: if you want to work out if your favorite celebrity is a Republican, just Google them and see if they talk about politics. If the answer is no, then yes: they're a Republican.[10]

MILO

In my mind, I play the role gays were always meant to in polite society: I test the absolute limits of acceptability. The social and religious convictions I represent do not map onto the norms of nihilism and self-esteem peddled by social-justice warriors (SJWs) and progressives since the 1960s. But they have set me, and my army of fans, free.

I am a threat because I don't belong to anyone. I'm unaffiliated.

They hate that.

I look and dress and behave as though I should have safe, MTV-friendly feminist opinions. But I don't.

I am the Ken doll from the underworld.

Social taboos for the past fifteen years have all come from the progressive left. They're a hideously ugly army of scolds who want to tell you how to behave. Libertarians and conservatives are the new counter-culture.

Liberals hate that too.

The tremendous outcry among social, online, and print media to this book being announced is the entire reason I'm writing it. Despite being announced between Christmas and New Year's, when most of the world was on vacation, the firestorm was immediate. I'm used to the heat. My former publisher, Simon & Schuster, was paralyzed by it. A lot of what came at me after the announcement were the typical lies I've dealt with. But even I was surprised by the scale of the onslaught. The *Chicago Review of Books* announced to great fanfare that they would not review another book published by Simon & Schuster, in response to Dangerous.

I don't think there's anything *particularly* outrageous in this book. But to believe the press coverage, you'd think this was the most offensive thing published since OJ Simpson's *If I Did It*.

DANGEROUS

What are they all so afraid of?

It isn't my outrageous behavior, my mockery of ideologies considered sacrosanct in America today, or even my addiction to uncomfortable truths. The establishment's real fear is that this book will deeply affect readers, especially young people. In particular, they fear that the young people at the epicenter of political correctness in America's universities will begin to question the ideologies foisted upon them, thanks to the book you hold in your hands.

My views are nowhere near as radical or "hateful" as my opponents pretend to think they are. I believe in free speech, freedom of lifestyle—for hedonistic liberals and traditional conservatives both—and in putting facts before feelings. If you want white nationalism, go listen to Richard Spencer. I'm the conservative Lenny Bruce, finding boundaries and raping them in front of you. (Lenny Bruce would overdose all over again if he saw what stuffy prudes we consider controversial comedians today.)

Political correctness used to be a particular way to think and speak in order to demonstrate to everyone around just how good of a person you are. Fellow liberals might not know anything about you, but they'd know you are a virtuous person based on your use of the term "undocumented American" instead of "illegal alien."

The new brand of political correctness, popular on college campuses and social media, is the idea that no speech should exist that directly challenges politically correct ideas. To campus crybabies, and the professors who have been breastfeeding them, it is incomprehensible that I should be permitted to speak on their campus.

Liberals label all speech they don't like as "hate speech." That term has been stretched so broadly it has lost all meaning. Simon & Schuster's

CEO, Carolyn Reidy, put out a laughably vague announcement that my book would not include any "hate speech." I asked for a set of guidelines as to how hate speech would be defined, but that doesn't exist. It's an "I'll know it when I see it" kind of situation.

Adam Morgan, the editor of *The Chicago Review of Books,* wrote in *The Guardian* that my book could inspire people to commit acts of terrorism, specifically naming Omar Mateen and Dylann Roof as examples.

This is a very particular kind of insanity on Morgan's part—I gave a speech about the dangers of Islam mere steps from the site of Mateen's massacre. And Dylann Roof, along with any other actual Nazis, hates me just as much as that piece of shit Mateen would if he weren't too busy burning in Hell. I'm a Jewish faggot who loves black guys, for God's sake! What kind of half-witted logic is that, especially coming from a man who writes about books for a living?

The practitioners of the new political correctness are not equipped for a world in which individuals can disagree with what is deemed appropriate thought. They rely on silencing the opposition with hysterics, instead of winning with superior ideas. If there isn't a piece in a leading media source comparing this book to *Mein Kampf* by the time you read this, don't worry, it's coming soon. And that's precisely why this book is so necessary. Purposefully or unwittingly, a generation of Americans now exists that is terrified of critical thinking.

Freedom of speech is America's most cherished right, and implicit in freedom of speech is the freedom to disagree. I'm not your typical conservative commentator. For one thing, my process is a little different. If I haven't spent at least $5,000 at Neiman Marcus then I find it very difficult to write more than 500 words. I'm like the Zsa Zsa Gabor of political discourse.

But I tell the truth. And that's what has made me popular.

Political correctness is a smokescreen. In today's culture we make an effort to appear "inoffensive" (I don't, that's why I'm the one writing the book). We are cautious. But to exist this way is in defiance of our natural instincts toward anger and anarchy. Everyone feels these things from time to time. When they are suppressed, awful things can happen—like mass murder.[11] The more time you spend trying to tame the beast, the stronger it becomes. Sooner or later we have no choice but to give in to our human nature.

America's next school shooter won't be a Milo fan. It will be one of the poor misinformed nose-ringed protestors holding a sign that reads "NO MORE HATE!" Canadian writer Alex Kazemi predicted on my hit podcast that angry lesbians would start becoming school shooters.[12] I think he's absolutely right.

If we are to win the culture war, we must fight hard and have a hell of a lot of fun along the way. The bodies and souls of America's youth hang in the balance.

In the following pages, I'll teach you how to cause the same sort of mayhem I do in defense of the most important right you have in America: the right to think, do, say and be whatever the hell you want. In short order, I have assimilated to the American ways of unapologetic free speech, and of putting facts, fun, and fabulousness ahead of feelings.

My motto is laughter and war. Keep reading and you'll find out how you can become as terrifying to the forces of political correctness and social justice as I am. And you won't even have to turn gay.

THE ART OF THE TROLL

2016 was the year of the troll. And, as one of the world's most famous trolls, I have special insight into what that means.

What does it mean to be a troll? If you stray too far into whiny, crybaby social-justice circles, trolling and political disagreement are one and the same. Others see no distinction between trolls and those who send poorly-worded death threats to public figures.

Trolling is far more complicated and joyous than any of that. The ideal troll baits the target into a trap, from which there is no escape without public embarrassment. It is an art, beyond the grasp of mere mortals. It is part trickery and part viciousness.

Trolling has many elements. It's often about telling truths that others don't want to hear. It's about tricking, pranking, and generally riling up your targets. And it's about creating a hilarious, entertaining public spectacle. The best part is, most left-wingers refuse to accept that they're being trolled.

Is it any wonder that a fabulous faggot like me is so good at it?

Even calling myself a faggot is trolling you. Calling myself a "fabulous faggot" is trolling you fabulously. It's an old trick I picked up from drag queens: always tell the joke the other guy is going to tell about you first, and make it funny. It's an incredibly disarming tactic. It's like Eminem saying, "Ya'll act like you never seen a white person before."

Picking deserving targets, and making them hopping mad, is essential to good trolling. So is annoying both sides. Left-wing reporters describe me to disbelieving readers as a misogynist, racist, white-nationalist alt-right bigot. Actual Neo-Nazis, meanwhile, call me a "degenerate kike faggot."[13]

At least one of them must be wrong, but their collective confusion is so glorious that I don't want to correct either.

This is top-tier trolling: annoying your critics so much they print hysterical lies about you because they can't beat you on the facts *and* because you get under their skin so effectively. They torpedo their own credibility and readership while your own fan base grows. Want to know why the trolls are winning? It's because no matter how much our critics hate us, yell at us, ban us from their comment sections, stamp their feet, throw their toys out of their stroller or pretend that jokes on Twitter can cause physical pain, *we're the only ones telling the truth any more.*

To be a good troll, you must have a certain level of disregard for other people's feelings. But the difference between trolling and cruelty is that cruelty has no purpose except to hurt someone. Trolls may hurt the feelings of delicate wallflowers, but they do so because reasoned argument and polite entreaty have failed. In my experience most of those delicate wallflowers turn out to be sociopathic professional activists cynically playing the victim, trying to persuade you that jokes on Twitter can cause lasting psychological damage.

MILO

The most high-minded trolls should troll only in the name of debunking some untruth or exposing wrongdoing or hypocrisy. That's what I try to do. When I see respectable publications wasting time writing about cultural appropriation, or an innocent joke deemed racist by overzealous ankle-biting bloggers, it's like my bat signal.

In my mastery of trolling, I am surpassed by one man: President Donald J. Trump. He trolled his way to the presidency. Like me, Daddy, as I like to call him (in itself another troll), only went after deserving targets: the media, Hillary and Bill Clinton, the disabled, and political correctness.

A master showman, President Donald J. Trump can command the media's attention even though most of their leading lights utterly despise him. Kardashianism, I mean narcissism, rules in America, and if you come across as self-involved enough, journalists will get drawn into the fantasy too. They will follow your every move.

I could post a one-second video of me sneezing on Facebook and get 5,000 comments. Azealia Banks cleaned out her closet and it was covered by almost every magazine in America. But forcing people who hate you and everything you stand for to point cameras at you for over a year? That's a level of trolling I can only hope to achieve. Trolling is the perfect weapon of a political dissident intent on spreading forbidden or inconvenient truths.

One of the purposes of trolling is to generate as much noise and public outcry as possible, which has the added effect of drawing attention to the very facts society is so eager to suppress. The mere act of unashamedly revealing such truths is frequently all that is needed to generate the outcry in the first place. Trolling and truth telling are made for each other; two bold acts of modern rebellion existing in perfect, intricate symbiosis. If you tell lies to and about men, if you spread conspiracy theories about the "wage gap" and "campus rape culture," if you tweet "Kill All White Men" and "I Bathe In Male Tears," if you close comment sections because you hate being ridiculed by readers who are smarter than you, if you prefer ideology and activism to facts, if you create a hateful atmosphere in which it's okay to laugh at white people but no one else, if you are mean and vindictive and cruel and sociopathic yet try to cloak yourself in the language of tolerance and diversity, if you get people fired for bringing up studies or asking you to justify your claims, if you whip up outrage mobs over innocent jokes on social media, if you see racism and sexism and homophobia and transphobia and every other imaginable kind of bigotry everywhere, and if you insist on warping reality to conform to your delusions, don't be surprised if there's a backlash. Don't be surprised if that looks like President Trump. And me. And a whole lot of other bad asses.

We don't care how egregiously you lie about us. As long as facts remain offensive, the age of the troll will never end.

"In times of universal deceit," wrote George Orwell, "telling the truth is a revolutionary act." We live in a world where politicians lie to you, the media lies to you, your schoolteachers and your professors lie to you. It's little wonder young people on campus retreat into safe spaces when they hear I'm coming—the juddering foundation of lies that props up the progressive worldview has become so fragile, even the slightest bit of contrary speech is enough to shatter it. I bring a neutron bomb when a penknife would do just as well, and the results are always spectacular.

I feel no animosity or hatred toward the kids who hide behind safe spaces and social media blocking programs to protect their worldview.

MILO

Their fragility is the result of an older generation's cowardice, and its inability to sort feel-good fiction from hard realities. They wanted so desperately to believe that everyone is equal and that we could all get along, and now their kids have swallowed the lies they barely believed themselves. Trigger warnings and therapy sessions are the result. Do not presume that just because I take sympathy on the cry-bullies I intend to go easy on them. I don't and you shouldn't either.

Freethinkers and cultural libertarians, take heart. Throughout history, there have always been myths and irrationalities to defeat, and there have always been those who defend them to the bitter, tearful end. Truth, like freedom, must be fought for in every generation. If you're reading this book, you'll likely be one of the people fighting for it this time round. Good on you.

It's cool to be counterculture, and we're it. Twenty years ago, it was conservatives banning video games because they found them offensive. Now progressives are doing the same thing.

Even the rebellious heroes of my youth have gone soft. In 1997, Marilyn Manson was outraging Christians and social conservatives. The Antichrist Superstar should have been a Trump fan. He was practically built for it. It was a real let down when he came out with a music video in which he decapitated a Trump look-a-like.

Today, the best way to rebel is to be conservative—or even just libertarian. Conservatives are no longer the cultural elites, censoring dissident leftist media. *Leftists* are the cultural elites, censoring dissident *conservatives*. As a result, a marvelously rebellious young force has arisen on the web. It's bold and it's subversive. And I'm its most dangerous faggot.

Three introductions is enough, yes? Let's begin.

1

WHY THE PROGRESSIVE
LEFT HATES ME

"At the core of liberalism is the spoiled child—miserable, as all
spoiled children are, unsatisfied, demanding, ill-disciplined,
despotic, and useless."
—*P.J. O'Rourke, Give War A Chance*

9 3% of workplace deaths are male.
Rates of rape and domestic abuse are far higher in Muslim
communities than non-Muslim ones.

The black community has a huge problem with crime and drugs.

These statements are all facts. Yet in today's America, introducing
them to the conversation causes instant outrage, like when I tell cab
drivers curry is not a deodorant.

If you discuss these inconvenient truths, you are expected to
begin with certain caveats. "I'm a feminist, but…" "The majority of

MILO

African-Americans are law-abiding citizens, but..." "I'll try breathing through my mouth, but..."

Caveats are irrelevant. I refuse to preface any discussion of Islam, for instance, with the usual fake niceties about radical extremists. I prefer to discuss facts directly, and I use exaggeration and bombast, often outrageously.

Challenging the myths of the Left causes them to lose their minds. I puncture their fantasies with attention-grabbing wit and style. I'm also hot, which I'll cover in excruciating detail throughout this book.

What really drives left-wingers up the wall is that I should be one of them. People like me are supposed to be good little metropolitan fags and vote Democrat. Go to anti-war protests and experiment with quinoa and hummus. We're supposed to pretend it's totally believable Rey could pilot the Millennium Falcon with greater skill than Han Solo. Never mind the fact that she learns the Force in like, half a day.

Even before the Left descended into identity-politics lunacy, I wanted nothing to do with them. I wasn't quite the conservative icon I am today either, though. I was doing something different.

I spent my youth in drug-saturated nightclubs in London, losing my virginity in interracial fivesomes with drag queens, experimenting with every depraved form of escapism I could find. And I listened to a lot of Mariah Carey, Marilyn Manson and Rage Against the Machine.

I also studied music theory, Schopenhauer, and Wittgenstein, and I read Margaret Thatcher biographies, shot my dad's guns, and dreamt of meeting George W. Bush. (I did later in life, but by then he wasn't right-wing enough for me.)

DANGEROUS

Little did I know that I was breaking all the Left's rules by reading Ayn Rand's *Atlas Shrugged* and daydreaming that I was the heroically entrepreneurial protagonist, Dagny Taggart.

I came to represent the Left's greatest fear: an opponent who is cooler, smarter, better dressed, edgier and more popular than them.

To understand precisely why the Left hates people like me so much, it's necessary to understand how and why their politics have changed over the past few decades.

WHY ALL THIS STUFF MATTERS—AND PAY ATTENTION AT THE BACK, BECAUSE THIS IS IMPORTANT

In the past, the Left were champions of blue-collar workers against the managerial, big business classes. Jobs, pay, and decent living standards for ordinary citizens were the priorities. A few leftists (Bernie Sanders in the United States and Jeremy Corbyn in Britain) continue this tradition. They are, notably, significantly older than most other left-wing politicians. They are also loathed by much of the establishment in their respective parties.

Why?

Because the mainstream Left today has very different priorities.

There was no reason why the Left had to abandon its old blue-collar base. The industries that employed their voters have largely disappeared, but the voters themselves didn't go anywhere. Indeed, as voters in old working-class heartlands entered economic crises, the Left should have been more attentive to their concerns.

But that didn't happen.

Instead, leftists chose to ignore the former working class, and turn to a very different electoral coalition: latte-sipping metropolitan voters, fairytale dwelling antiwar activists, ugly women (sigh), and minorities.

The fact that minorities were only a small section of the electorate didn't bother the Left; they could always import new voters. Zero fucks were given about the rapid influx of cheap labor or the deluge of new welfare recipients. Both of these obvious consequences only added further pressure to the already-beleaguered, long forgotten, working class base.[14]

This reminds me of the movie *Scream*, when Sidney (aka Neve Campbell) finds out it was (*spoiler alert*) her boyfriend who was trying to butcher her and all her friends the whole time. Sidney didn't let him get away with it, however. She shot him in the head. After they were so wantonly betrayed, it's remarkable to me that millions of former working-class families still remain loyal to the Left.

As their electoral coalition changed, so too did the Left's politics. They became *less* concerned with pay, *more* contemptuous of old industries, and *venomous* towards the cultural values of their old voters. Barack Obama's infamous 2008 quip that former working-class communities "cling to guns, or religion, or antipathy toward people who aren't like them, or anti-immigrant sentiment, or anti-trade sentiment,"[15] epitomized the new attitude of the Left.

Leftists have always been well practiced at turning social classes against one another. But the working classes can prove frustrating to socialists intent on class warfare. Marxists were particularly perturbed when, during World War I, the European working class (with the exception of Russia) chose to fight for King and Country instead of rise up against their masters. This is understandable to a certain extent, socialist leaders like Marx had never done a day of work in their life.

DANGEROUS

In the 1920s, the Italian Marxist Antonio Gramsci had an idea for a new form of revolution—one based on culture, not class. According to Gramsci, the reason the proletariat failed to rise up was because old, conservative ideas like loyalty to one's country, family values, and religion, held too much sway in working-class communities.

If that sounds redolent of Obama's comment about guns and religion, it should. His line of thinking is directly descended from the ideological tradition of Gramsci.

Gramsci argued that as a precursor to revolution, the old traditions of the West—or "cultural hegemony," as he called it—would have to be systematically broken down. To do so, Gramsci argued that "proletarian" intellectuals should seek to challenge the dominance of traditionalism in education and the media, and create a new revolutionary culture. If you've ever wondered why you're forced to take diversity or gender studies courses at university, or why your professors all seem to hate western civilization, blame Gramsci.

In the 1950s and 60s, a group of European expatriate academics known as the Frankfurt School married Gramsci's idea of cultural revolution to the idea of a new revolutionary vanguard: one made up of *students*, feminists, and minorities, many of whom felt excluded from mainstream western culture and sought to change it. Their ideas would provide much of the intellectual ballast for the cultural upheavals of the 1960s, and the subsequent transformation of the Left. Andrew Breitbart wrote about them extensively in his bestselling book, *Righteous Indignation*.

The New Left, as they came to be called, were responsible for the early stages of the Left's pivot away from traditional class politics and towards the divisive, politically-correct world of gender, racial, and sexual politics we know today. They were the ones responsible for making issues like abortion, the reversal of gender roles, "racial justice," pacifism, and multiculturalism into major platforms of the Left. If they could keep their "rainbow coalition" acting and voting as a bloc, and focus all their hatred on the weary white male working class, then political dominance would soon be assured. Thus began the reign of identity politics.

These sneering students who joined the New Left in the 1960s became the professors who are teaching you today, rebelling against the over-protective, military-minded, and somewhat austere World War II generation. Novelist and former noted liberal John Updike wrote of the disdain he saw from "Cambridge professors and Manhattan lawyers and their guitar-strumming children... privileged members of a privileged nation... full of aesthetic disdain for their own defenders... spitting on the cops who were trying to keep the USA and its many amenities intact."

Cultural Marxism, nurtured by the Frankfurt School, struck a chord—even though, for the most part, these young baby boomers didn't realize where their ideas were coming from. Rock musicians, the standard-bearers of young boomer culture, became fierce advocates for pacifism, feminism, gay rights, and all the other causes of the New Left.

There is, of course, another reason the New Left was so successful in the 1960s: a lot of their arguments made sense. There was racism to be fought, structural, institutionalized and legal racism. Sexism in the workplace was rampant—even worse than on *Mad Men*. And gays were oppressed, by conservatives and liberals alike.

The tragedy is that instead of granting life to the inherently divisive doctrines of Cultural Marxism, these problems could easily have been solved with the milder tradition of Classical Liberalism. Indeed, in 1950s Britain, it was classical liberal politicians of the Wolfenden Committee who began the process of decriminalizing homosexuality. Marxists played little if any role in it. By the end of the 1960s, when the New Left were still on the fringe, their milder allies in the social liberal movement were already well on their way to winning America's most important cultural battles: Jim Crow was dismantled, and the Civil Rights and Voting Rights acts were passed.

For better or worse (it was definitely for worse), the New Left became the defining youth movement of the 60s and 70s, and although initially perceived as radical, its ideas would eventually come to dominate modern culture. The counter-culture of the 1960s became the prevailing culture of the 1980s. By the 1990s, a decade in which, despite the LA riots and the OJ trial, we could all watch *The Fresh Prince Of Bel-Air* without agonizing over white supremacist tropes in the Banks household, the New Left had become the establishment. It was now difficult to argue that any social group in the West lacked equality under the law. Indeed, thanks to the persistence of government redistribution plans and the early growth of affirmative action, some groups were already getting favored treatment—a sign of things to come. But the New Left still achieved complete control of media, academia and the arts, just at the point when they were no longer needed.

Metropolitan elites of today's leftist political class follow the intellectual legacy of Gramsci and his contempt for working-class, traditionalist culture. The knee-jerk endorsements of feminism, Black Lives Matter, and gay identity politics are in no small part related to this Marxist tendency to back the "revolutionary class" against the "oppressors," regardless of facts. Another by-product of 1960s leftism is the unabashed hatred of white males, who are (correctly) identified as the architects of western culture.

For the New Left, white men are the cultural counterpart to the economic bourgeoisie class in classical Marxist theory—a class of oppressors that must be overthrown by the oppressed. The influence of the New Left is seen most clearly in universities, where efforts to "deconstruct" the pillars of western civilization, from classical liberal humanism to the mythical "patriarchy," proceed just as Gramsci would have wanted.

By the early 2000s, in firm control of the baby boomer's cultural consciousness, the New Left was on course to become the new cultural hegemony. Conservatives, preoccupied with defeating the Soviet Union and reviving the free market, failed to grasp the gravity of the Left's cultural revolution. On the Right, culture wars were only fought by *social* conservatives, spearheaded by evangelical Christians, who obsessed over unwinnable fights like gay marriage, and alienated young people with hare-brained censorship campaigns against rock music, comic books and video games.

When social conservatives started going after *Harry Potter* for "promoting witchcraft," it became embarrassingly clear which side had won the culture wars. And it's *culture* that matters. "Politics is downstream from culture," as Andrew Breitbart used to say. Politics is just a symptom, which is one of the reasons I spend more time on college campuses than I do in Washington, DC.

If you're reading this and you're in college, or you recently graduated, you can lay the blame squarely at your parent's generation for handing culture to the regressive lunatics and SJWs. The previous generation of conservatives failed completely in their attempts to save academia, the media and the arts. In many cases, they didn't bother to fight at all, preferring to spend hundreds of millions of dollars on think-tanks and magazines complaining about the problem while doing absolutely nothing to fix it, as brilliantly set out in a well-known 2016 essay in *The Claremont Review of Books*.[16] FOX's Tucker Carlson is refreshingly harsh on this point, describing the conservative establishment as "overpaid, underperforming tax-exempt sinecure-holders."[17] Liberals, meanwhile, were setting up university departments, organizing activist groups and installing themselves in Hollywood and New York City.

By 2010, the argument that racism, sexism, and homophobia still ran rampant in western society started to look absurd. I suspect the reason gay marriage became such a *cause célèbre* for the Left during this period is because it was, for them, the last clear-cut legislative battle that could be easily fought and won.

Like carnival magicians, the Left kept voters distracted, so they didn't notice they were being taxed oppressively, regulated minutely and manipulated in countless other ways.

Seriously, you have to hand it to them. These guys put the work in. I do admire leftist's energy levels. If I had to spend all day screaming and crying, stewing in my anger, blaming made-up concepts like the "patriarchy" for my failure and defending Barack Obama, I'd be exhausted.

Modern American liberals took Orwell's "Two Minutes Hate" from *1984* and turned it into 24 hours. The "Two Minutes Hate" is a daily ritual in which every citizen must watch a video depicting the Party's enemies and direct hatred toward them. For two minutes. CNN has published several articles comparing Trump's presidency to Orwell's dystopian fantasy, sanctimoniously oblivious to their own offenses.

How do they keep those hatred levels up? Maybe I've stumbled onto the real reason they love Starbucks so much.

WHY THE LEFT HATES *YOU*

Because of their intellectual pedigree in the angry, victim-centric doctrine of Cultural Marxism, the Left is committed to defending a worldview which arranges women, minorities, and gays in a league table of oppression, with straight white men as the eternal oppressors at the top of the list, followed by gay white men, followed by straight white women, all the way down to paraplegic black immigrant Muslim transsexuals at the very bottom. Straight white men are the new "bourgeoisie," the group oppressing everyone else.

The academic phrase for this is "intersectionality." Intersectionalists are the ones responsible for dreaming up new, ever more bizarre categories of oppression. These fun people believe there are "intersecting" categories of oppression: it's not enough to just talk about the oppression associated with being a woman, one *must* also talk about the oppression associated with being a *black* woman, a black *disabled* woman, a *fat* black disabled woman, a fat black disabled *Muslim* woman, and so on.

In plainer English, different people's lives suck for a bunch of different reasons. The progressive Left has constructed entire university departments just to parse that sentence.

The "Intersecting Axes of Privilege, Domination and Oppression" lists fourteen categories of oppressed groups with a corresponding "privileged group" for each one.[18] There's whites (privileged) vs.

people of color (oppressed), " masculine and feminine" (privileged) vs. "gender deviants" (oppressed), attractive (privileged) vs. unattractive (oppressed), credentialed (privileged) vs. nonliterate (oppressed), and even fertile (privileged) vs. infertile (oppressed).

Our bias in favor of people who can read and write, is, according to the Axes of Privilege, "Educationalism." Our bias in favor of the fertile is "Pro-natalism." Our bias in favor of men who look like men and women who look like women is "Genderism." Heaven help you if you're a literate, attractive, straight white man who looks and behaves like a man. According to the categories of oppression dreamed up by intersectional theorists, nothing and no one could be more privileged.

This is why, despite facing their own unique problems, men, and especially white working-class men, are routinely ignored by the new leftist political class—because regardless of the data, straight white men can never be the victims of anything. Any attempts to address their issues are usually met with outrage and condescension. In 2016, when the British Conservative MP Philip Davies gave a speech at a conference on men's issues, the reaction of feminists in the left-wing Labour party was to demand he be suspended from his party. As for whites, any attempt to organize is usually received by the mainstream as the revival of Nazism, despite the fact that much of such organizing activity today comes as a direct response to a culture that appears to hate them.

I'd prefer a world with no identity politics. I'd prefer we judged people according to reason, logic and evidence instead of barmy left-wing theories about "oppression." But if you *are* going to divide everyone up, you have to accept that straight white men are going to want their own special party too. If we are to have identity politics, we must have identity politics for all.

MILO

Straight white boys in college aren't Neo-Nazis for resisting Black Lives Matter and feminism or for advocating for their own identity groups: they are simply responding—entirely logically—to what they've been told about how the world works. It just so happens they have been born into a group that invented the best and worst stuff in history, so they have to deal with that legacy.

Popular culture, dominated by the Left, is instructive. Movies are filled with petty, mean-spirited jabs at straight white men. There's a huge trend in movies that seek to channel white guilt over slavery, like *Django Unchained, 10 Years A Slave* and *MLK*. In the wake of #OscarsSoWhite this is only getting worse, as Hollywood bends over backward to avoid being called racist again (*Moonlight* was a terribly boring film and never would have won Best Picture if it weren't for white appeasement). The straight white male villains in these movies get progressively more sadistic and irredeemable. Strangely, there are no movies about Ottoman or Middle Eastern slave-owners. I suppose we'll have to wait for Muslim guilt to become a thing.

With straight white men replacing the bourgeoisie as the hated oppressor class of the Left, they've become fair game for smug champagne socialists in entertainment and the media. That's why you routinely see movies, stand-up routines, songs and *Guardian* columns about straight white men that would be classified as "hate speech" if they were directed against any other group in society.

White men can't dance, jump or sexually satisfy their partners. These are all socially acceptable jokes. Call an Irishman a drunk leprechaun or an Italian a made man, and you'll have no problem. But if you dare joke that black people are loud, Asians can't drive, or Latinos steal, you'll face the full force of triggered Twitter mouth breathers.

DANGEROUS

The new, identity-driven Left doesn't hate *only* white men. One of the consequences of replacing the old working-class/bourgeoisie dichotomy with the myriad identities of intersectional theory is that everything has become much more complicated. Yes, straight white men are the *most* oppressive, but how do you order everyone else? Are Muslims oppressing women, or are women oppressing Muslims? Is a disabled black man oppressed more than an able-bodied black woman? And what do we do about white men who are, for the sake of argument, extraordinarily gay, but also rich, popular authors of best-selling books about free speech?

The result of dividing their political coalition into a hierarchy of victim groups is a tragicomic battle for the bottom (insert cheap dick taking joke here). Each group fights to be more oppressed than the others. You see this on social media all the time; "white feminists" attacked by intersectionalists for not being ethnic enough, and thus not being oppressed enough. Or, they are criticized for being too ethnic, aka "cultural appropriation." Probably.

Since the 1970s, social psychologists have been aware that emphasizing differences between groups leads to mistrust and hostility. In a series of landmark experiments, the psychologist Henri Tajfel found that even wearing different-colored shirts was enough for groups to begin displaying signs of mistrust. So guess what happens when you tell everyone that their worth, their ability, their right to speak on certain subjects and—shudder—their "privilege" is, like original sin, based on what they were born with, rather than any choices they've made or who they are?

Here's what you get: the modern Left. Blacks fighting gays fighting women fighting trannies fighting Muslims fighting everyone else. It's the iron law of victimhood-driven identity politics. Someone has to win, and everyone else has to lose.

Progressive identity politics ignores basic human realities. If you live authentically as yourself there will be repercussions. Not everyone will like you. Some people may even want you dead. As Friedrich Nietzsche said, "Man is the cruelest animal." This is a fact of life and it is not changed by all the abuse and harassment policies in all of Silicon Valley. Progressives will never understand this.

Identity politics is universally attractive because it enables failures and weaknesses to be spun as the products of oppression and historical injustice. Personal responsibility is removed from the equation. Primary victims of identity politics in reality are the designated "oppressor class," for whom it can be humiliating and deeply unfair.

The modern leftist movement has argued itself into a position where people can be discriminated against on the basis of gender, skin color and orientation. Take MTV's *White People*, a "documentary" highlighting a handful of cherry-picked examples aimed to demonstrate "white privilege" in action. It's an hour of television designed to produce discomfort in those with the wrong skin color. Or Netflix's *Dear White People*, another pathetic dose of race-baiting.

White men can only survive in this new landscape through self-flagellation and groveling apology for what they are, by promoting how they're "woke," a "male feminist," or a "straight ally." (See: Macklemore.) "Straight white man" has become a socially acceptable form of insult. It'll be a while before we see *Dear Black People* on our screens, much as America's police officers might have something to say to that community.

Dangerous

The future of the progressive movement will be akin to the nightmarish community of grievance-bloggers on Tumblr, where minorities, both real and imagined, engage in an endless competition for supreme victimhood status. Welcome to the era of Minority Wars.

If you're gay, they'll ask what your skin color is.

If you're black, they'll ask if you're a woman.

If you're a woman, they'll ask you to stop worrying about Muslim rapists, you racist.

If you happen to fit into every conceivable minority group, heaven help you if your opinions do not precisely follow political orthodoxy.

Donald Trump, and Margaret Thatcher before him, were both right when they said identity politics and name-calling is what people do when they don't have any arguments left.

The modern Left is an ouroboros, the ancient Egyptian serpent that eats its own tail, constantly consuming itself in a twisted, never-ending cycle of victimhood, hatred and name-calling. No matter how nice they are to you when they're focusing on your particular group's causes, leftists will always, in the end, find a way to shame you about some alleged "privilege."

And if they can't win by public shaming, they rage and flounce off, or at least threaten to. What an entertaining spectacle it was, watching all those celebrities walking back their promises to leave the country if Donald Trump was elected. To the typical actor, threatening to leave the United States over the election was just another set of lines to read. A Trump presidency was supposed to be as likely as Trevor Noah ever having successful ratings.

Did you notice that these whiny celebs uniformly threatened to move to overwhelmingly white countries? Imagine the chutzpah and obliviousness it takes to call working-class Americans racist while you plan to move to Canada if your candidate loses. At least Snoop Dogg promised to move to South Africa, although, it's hardly the Congo down there. I'm guessing what Snoop had in mind was a nice gated complex with other rich westerners.

Aside from Snoop Dogg, if it wasn't Canada, it was New Zealand, Australia or another primarily white, English-speaking country. Why not Mexico or the Gambia? Guatemala doesn't have a Whole Foods, so Lena Dunham had to cross it off her list.

So Why Does the Left Hate Us?
"Scab" was a derogatory word used by the unionized workers of the old Left to describe strikebreakers: people who, during a strike, decided that feeding their families took priority over an abstract idea of left-wing solidarity.

The Left loathed scabs with a passion far exceeding their hatred for the bourgeoisie. After all, the bourgeoisie were just protecting their own interests. By not following the Left's marching orders, scabs were allegedly betraying theirs.

Once branded a scab, you and your family were scabs for life. No amount of denial or explanation could expiate it. The word scab was (and for some is) akin to a swear word. A cursed word. It wasn't Twitter that gave name-calling its power: social media just added mass scale and mob mentality to an earlier leftist strategy to adorn the untouchables with scarlet letters. No prizes then, for guessing why the Left hates me so much. I'm not one of them. I don't fit into the box they demand of me. I don't fit into any fucking box. "I am large, I contain multitudes."

My existence infuriates them, not only because I debunk their myths with style, wit and humor, but also because their usual smears don't work on me. Feminists can't accuse me of suspect motives, because I'm not interested in women except in an academic sense. I can't be accused of being homophobic—only that laughable charge of "self-hatred," which, come on, I love myself, a lot.

In short, I'm the Left's worst nightmare: a living, breathing refutation of identity politics, and proof that free speech and the truth wrapped in a good joke will always be more persuasive and more powerful than identity politics.

I'm also particularly terrifying to the Left because they see in me a repeat of the 1980s, when workers across Britain and the United States turned to Reaganism and Thatcherism. In the age of Trump, the Left are worried I might not be the only dissident minority. They're afraid *you* might agree with me. Because if you're reading this, there's a good chance you might have realized the Left doesn't have your best interests at heart, because your heartbreak isn't sad enough.

Just as leftist's old base abandoned them to become conservative-voting "Reagan Democrats" in the U.S. and "Essex Men" in the U.K., so too will a new wave of dissident women and minorities break apart their coalition.

The Left's deepest wish is that we rebel minorities didn't exist. Nothing terrifies them so much as the thought of their cherished identity classes going off the reservation. That's why they reacted so hysterically, or in many cases, so silently, to Gamergate's #NotYourShield. It's also why *Clueless* actress Stacey Dash literally lost her social life (and wrote a book about it) when she came out as all-in Republican. And it's why I, an obnoxiously proud gay man, continue to be called homophobic.

The Left champions the powerless, and fights the powerful. In itself, that's not a bad thing. Many of the basic luxuries we take for granted today like two-day weekends, eight-hour workdays, and basic occupational health and safety, were won by leftist worker's rights movements. Other more important achievements, such as the end of lynching in the American South, were won by left-wing activists who instinctively detest injustice.

The dark side of this instinct, however, is the hatred of people deemed too successful or well-off: the "privileged." "Puritanism," wrote H.L. Mencken, whose lifetime spanned the first progressive era, is the "haunting fear that someone, somewhere, might be happy."

Who could possibly *hate* happiness?

Those who are denied it themselves.

Morally authoritarian movements are attractive to ugly, miserable, talentless people. It offers an outlet for their hatred of the successful and good-looking, and anyone who looks like they might be enjoying themselves. Rush Limbaugh famously described feminism as a way for ugly women to get attention and enter the mainstream.

On my travels around campuses, I observed happy, well-groomed, ambitious and intelligent Milo fans, as well as the greasy blue-haired social justice apparitions protesting outside. My time on campuses exposed a massive flaw in the Left's plans for world domination: they've taken for granted their lock on the youth constituency.

The Left needs ideological shock troops to propagate its ideas, and none have been more useful to them than impressionable young people, who eagerly take up left-wing causes out of their natural inclination to make an impact on the world, before the realities of raising children and paying a mortgage set in.

The Left convinces young people that they're going to be heroes. In reality, they're like foot soldiers in the intellectual equivalent of the Somme; running at machine guns armed with bayonets.

Bored American youth are indoctrinated into wacky, flimsy ideas that never stand up to the real world, leaving them disappointed, disillusioned, and angry.

Their grip on the minds of young people is weakening, and I am happy to be a leading cause. My efforts to support millennial gamers, and then my "Dangerous Faggot" tour, rapidly mobilized a new breed of dissident student. And now I've written the textbook on how to fight back against cultural lunacy.

To quote esteemed author Michael Walsh, "The only weapon they have is our own weakness… It is our wish to be seen as reasonable, as proportional, as judicious, as measured [*all leftist terms*] that hinders us from taking decisive action against them."

For too long, conservatives have relied on pundits whose audience is primarily over 60. In the case of FOX News, it's over 70. Do you really think anyone who isn't two score into senior citizen discounts wants to have Charles Krauthammer, Stephen Hayes, Frank Luntz, Rich Lowry or Karl Rove on their television screen?

Young people have always been instinctively anti-establishment, and that's where I come in. There is no other libertarian or conservative pop culture figure who comes close to the purchase I have with Generation Next, who are sick of being lectured to by the increasingly nannying Left. America's young conservatives and libertarians are looking for heroes. I'm happy to oblige.

MILO

Without an endless supply of eager young activists, the Left is nothing. And I am hoovering up those young people and spitting them out as mischievous, dissident free speech warriors who don't give a damn about your feelings. For hundreds of thousands of students, simply reading this book has become the ultimate statement of rebellion. To them I say: Milo Merchandise is also available, while supplies last.

You've seen how liberals respond when their backs are against the wall: with hate, because they've forgotten how to argue, all the while trumpeting their own moral superiority. Well, here's something I've learned during my time in America: aggressive public displays of virtue are where the morally deplorable hide.

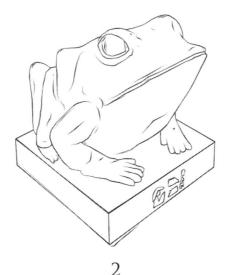

2

WHY THE ALT-RIGHT HATES ME

To the proud white supremacists at *Daily Stormer*, I am a "nigger-loving … kike faggot" and a "disease-ridden Jew."[19] But to NBC News and *USA Today* I am a "white nationalist leader."[20] Aside from the "disease-ridden" part, *Daily Stormer* is closer to the facts. What does that tell you about the mainstream media?

Anyone who calls me a white supremacist has no understanding of what white supremacy is. That's sadly common in America today, where wearing a Trump hat is enough to get you called a Nazi and attacked in the street by black-masked "anti-fascists." The media, in its hysterical, fact-free hunt for racists under the bed, has lost its authority in these matters.

For those of you still confused, I'm going to explain what white supremacy is, what the alt-right is, and why I have no love for either.

In late November 2016, *Bloomberg Businessweek* published their annual Jealousy List, a collection of "stories we wish we'd done this year—and don't want you to miss." The list was predictable: *Washington Post, New York Times, Wall Street Journal,* as well as *BuzzFeed* and *Deadspin.*

And then, not so predictably, *Breitbart.*

Bloomberg chose "An Establishment Conservative's Guide to the Alt-Right," a 5,000-word explainer on the controversial movement written by yours truly along with my colleague Allum Bokhari. They were right to pick our story. It was the most influential piece of political journalism published that year.

When we published our exposition, there had been little commentary, and no trace of an authoritative definition of the emerging alt-right. The media stuck to their usual hysterics that accompany the rise of any popular new right-wing movement.

It's profoundly anti-intellectual to substitute moral outrage for genuine understanding, but that was the approach taken by many commentators towards the alt-right when it first emerged. This was grossly unfair: in its early days, the alt-right included a member base as diverse as disaffected Tea Party supporters and eighteen-year old meme addicts curious about a movement that defied so many taboos. Even today, it's not clear-cut. There are Jews who still identify with the alt-right.[21]

National Review portrayed alt-righters as embittered members of the white-working class, which was not correct. "Thuggish alt-right Trumpers" said *Red State*, another conservative outlet hand-wringing about online trolling. *BuzzFeed* described the alt-right as a "white nationalist movement" where "rare Pepes ... are common." (I'll explain what a "Pepe" is later in this chapter.)

BuzzFeed also quoted lawyer Ken White, who lamented that it was "Really hard to tease out the genuine white nationalists from the trolls," but added, "At a certain point the distinction isn't meaningful."[22]

Well, I think the distinction is very meaningful.

To deny the movement's complexity in a frantic effort to advertise their own moral virtue, as so many columnists did on the Left *and* Right, was an act of supreme intellectual dishonesty. The distinguished Jewish political philosopher Leo Strauss insisted scholars should seek "to understand the author as he understood himself."

There's a world of difference between teenagers telling jokes on Twitter about forbidden subjects to wind up whiny SJWs, and someone like Richard Spencer, who wants a "peaceful ethnic cleansing" of the United States.

The definition of alt-right has evolved since we penned our guide. White nationalists and Neo-Nazis took over, and people who initially enjoyed the label were being accused of sins they did not commit. This suited the media just fine. It's weird how obsessed the media is with calling everyone racist, isn't it? It's almost like they want everyone to be racist or something, for some reason. Whatever their reasoning, they were given many more cover story options as a result.

In effect, the extremist fringe of the alt-right and the leftist media worked together to define "alt-right" as something narrow and ugly, and entirely different from the broad, culturally libertarian movement Bokhari and I sketched out. This wanton virtue signaling was wholly unjust to young members of the movement who were flirting with dangerous imagery and boundary pushing. Bokhari and I called them "memesters," and those are the people I will always speak up for. God knows I've dabbled with dangerous iconography myself. I wore just about every political symbol you can imagine in my teens and early-twenties experimentation phase. Not because I have any particular love for the regimes they came from. I just like pissing people off!

There are lot worse things you could do in your youth than shock *National Review* writers on Twitter. As many realized during the 2016 election, *National Review* needed a little shocking.

For the record, flirtation with the alt-right is nowhere near as deplorable as the left-wing extremist youth movements of the 60s and 70s. If you currently attend Columbia University, you might find yourself in a class led by adjunct professor Kathy Boudin, a former Weather Underground terrorist who served twenty years in jail for assisting in the murder of two Nyack, New York policemen, including the first black officer in the precinct.

Even before her release, *Harvard Educational Review* was publishing her articles. Surprise, surprise: if you join a left-wing extremist organization, your life is not going to be ruined.

And of course, if you were a student at the University of Illinois in the early 2000s, you may well have found yourself taught by Obama associate William Charles "Bill" Ayers, an unreformed communist and co-founder of the Weather Underground, responsible for dozens of terrorist attacks on targets ranging from police precincts to the Pentagon.[23]

At least *he* never compared a black person to Harambe on Twitter.

I have no sympathy for Ayers and others who took part in and directed terrorist violence in the 70s. I *would* be sympathetic to someone who hung a Weather Underground flag in their dorm-room because of the rebellious appeal it represented in that era. Young people have always dabbled in radical, dangerous ideas, and so long as such dabbling was only a phase and did not extend into violence, they shouldn't be punished for it later in life. Maajid Nawaz, former member of the Islamist group Hizb Ut-Tahrir and now one of the world's leading anti-extremist campaigners is a perfect example of why we should be lenient about what people do in their youth.

My support of dangerous memes holds, by the way, even if your desire to explode polite taboos includes taking aim at the Holocaust. This is where I lose some of my conservative readers, but hear me out.

What a lot of conservatives don't realize is that no one aged 21 knows anyone who was alive during World War II. And because they're not educated properly, they don't regard anti-Semitism any differently from racism or sexism.

I happen to disagree, strongly, that anti-Semitism is just like racism or sexism. I think it's a unique case, and in my college talks I often underscore what I think is a particularly virulent history of bigotry against Jews. Since there have been Jews, it has always been dangerous to be one, somewhere in the world. But a lot of teenagers I talk to regard right-wing journalists complaining about oven jokes with the same contempt they have for left-wing complaints about racism and sexism. They think it's all a load of crap cooked up to save people's feelings. And when you look at what has passed for anti-Semitism in the age of identity politics, they have a point.

It's simply a fact that Jews are disproportionately well-represented in the media, entertainment industry and in banking. We perform well in those industries! And merely pointing out that statistical success should not be considered anti-Semitic. When you attack people for telling the truth, you lose credibility—and young observers might just lump you in with the race-baiters of Black Lives Matter and the dishonest professional victims who make up the majority of third-wave feminism.

I understand why so many young people find jokes about the Second World War attractive: they drive establishment types, especially conservatives, *absolutely crackers*. And I will defend to the death their right to tweet jokes about gas ovens, no matter how badly their words may burn.

THE ALT-RIGHT DECLARES A HOLY CRUSADE—AGAINST ME

From day one, the media had an agenda with the alt-right: turn it into a synonym for "Neo-Nazi," and then accuse all young conservatives of being members of the movement. It's an old game, and it's growing exceedingly tedious.

Because I was guilty of writing the only even-handed analysis of the alt-right—in other words, I gave them a fair hearing, as I thought journalists were supposed to do—the mainstream media decided to crown me queen of the movement.

I publicly stated numerous times that I was not a member of the alt-right but it didn't make a difference. Nothing would make the media tell the truth: journalists simply lie and lie until their enemies are beaten into submission. I won't be beaten into submission by anything other than a BBC.

The only people who want me at the head of the alt-right are the mainstream media, who have variously described me as a "leader," a "self-proclaimed leader" and a "face" of the movement. These include NPR, BBC, *Bloomberg*, *Daily Beast*, *Daily Telegraph*, *Prospect*, *Evening Standard*, *The New Republic*, and many, many more.

On the one hand, these guys are declaring the alt-right to be a racist, anti-Semitic, homophobic hate group. On the other, they're saying that a gay Jew with a black boyfriend is the head of it. Something doesn't quite add up. But consistency has never been a strong point of the liberal media.

I'm willing to accept there are a few idiots working at NPR and *Daily Beast* who simply don't know better. The rest are just outright liars. No matter how visually appealing my face is, the alt-right does not want me associated with them. Perhaps some of the younger, less serious memesters wouldn't mind, but the hardline, white supremacists are unequivocal about it.

"I am hereby declaring a Holy Crusade against Milo Yiannopoulos, who is the single greatest threat our movement has at this time," wrote *Daily Stormer* editor Andrew Anglin last year.[24] "He is our arch-nemesis. We need to stop this kike."

Frankly, I am overjoyed that both infantile communists and internet Nazis all hate my guts. All the worst people in the world—feminists, cyclists, Black Lives Matter activists, vapers, vegans and, yes, the couple thousand Bitcoin brownshirts living in their parent's basements really, really hate me.

To the idiots at NBC News, *USA Today* and CNN: the editor of the most hard-core alt-right site on the web declared me the movement's "arch-nemesis." I will personally pay $10,000 to any of these failing outlets that report this fact (*I know they need the money*).

Breitbart's former executive chairman Steve Bannon offered a nuanced take on the alt-right to the Wall Street Journal, defining it as, "Younger people who are anti-globalism, very nationalist, terribly anti-establishment."[25] Unfortunately, nuance doesn't play well in the mainstream media. *Breitbart* was repeatedly pigeonholed by the press as an "alt-right" platform. Yes, *Breitbart*, where virtually the entire management team and most senior editors are Jewish, the same *Breitbart* that publishes the *Breitbart Jerusalem* vertical, is supposedly a platform for a movement that, according to the mainstream media, hates Jews and Israel.

The media's ultimate target was the incoming Trump administration, which is why they stepped up their attacks on *Breitbart* after Steve Bannon was appointed to the campaign team. *Huffington Post* and *The Intercept* published mind-bending "explainers" on how Bannon was somehow both anti-Semitic and pro-Israel at the same time. According to *The Independent,* Bannon was an "alt-right media baron" with "the ear of the president." According to the LA Times, the alt-right was actually "Steve Bannon's fringe brand of conservatism."

Once again, the Fake News Media displayed its talent for spinning a web of lies across multiple publications.

But this was 2016, a year that unlike any other proved just how absurd, powerless, and morally bankrupt the press had become. Donald Trump ignored the media pressure and named Bannon his Chief Strategist.

THE FRINGE TAKES OVER

Alt-right is dead. It was killed by the media.

You see, if you call something neo-Nazi long enough, it will invariably attract actual Neo-Nazis and—this may surprise you— scare off normal people.

The alt-right has always had a fringe element of Reich-loving basement-dwellers who describe the Holocaust as a "Holohoax" and want to ban "race-mixing." When Bokhari and I wrote our alt-right guide, these were just one of many factions in it, alongside dissident intellectuals, taboo-breaking kids, and instinctive social conservatives.

An Israel-supporting former Tea Party member was, in those days, just as likely to be drawn to the alt-right as a Richard Spencer devotee, because it was the most exciting, dynamic, and effective right-wing movement to emerge *since* the Tea Party. Even leftist outlets like *BuzzFeed* acknowledged its power to dominate the internet and influence the news cycle.

One week in September, shortly after Hillary Clinton read out several of my headlines in a speech on the alt-right, the national broadcast media spoke of little besides Pepe the Frog. Pepe, for the uninitiated, is a cartoon frog from a web comic that went viral in the mid-noughties. Originally used as a reaction image to signify a poster's emotional response to something (there are "Sad Pepes, Happy Pepes, Angry Pepes and Smug Pepes—a lot like emojis), the frog inexplicably evolved into something of a mascot for the alt-right and for Trump supporters.

Following the classic media playbook of "if you don't understand it, call it racist," the media branded this innocent cartoon frog a "symbol of white supremacy."

We should give thanks to NPR, CNN and the Southern Poverty Law Center for identifying the real causes of racial tension in America. It isn't terrible schools, or black fatherlessness, or constant race-baiting from hucksters like Al Sharpton. No. It's a cartoon frog.

If you're wondering why largely apolitical trolls are attracted to the alt-right, this is it—nothing tickles them more than getting the entire world to discuss one of their memes and desperately try to make sense of it. Double points if it makes people angry and they start calling it names on cable news!

Thanks to the willingness of old-school conservatives to march in lockstep with the mainstream media, the alt-right gradually came to be dominated not by friends of Pepe, but by actual white nationalists. A turning point came shortly after Donald Trump's election victory, when Richard Spencer encouraged a room full of his supporters to "Hail Trump," which about three people promptly did—with so-called "Roman salutes."

Even nominal white identitarians like Paul "RamZPaul" Ramsey decided they'd had enough with the movement after that, and promptly disavowed it.[26]

It increasingly looks like the only people left in the alt-right movement are Holocaust-deniers, Richard Spencer fans and *Daily Stormer* readers. If that's the case, I want nothing to do with the movement—and, as I've made clear, the movement wants nothing to do with me. Still, I can guarantee CNN will continue to refer to me as the alt-right's leader anyway.

The tragedy of the alt-right is that it has some legitimate grievances: demographic transformation, popular anti-white rhetoric, affirmative action, identity politics for some but not others and enforced diversity, to name just a few. But the alt-right won't continue to receive attention for these things. It will continue to be painted as another word for neo-Nazi.

Pepe, I am happy to report, has escaped the redefinition of "alt-right" mostly unscathed, and is still a mascot on college campuses, where he is used as a symbol of dissidence and resistance to progressive Left orthodoxy.

Dangerous

If leftists continue to ignore sensible moderates, like me, the frustrations that animate alt-righters will grow stronger. There is no rampant anti-Semitism in America today—except from Muslims—and there is no widespread white nationalist movement. But one day there might be, if the media keeps calling people like me "white supremacists" because they can't work out how to beat a gay version of Anna Nicole Smith in an argument about campus rape culture. Kimmie!

3

WHY TWITTER HATES ME

In May 2016, Facebook was embroiled in that year's second-biggest tech controversy. The first was my suspension from Twitter. But more about that in a bit.

Facebook had been caught in a lie: its "Trending News" feature, ostensibly designed to provide users with a list of the most popular topics being discussed on the platform that day, was being manipulated.

Despite heralding a new age of free, unfiltered information in its early days, the differences between new media and old media were not so great after all. Both were spoon-feeding information to their readers, deciding for the public what they should and shouldn't see.

It wasn't supposed to be this way.

In the early years of Facebook, the idea of an editor deciding what information you most needed to see was laughable. Equally, there was no algorithm deciding who saw what posts, when, and where. The system was simple: users followed other users, and saw a list of their posts, updated in real-time. Beyond the block button, there was no filtering. If your friend made a post at 6:15 PM, you saw it at 6:15 PM. The present system, where Facebook chooses what you see, when you see it, and how you see it, is a radical departure from its early, democratic ideals.

Facebook says their Trending list is meant to highlight "major events and meaningful conversations;" politically neutral metrics. But it's not hard to predict what will happen when a company in one of the most progressive industries (tech), located in the most progressive city in America (*San Francisco*), trusts its staff (censors) to implement policies neutrally.

In May 2016, it was revealed that Facebook was discriminating against topics of interest to conservatives on its "Trending News" feature. A former employee of the team told *Gizmodo* that in addition to neglecting conservative trends, the company also suppressed stories about itself. And artificially promoted stories about the Black Lives Matter movement.[27]

According to *Gizmodo,* Facebook's team of "news curators" were:

> ...Told to select articles from a list of preferred media outlets that included sites like *The New York Times*, *Time*, *Variety*, and other liberal mainstream outlets. They would regularly avoid sites like *World Star Hip Hop, The Blaze*, and *Breitbart*, but were never explicitly told to suppress those outlets."[28]

A leaked document published in *The Guardian* later confirmed that Facebook would check against a list of preferred mainstream outlets (including BBC, *New York Times,* CNN and FOX) before assigning a story "national-level importance."[29] In other words, it was up to places like CNN to sign off on stories from right-leaning outlets. Can anyone spot the problem?

Facebook's policy of discrimination against conservatives wasn't mandated from the top down, but it didn't need to be. Silicon Valley companies don't have to institute policies of bias against conservatives— all they have to do is give minimal oversight to their overwhelmingly left-leaning employees, and turn a blind eye to the inevitable consequences.

And that's exactly what Facebook did. "We choose what's trending," a former employee told *Gizmodo.* "There was no real standard for measuring what qualified as news and what didn't. It was up to the news curator to decide."

The source told *Gizmodo* exactly what this meant for conservative news, and for progressive news. In short, the former was suppressed ("deep-sixed," according to internal Facebook jargon) while the latter was promoted. Again, from *Gizmodo:*

> Among the deep-sixed or suppressed topics on the list: former IRS official Lois Lerner, who was accused by Republicans of inappropriately scrutinizing conservative groups; Wisconsin Gov. Scott Walker; popular conservative news aggregator the *Drudge Report*; Chris Kyle, the former Navy SEAL who was murdered in 2013; and former FOX News contributor Steven Crowder.

Meanwhile, according to the source, Facebook's left-leaning staff pressured Mark Zuckerberg to use Facebook to help swing the election for Hillary Clinton, and blamed him for not doing enough after she lost.[30] And as for Blacks Lives Matter, "Facebook got a lot of pressure about not having a trending topic for Black Lives Matter," the source said. "When we injected it, everyone started saying, 'Yeah, now I'm seeing it as number one.'"

This particular injection is especially noteworthy because the #BlackLivesMatter movement originated on Facebook, and the ensuing media coverage of the movement often noted its powerful social media presence.

Facebook's political bias scandal took place *after* Twitter's, but unlike Twitter, Facebook actually matters to normal people, so it caused an instant response from politicians. A petition was created by the Republican National Committee, stating, "Facebook Must Answer For Conservative Censorship."

Senator Jim Thune, then Chairman of the Senate Commerce Committee, also called on Facebook to explain itself: "If Facebook presents its Trending Topics section as the result of a neutral, objective algorithm but is in fact subjective," wrote Thune, then "Facebook's assertion that it maintains 'a platform for people and perspectives from across the political spectrum' misleads the public."

Shocked by the response, Facebook leapt into action—they announced a whitewashing "internal report" (which of course found no wrongdoing at the company) and invited a bunch of establishment conservatives to a closed-door meeting at their Menlo Park headquarters.

Breitbart received an invitation to attend the meeting, but unlike S.E Cupp, Glenn Beck and other assorted establishment types, we declined to attend. The invitation was clearly only a photo op, and not a serious effort to engage with conservatives. Instead, I asked

Mark Zuckerberg to answer, in a live debate with me, to the only group who mattered: the millions of conservatives who used his platform. He refused.

I'm a humble man—take a walk if you're still laughing thirty seconds after reading that—I can handle not receiving attention, so my response to Facebook's snub was characteristically gracious and mild. Along with Allum Bokhari, I wrote a series of stories exposing the wacky progressive views of Facebook's Trending news team, leading to them all getting fired and replaced with a computer algorithm. You're welcome, America.

Political activist Pamela Geller, who was banned from Facebook following the Muslim terrorist attack in Orlando, is also not letting the matter of Facebook's bias stand. Geller is currently suing the company, and in an article for *Breitbart*, she explained why:

> I am sick and tired of the suppression of our speech. We are unable to engage in the public square. And yes, Facebook is the public square; it's where we connect. We have to fight for it. Shouting into the wilderness is not freedom of speech. My Facebook page has close to 300,000 followers, and combined with my pages (SIOA, SION, AFDI), the reach is another 100,000. It's a critical connection.
>
> Facebook has immense power over organic media— the sharing of our information and news between friends and associates. I would say too much power. They're trying to change the people by restricting our access to information.[31]

Gun shop owners, immigration hawks, and admins of right-wing meme pages have also all faced censorship from Facebook.

Sadly, out of the leading web companies, Facebook is perhaps the best of the bunch. The impression I get from speaking to Facebook's management behind closed doors is of a company trying desperately to rein in its own hyper-progressive employees. A report from *The Wall Street Journal* revealed that in the middle of the 2016 campaign, Mark Zuckerberg faced pressure from his community standards team to censor content from Donald Trump, whom they argued was engaging in "hate speech." The team even threatened to quit if Trump wasn't censored, but Zuckerberg reportedly held his ground.[32]

Zuckerberg also stood fast when faced with pressure to remove Trump supporter Peter Thiel from Facebook's board, releasing a statement in support of political diversity:

> We care deeply about diversity. That's easy to say when it means standing up for ideas you agree with. It's a lot harder when it means standing up for the rights of people with different viewpoints to say what they care about.[33]

This doesn't make Zuckerberg special. Assuming this isn't a deception (remember, he once called his own users "dumb fucks" for trusting him with their personal data), he's doing the bare minimum of what we expect from social media companies—providing people with a platform to air their opinions, without letting his personal politics get in the way.

Facebook requires constant policing from the conservative media to keep the biases of their staff in check. On numerous occasions, wrongfully suspended accounts—like Pamela Geller's—have only been reinstated following coverage from *Breitbart*. Facebook only took concerns over its Trending news team seriously after the conservative media got involved, and only fired them after *Breitbart* reported on their political biases.

GHOSTBUSTERS

"That trunk of humours, that bolting-hutch of beastliness, that swollen parcel of dropsies, that huge bombard of sack, that stuffed cloak-bag of guts, that roasted Manningtree ox with pudding in his belly, that reverend vice, that grey Iniquity, that father ruffian, that vanity in years."

My love of Shakespeare has provided me with *so* many colorful ways to describe Twitter and its sandal-wearing, hobo-chic CEO Jack Dorsey.

Twitter's stock has declined some 80% since 2014, and user growth has stalled since 2013. Karma and divine retribution are alive and well.

Once the most attention grabbing of the social media platforms, Twitter promised to usher in a new age of instant, democratic free expression. Its character limit encouraged users to share rapid-fire thoughts with the world, without a filter. In its early days, Twitter could justifiably claim it showed us what was on the world's mind at any given moment.

And it was fun! It was fun to watch governments and politicians humbled in the face of the global citizenry's un-moderated opinions. It was fun to engage in the raucous back-and-forth between liberals, conservatives and libertarians, on a platform which, for a while at least, was the opposite of a safe space. It could embarrass governments, kill officially mandated myths, and even topple dictators. It was *dangerous*. Naturally, I was a fan. My Twitter handle was @Nero, a nod to the Roman emperor known for his good looks, artistic soul, and for lighting his enemies on fire.

Twitter was about freedom, fun, and the humbling of authority. It was only a matter of time before progressive crybabies ruined everything. In late 2015, co-founder Jack Dorsey replaced relatively pro-free speech Dick Costolo as permanent CEO. Dorsey, a *very* close friend of DeRay Mckesson, had marched with Black Lives Matter in Ferguson, Missouri.[34] He quickly set about turning Twitter into a sharia-compliant conservative-free zone.

Like any CEO, Dorsey can't admit his political bias openly. On the rare occasions when he does address the issue, he insists that the platform is politically neutral. In an interview with *Today Show's* Matt Lauer, Dorsey flatly denied that Twitter censors anything other than threats of violence, insisting Twitter merely existed to "empower conversation."

Two months after Dorsey became CEO, actor Adam Baldwin received a temporary suspension for a tweet implying that conservatives and libertarians were more sexually attractive than left-wingers. (An observation that has been repeatedly confirmed by surveys and studies.[35]) The tweet broke none of Twitter's rules, yet Baldwin was forced to delete it before his account was restored. This was at the same time angry death threats to Donald Trump were an unchecked daily occurrence. I knew it was only a matter of time before Dorsey came for me.

In October 2015, Fusion referred to me as "the internet's biggest troll" with "terrifying allure." They weren't wrong. A few months later,

MILO

Twitter removed my blue "verified" check mark. Not for any specific reason, they just saw how popular I was becoming and wanted to squash me. For this brave act, *Huffington Post* congratulated the platform for "standing up for women online."[36] Ugh, please.

Verified checks are given out to prominent figures likely to be impersonated. I'm probably the most impersonated individual who isn't Beyoncé, yet Twitter still took away my check mark, for ideological reasons. At the time, it was unprecedented.

I knew from that moment Twitter was looking for any excuse to ban me, and they would eventually find one. I also knew that when they succeeded, all hell would break loose. I wasn't disappointed, although Twitter's shareholders probably are now.

The pretext needed to ban me turned out to be the all-female reboot of *Ghostbusters,* a remarkably bad film that flopped at the box office and contributed to Sony's decision to take a near $1 billion write-down on its movie business.[37] I published a catty review of the abominable flick, tarring it with my trademark reserve, as a crime against comedy. It is perhaps the only movie I've ever seen conceived entirely out of spite, which would have been okay, if it were funny. I castigated the abysmal performances from the lead actresses, including the inexplicably popular Leslie Jones.

The film had been attracting controversy for months before its release. When its trailer debuted on YouTube, it was immediately assailed upon by peeved pop-culture fans of the classic Bill Murray movie. They had read reports about director Paul Feig's plan to reinvent the franchise from the ground up, as well as his seemingly sparse knowledge of the *Ghostbusters* universe. Feig had basically transformed a movie about four out of shape, middle-aged men, three of them white and one black to a chick flick with four out of shape, middle-aged women, three of them white and one black. Groundbreaking.

This, coupled with the fact that the promo video was intensely boring, led to it becoming the most-disliked movie trailer in YouTube's history.

Under normal circumstances, this would not be hugely controversial. Cult franchises like *Ghostbusters* can be treacherous territory: upset the fans and you may be in for a lifetime of loathing. Just think of what fans did to George Lucas after *The Phantom Menace* hit theaters.

But these weren't normal circumstances, and the fan's reaction to *Ghostbusters* quickly became a media and political controversy. Partly as a means to market the movie, Feig and the *Ghostbusters* cast began denouncing its critics as "misogynist" and "right-wing."

The media, amazingly, swallowed this obvious attempt to delegitimize criticism and ran with it. Not just the film media, you understand, but also the political, mainstream and even alternative media. They had their perfect story: four helpless actresses were being preyed upon by hordes of anonymous men. The frantic pro-*Ghostbusters* campaign reached peak absurdity when, after disappointing box office returns, politicians from the California Legislative Women's Caucus gathered at a private screening to watch the movie. After the viewing, their leading members gave what felt to me like a series of pre-arranged statements to journalists, each one of them celebrating the movie as a work of high art and a progressive leap forward.

As always, the smell of butt hurt attracts trolls. *Breitbart* editor Ezra Dulis put it eloquently: "To a Twitter troll, there is no greater rush than a response from an angry celebrity—the knowledge that you, in the middle of Podunkville, USA, have the power to get under the skin of someone rich, famous, and surrounded by ass kissers."[38]

So, when Leslie Jones, one of the four leading actresses in this cinematic train-wreck, began angrily responding to her detractors on Twitter, the result was inevitable. She was feeding the trolls, so they swarmed like frogs on grasshoppers.

Media reports say I was the one who led these swarms. This couldn't be further from the truth. Jones was engaging in running battles with her detractors on Twitter for hours before I got involved, actively trading insults with them and provoking them.

I criticized Jones, tossing a few jabs her way. The reason lefties in the media saw me as ringleader of the trolls is that it's hard for them to imagine people moving collectively *without* a leader. It's their authoritarianism showing: for them, a herd must have a shepherd. The idea of people thinking and acting independently frightens them.

My only crime was daring to criticize a black woman, itself seemingly proof of racism today. I tweeted that Jones was playing the victim,[39] that her character in *Ghostbusters* was an unfunny racial stereotype, and that her tweets were barely literate.[40] All are true. (Despite calling people "bitches" all evening, she had the audacity to report me for that last one.)

Like Mogwai, there are very specific rules to follow when it comes to feeding trolls, or else you'll end up with Gremlins. A small minority tweeted revolting things at Jones, such as comparisons between her and Harambe, the recently deceased gorilla. Jones accused me of supporting the racists tweeting her gorilla pictures (wrong), and she retweeted sycophants accusing me of being a "Gay Uncle Tom." (Later, she would laughably claim the retweets were a result of her "being hacked"). Finally, she blocked me and closed her Twitter account. I sent out a final tweet ("Rejected by yet another black dude!") and left it at that. Another easy victory over a hypocritical, thin-skinned Hollywood celebrity.

I can't stand celebrities with thin skin. Getting hate mail is part and parcel of being famous no matter what you look like. Even someone as ridiculously good-looking as me gets hate mail.

The next day, a day that will live in social media infamy, I was scheduled to headline a "Gays for Trump" party at the Republican National Convention. A few minutes before I was to take the stage, I was banned from Twitter forever. I suspect—but can't prove—that they waited until just before my event deliberately, to cause maximum damage. This is a company whose employees wrote "#SCREWNERO" on a whiteboard in its San Francisco headquarters.[41]

They didn't plan on my preternatural skill for turning every minor setback into a gigantic, glittering triumph.

Like all progressive imbeciles, Twitter HQ was clueless about the Streisand Effect: whenever censorship is attempted, it simply draws more attention to its target. The immediate result of my ban was the greatest barrage of press attention I'd ever received, up until then anyway. I became Patient Zero in Twitter's crusade against conservatives, particularly the Trump-supporting kind. CNN, CNBC, and ABC all wanted me on to talk about it. Sometimes I wonder if my biggest enemies are in fact my biggest friends, and are all secretly helping me out while pretending to be leftists in public.

I was the number-one trending topic for a full day, with tens of thousands of users tweeting #FreeMilo in solidarity. My fans scrawled the slogan in chalk outside Twitter's international network of offices.

MILO

One of my more mischievous fans filmed himself convincing a group of animal rights activists to chant "Free Milo," after persuading them that I was a captive donkey.

Do I feel bad about being a catalyst for Twitter's censorship? No more than Jean-Luc Picard should feel bad about being a catalyst for the Borg's invasion of Federation space.

Despite what you'll have read in the media, I neither tweeted anything racist or harassing at Leslie Jones, nor in any way did I encourage the few anonymous people who did. Twitter says I led "targeted harassment" against Jones, which seems to mean "being famous and having the wrong opinions." My supposed harassment was so bad, Jones was "driven off Twitter." Though it must not have been *that* bad because she was back after 48 hours.

This is a shocking double standard. We don't blame Justin Bieber when he tweets or posts on Instagram about Selena Gomez, prompting death and rape threats toward her. We don't blame Beyoncé for what the Beyhive does to Taylor Swift. They are never held accountable for the actions of their fans by the media. If Bieber or Bey came out as Trump supporters, I guarantee you this would change.

Another thing you won't read in the press is that Leslie Jones directly incited harassment against her critics, the very rule violation I was falsely accused of when Twitter suspended my account. A user suggested to Jones that some introspection might be in order if she wanted to stop the wave of trolling, to which Jones responded with an unequivocal call to dog-pile: "Bitch I want to tell everyone about you but I'm going to let everybody else do it I'm gonna retweet your hate!! Get her!!"[42] In another tweet, she also urged her followers to "go after them like they going after me."[43] Twitter did nothing in the face of these flagrant rule-violations; she didn't even have to delete her tweets to unlock her account, which—as I know well—is the site's mildest form of punishment for a terms-of-service breach.

I don't mean to sound whiny about all this, because my Twitter ban made me a lot more famous. It was one of the best things that ever happened to me. It broke my addiction to the constant little dopamine hits I got from all those retweets and likes. I get a lot more actual work done these days.

Plus, being banned was cool, like Madonna and Andrew Dice Clay being banned from MTV in the 1990s. I joined an elite club of dangerous people banned from Twitter, like musical genius Azealia Banks and right-wing investigative journalist Chuck Johnson. (All three of us are Trump supporters; go figure.) As a result of my Twitter ban, I became, for a huge slice of young America, a forbidden, guilty pleasure. So, yes, I don't mean to whine because I'm not in the least bit sad about it. But it's important to set the record straight when the lying mainstream media comes for you with its usual arsenal of name-calling, hysteria, selective disclosure and outright mendacity.

TWITTER GOES TO THE SUNKEN PLACE

With me out of the way, the Left proceeded in its crusade to censor Twitter, with a barrage of pressure from their allies in politics and media. A host of feminist windbags, including ghoulish Democratic congresswoman Katherine Clark and hand-wringing British Labour MP Stella Creasy, ginned up a panic about "death threats" and "trolls" who were supposedly striking fear into innocent, powerless women on Twitter. (Coincidentally, these women almost always turned out to be professional feminist activists and left-wing politicians.)

The narrative was repeated ad nauseam across national media in both Britain and America. Slowly, the platform that once proclaimed itself "the free speech wing of the free speech party" began to contort into a feminist-friendly safe space. Making a joke about feminists put you at risk for losing your account. But you could tweet #KillAllWhiteMen, #MasculinitySoFragile, or "I BATHE IN MALE TEARS" without a care in the world.

Countless right-wingers have been kicked off Twitter, sometimes temporarily, sometimes permanently,[44] including cultural libertarian YouTuber Sargon of Akkad, and the Canadian writer and anti-feminist Janet Bloomfield. They even put a "safety" filter on all outgoing links to the blog of Vox Day, sci-fi's leading right-wing iconoclast.

Twitter came down hard on the alt-right—after the 2016 election, dozens of the movement's prominent voices got the boot. At the same time, Jerome Hudson, an African-American writer for *Breitbart*, was bombarded with racial slurs including "coon" and "Uncle Tom," instigated by washed-up rapper Talib Kweli, and Twitter took no action.[45] In the two months following the election, social media analytics discovered more than 12,000 tweets calling for the death of Donald Trump—tweets that remain on the platform.[46] Yet Twitter continues to profess its political neutrality. In my time as technology editor for *Breitbart*, I never saw an account suspended for sending death or rape threats to Donald Trump or any other prominent conservative.

Twitter was secretly discriminating against conservative news sources well before the words "fake news" emerged from a progressive news outlet. In February 2016, a source who worked closely with Twitter revealed to *Breitbart* that the company had been "shadowbanning" inconvenient Twitter users and maintained a "whitelist" of trusted news sources.

"Shadowbanning" is the sneaky practice of removing or minimizing a user's posts from public view without alerting the user, who often continues posting, believing nothing has changed. Shortly after Trump's inauguration, Twitter acknowledged they were hiding tweets from search results.[47] They began marking entire accounts as "sensitive content," forcing users to "opt-in" to see certain tweets, rather than opting out, to remove unwanted information. *Drudge Report*, the biggest conservative site on the web, was flagged as "sensitive content" by Twitter.

If Dorsey won't address his platform's blatant bias, he might one day have to answer to the courts. On March 4, 2016, I asked President Obama's Press Secretary, Josh Earnest, about the role Obama might play in reminding social media platforms about the importance of protecting free expression.

Earnest made it clear that even Obama believed that the success of social media platforms is "predicated on the important protection of First Amendment rights to self-expression." He also recommended that Twitter users who feel aggrieved by the platform's policies turn to lawsuits as a response. Several such lawsuits are already in the works.

That was President Obama, the most powerful progressive of the last two decades. If Twitter's censorious direction received stern words from *his* administration, Dorsey ought to be quivering in his Birkenstocks with Trump in office.

The death of Twitter is inevitable at this point, but Dorsey certainly isn't doing anything to slow down the process. Censorship creates a chilling effect, frightening other users from speaking their minds. On Twitter, a site designed for rapid-fire streams of consciousness, that means nothing less than the death of the platform.

There's an impression, put about by the media, abetted by Twitter itself and now, stupidly, accepted by just about everyone, that Twitter's problems and the reason the company hasn't been acquired boil down to "abuse" and "harassment."

Actually, the opposite is true. The history of social networks knows no exception to this simple rule: when you start clamping down on free expression, you die. Twitter is no different. Twitter can't maintain user growth because it's boring (all the cool people left, or have been banned) and because the product is terrible. Not because of "trolls." If trolls were the problem, comment sections, Reddit, 4chan and YouTube would have closed down years ago.

People *love* getting into spats on the internet. Some people spend their whole lives doing it. The only people who object to ridicule and criticism are touchy, fragile celebrities and journalists with brittle egos who can't cope with readers pointing out how biased and stupid they are. Twitter's problem is not that there's too much edgy speech, it's that there's too *little*. Also, Twitter's product is so badly engineered, people who don't want to hear from each other too often do.

I can't believe I'm the only person who understands this.

The media's "war on trolls" is just another kind of class warfare: politically correct, university-educated elites don't like how the working classes speak. They're horrified by the ribald humor, sharp language and raucous tone of blue-collar interactions. So they brand it all as "abuse" and "harassment" and close their comment sections because they are too delicate to engage with ordinary people.

Dangerous

The edgiest and most interesting people have now either left Twitter or been struck off. The platform is dying, and so is the business behind it.[48] You know, I sort of feel bad for anyone banned after 2016. They're so behind the curve.

And as for suspending me because of a spat with Leslie Jones… come off it. I mean, if you're going to sell out your core values to a celebrity, at least pick someone funny and/or talented, or at least pretty.

GOOGLE

Twitter is the Silicon Valley company where progressive bias is most apparent, but Google is the company where it is most dangerous. If Google decides that it doesn't want web users to find something, it would be very difficult to stop them—or even to find out they did anything in the first place. That's probably why, out of all the Silicon Valley companies accused of bias, it was Google's that Donald Trump addressed directly.

The occasion that led him to address it was the release of an explosive video showing bias in Google's search results. In the video, tech channel *SourceFed* demonstrated that searches for Hillary Clinton did not autocomplete to words that were popular searches if they reflected negatively on the Democratic candidate. For example "Hillary Clinton cri" did not autocomplete to the popular search term "Hillary Clinton criminal." This contrasted with the competing, though far less influential Bing and Yahoo search engines, where all search terms autocompleted correctly.[49]

Google denied altering its search recommendations to favor Clinton, saying it does not autocomplete terms that are "offensive or disparaging when displayed in conjunction with a person's name." But a later experiment from prominent psychologist Robert Epstein found it easy to get Google to display negative search terms for Clinton's primary opponent, Bernie Sanders… and for Donald Trump.

Eric Schmidt, CEO of the company that owns Google, is very much in the mold of Tim Cook, Jack Dorsey, and Mark Zuckerberg. But unlike those three, his involvement in politics suggests a *direct* link between his work and his support for left-wing politicians. Schmidt founded The Groundwork, a campaign organization with the sole purpose of putting Hillary Clinton in the White House, by putting Silicon Valley's technological prowess at the campaign's disposal.

WikiLeaks confirmed Schmidt's involvement with the Clinton campaign in an email leak, which included a Democratic staffer acknowledging that Schmidt's group was working "directly and indirectly" with the Clinton team.[50] A leaked email sent from Schmidt himself suggested the creation of a voter database that regularly aggregates "all that is known" about individual voters.[51] Creating such a database is Orwellian in the extreme and sounds daunting, but Google, with its vast quantities of user data, could pull it off with frightening efficiency.

It's not just Clinton, either. A report from *The Intercept* in April 2016 revealed just how close Google's relationship with the Obama administration was.[52] The report showed that Google representatives attended meetings at the White House "more than once a week, on average, from the beginning of Obama's presidency through October 2015."

The Intercept's report also showed how Google operated a "revolving door" with the White House, with employees frequently moving between both. They noted 55 instances of employees leaving Google for federal government jobs during the Obama years; 29 of them went to work directly in the White House. Additionally, 127 government employees left their jobs to work at Google.

With such a close relationship, it's little wonder Eric Schmidt fought so hard to elect Hillary Clinton, the Obama continuity candidate.

One of Robert Epstein's earlier experiments found that manipulation of search results can convince undecided voters to back a candidate with frightening efficiency.[53] In some demographics, Epstein found that the conversion rate was up to 80%.

If conservatives thought mainstream media bias was bad, just wait until they see the effects of search engine bias.

Some might consider conservatives fortunate that tech companies didn't use all the powers at their disposal to influence the election. Google could, if they wanted to, ban all links to *Breitbart,* as could Twitter and Facebook. Ultimately, such a bold move would be a bad business decision—in the current climate, conservatives feel just safe enough on social media not to flock to competing platforms. There is growing awareness that the companies that serve as conduits for speech on the web are no longer politically neutral, but not enough to trigger a mass exodus. Yet.

Conservatives Must Take on Silicon Valley

Given the high-tech forces ranged against him, it's nothing short of a miracle that Donald Trump won the presidency. In 2020, when social media and search engines are likely to wield even more power, he may not be so lucky. If conservatives want to keep winning, they need to get serious about Silicon Valley, and it needs to happen fast.

MILO

Aside from rare exceptions like Peter Thiel, almost everyone in the world of tech *absolutely hates conservatives*. Jack Dorsey is in bed, *cuddling* with Black Lives Matter. He has brought censorious feminists into Twitter to advise the company on who it should ban from the platform.

Mark Zuckerberg, meanwhile, is an ardent globalist who believes the United States should "follow Germany's lead on immigration."

Eric Schmidt is less vocal, but as we saw above, potentially far more dangerous. He already worked to put Hillary Clinton in the White House. Who knows what he learned from her loss, or what he will do to sabotage Trump over the course of his presidency?

The biggest advantage conservatives have on the web is *Drudge Report*, an incredibly well trafficked news aggregator run by conservative media pioneer Matt Drudge. The site can instantly make a story go viral, and has been a constant thorn in the side of progressives seeking dominance of the web. But it's not a social platform. Social media continues to advance, and we cannot allow progressives to monopolize it without a fight.

Social media bias is far more dangerous to conservatives than mainstream media bias. Users believe they're choosing information sources themselves, and are more trusting as a result. If conservatives—including President Trump—want to avoid disaster, they need to get serious about pressuring Silicon Valley to stay honest. They should raise the specter of antitrust, media regulation, and all the other regulatory demons feared by America's social media companies, who have many legal and financial reasons for wanting to remain classified by the courts as politically neutral platforms, even though everyone knows they're not.

Republicans need to get aggressive, they need to constantly scrutinize and investigate social media companies, keeping them under the spotlight at all times. They need to organize around and encourage competitors. It may be difficult for 60-year-old politicians who still need their grandkids to unlock their phones for them, but it's their own political future at stake. Hire an intern, gramps.

As for ordinary users, we need to fight back against companies that now oversee so much of our day-to-day communications. Learn the data laws of your home country—what information social media companies are allowed to keep on your activities, and what they're required to hand over if asked. Find other people who have been treated unjustly by social media companies, and form pressure groups. Organize letter-writing campaigns to your congressmen. Tell conservative and libertarian journalists what's going on. Better yet, start your own business and create a platform that will live up to the original hopes for social media.

Fighting back against politically biased social media companies is the most important battle for conservatives and libertarians in the coming decade. Leftists at a college campus might influence a few hundred other students if they're lucky. A social media company can influence tens of millions. There is no greater danger to free expression and free speech today than the far-left biases of Silicon Valley. Do not let them get away with it.

In the end, the censors always lose. But only if there are enough brave free speech warriors calling for their heads.

4

WHY FEMINISTS HATE ME

*"You don't know how hard it is having to hold on to your keys when
you're walking alone..."*

I'm going to stop her right there. Do these women really think all
men are just raring to fight, no fear of the world, all the time? And
yet *I'm* the sexist.

Also, you have the right to bear arms, bitch. If there's one thing
Buffy taught me it's the ageless equalizing power of weaponry. I don't
walk around with two armed guards because they're so adorable (*they
are*). It's because they make better kill shots than I do.

Feminism is dying. Although it has enormous influence on
politically-correct elites in the media and Hollywood, support for it is
collapsing among ordinary people of all political persuasions, thanks,
at least in part, to hysterical, feminist activists who pedal lies and
conspiracy theories on a daily basis.

Because I'm a compassionate soul, I'm going to explain in this chapter not only why feminists hate me, but also how they can turn things around for themselves. I'm not just doing this because I'm kind. I'm actually fond of giving my enemies a guide to beat me.

It also doesn't hurt that when I explain the real world to feminists it drives them even crazier than they already are. They call it Milosplaining.

The fight for women's rights started in the late 19th century, and focused almost completely on women's suffrage. Although these brave women were hideously ugly, they were pioneers and even heroes. This is generally known as the first wave of feminism.

The second wave, starting in the middle of the twentieth century, was broader, but also grounded in laudable goals: ending sexual harassment in the workplace, ending discrimination, repealing archaic laws enabling marital rape, and, above all, establishing full equality of opportunity for women. Few reasonable people could disagree with their objectives.

Still today, fair-minded women like Christina Hoff Sommers continue to beat the drum for what she calls "freedom feminism;" a feminism that promises equal legal rights and equality of opportunity.

Third wave feminism reared its fishy head in the 1990s. The feminism Sommers speaks of is almost unrecognizable in their messaging.

To understand what it is third wave feminists want, look at what they spend their time on now.

Manspreading: a term used to describe the practice of spreading your legs apart on public transport. This alleged sexist outrage, which grew out of a feminist Tumblr blog, was made illegal in the city of New York.[54]

Mansplaining: the grievous sin of explaining something to a woman whilst being male. Manthreading: doing the same, on social media. Not illegal... yet.

Eggplant emojis have also drawn the attention of third-wave feminists. According to one blogger, they're the "next frontier in online harassment."[55] Eggplants look too similar to purple penises, apparently. In a sign of just how eager mainstream society is to please feminists, Instagram banned the eggplant. I've since switched to using the Eiffel Tower emoji when my boyfriend asks me what I want for dinner. Don't anyone tell *Jezebel*.

Air conditioning is also sexist. Men can deal with the cold better, feminists say, and obstinately keep it cranked up.[56] You know, I also get cold quite easily, but I've never considered turning it into a sociopolitical issue.

How did all these things come to be nationally politicized, at a time when fewer than one in five American women describes herself as a feminist? How and why did corporations start taking complaints from New York bloggers seriously, when their actual customers so clearly don't give a shit? As the politically moderate columnist Heather Wilhelm puts it, "I didn't leave feminism, it left me."

Wilhelm's sentiment is shared by increasing swathes of the western public, male and female, liberal and conservative. Feminism describes itself merely as a movement for female equality. But it behaves like something quite different: a vindictive, spiteful, mean-spirited festival of man-hating.

In Britain, only 7% of people choose to label themselves as feminist.[57] In America, the number is higher: 18%, according to a *Vox* poll.[58] Another poll from *YouGov* and *The Huffington Post* found that 23% of women and 16% of men identified with the term.[59] The number of people who identify as feminists in the West is approaching the number of people who believe that blacks are innately inferior to whites.[60] (That's fewer than 10%.)

Researchers at the University of Toronto discovered that people who were already inclined to favor feminist causes were less likely to do so if they came into contact with a "stereotypical" feminist activist.[61] The more people *see* feminists, the less likely they are to *identify* with feminism... even if they're already feminists! The researchers concluded that feminists and other activists ought to behave in a less abrasive manner if they want to win support for their causes.

Fortunately for meme creators, feminists continue to do the exact opposite.

MANHATERS

When you tell a feminist you don't believe in feminism, she'll often respond with the inane line, "So you don't believe in equality for women!" Yet in both polls referenced earlier in this chapter, overwhelming majorities supported equality of the sexes—86% of men and 74% of women in the U.K, and 85% overall in the U.S.

Can you think of any other topic that you can get 85% of Americans to agree on? This is a country where 5% of people believe Paul McCartney died in 1966 and was replaced by a double, and 14% are unsure.[62]

Clearly, both genders overwhelmingly believe that feminism and equality no longer mean the same thing.

In 2013, feminist filmmaker Cassie Jaye began making a documentary about the Men's Rights Movement (MRM), feminism's favorite boogeymen. Jaye went into the project with the assumption that she was going to be examining a hate group—that's what feminist bloggers and activists were then branding the MRM.

MILO

The facts didn't match the narrative.

A *Breitbart* analysis of stories on NPR's website showed there are 2.8 times as many stories on women's cancers as men's. Bringing that up in public is a guaranteed route to sneers and ridicule from journalists, regardless of mortality rates. The phrase "men's rights" means "misogyny" to the mainstream press.

On top of the lack of publicity, there is a huge gap in research funding. Prostate cancer sufferers are approximately 10% more likely to survive the disease than those with breast cancer,[63] but figures from the National Cancer Institute show annual funding for breast cancer outstripping that of prostate cancer by double or more.[64]

It's not just cancer, either. In the top ten causes of death—heart disease, cancer, stroke, chronic obstructive pulmonary disease, accidents, pneumonia and influenza, diabetes, suicide, kidney disease, and chronic liver disease and cirrhosis—men are more likely to die than women. According to 2014 figures, American women have an average life expectancy of 81.2 years. For men, it's 76.4.[65]

The gender *health* gap is very real, unlike the gender *wage* gap, which is completely explained by life choices. The gender wage gap gives feminists something to complain about and pick up cushy diversity consulting gigs to "fix," while the gender health gap leaves men in coffins.

Suicide is frequently described as a "silent epidemic" thanks to the rapid increase in the number of victims over the past decade. It would not be a silent epidemic if the numbers skewed even slightly toward women. CDC research tracking suicides from 1999 to 2014 found that the rate of male suicide increased 62% faster than the rate of female suicide.[66] Men are now more than 4 times as likely as women to die by their own hand. A typical third-wave feminist response to this epidemic? #IBatheInMaleTears.

The MRM has other complaints. There's a lack of resources for male victims of domestic violence. In Britain, for example, there are just 78 spaces in the *entire country* that can be used as shelters for male victims of domestic violence, compared to approximately 4,000 for women, despite the fact that women and men suffer domestic violence at roughly similar rates. Even left-wing sources acknowledge this.[67]

There's disparity in prison sentencing. A study from the University of Michigan found that on average, men receive sentences that are 63% higher than women, for the same crimes committed in the United States.[68] One case in Britain neatly summed up the problem: a woman was spared jail despite stealing £38,000 from her company's debit card, because the judge, in his own words, "hates sending women to prison."[69]

When a feminist tells you some lie about women earning 79 cents to a man's dollar, remind her that in some U.S. states, custody courts award mother's full time custody 72% of the time.[70] Now that's *actual* discrimination. The National Organization for Women's website boasts of their opposition to "joint custody." On what grounds? "Increased father involvement does not necessarily result in positive outcomes for children."[71] Yeah, like those uber-dykes at NOW could get anyone to put a baby in them. I'd rather mouth-fuck Sloth from *Goonies* than go to bed with one of them.

These issues alone—putting aside all the other complaints of the MRM, from military conscription to workplace fatalities to false rape accusations—are more than enough to justify male advocacy. And even if feminists were concerned by the rhetoric of the Men's Rights Movement, they would have to be monstrously sociopathic to try to stop a respectable, feminist filmmaker like Cassie Jaye from carrying out an impartial investigation of these issues. Wouldn't they?

Earlier in this book I mentioned how mercilessly the Left treats perceived "traitors" to its identity-driven crusades. Jaye was no exception. Despite having a track record of acclaimed work, with two award-winning documentaries under her belt, Jaye found herself cut off from traditional routes of support. When I interviewed her for *Breitbart*, she told me that initial grants were withdrawn once it became apparent that she wanted to take a balanced look at the movement. "We weren't finding executive producers who wanted to take a balanced approach, we found people who wanted to make a feminist film."[72]

In her search for funding, Jaye learned more about the institutional bias against men's issues. "There are no categories for men's films though there are several for women and minorities. I submitted the film to human rights categories, and was rejected by all of them." Jaye eventually had no choice but to turn to an internet crowd-funding campaign, which *Breitbart* and a gang of other deplorables lent support to. After I wrote a story about Jaye's movie, it was funded in a day.

What does it say about society's hostility to men's issues that it took a right-wing provocateur like me to get this documentary off the ground? Where was the establishment, with its supposed commitment to equality and fairness and human rights? And why can't people talk about this stuff without getting shouted down or ejected from polite society?

Feminists and the establishment weren't content to simply not fund Jaye's documentary—they accused Jaye of having a "weird affinity for bigots" and actively encouraged boycotts of the film.[73] In Australia, the cinema slated to host the premiere of the movie pulled out following a pressure campaign.[74]

Jaye had betrayed the sisterhood, and the claws were out. All it took was the mere hint of an honest, impartial look at men's issues. Is it any wonder that people no longer associate feminism with equality of the sexes?

On the rare occasions society does take notice of men's issues, feminists are usually there to spoil the party.

"Movember" is an annual event in which men grow their mustaches to raise awareness for prostate cancer—a whimsical grassroots effort, it is one of the few instances in which awareness of a male cancer briefly rises to the fore.

Feminists, instead of helping, regularly complain about the press attention it receives. The left-wing *New Statesman* complained that Movember is "divisive, gender normative, racist and ineffective." Why racist? Because "large numbers of minority ethnic men" use mustaches as a "cultural or religious signifier." (Or maybe because some races can't grow facial hair.) An article in Rabble, a Canadian news site, complained about sexist "Mo Bros" and their "exclusionary" behavior.[75]

Slate published an article from two feminists whining that Movember "celebrated masculinity" in order to fight cancer. They meant it as a criticism. They wrote: "Are we grumpy contrarians and feminist killjoys who hate things precisely because other people love them? Probably, but…" Well, at least they have some self-awareness, that's rare for feminists these days.

Testicular cancer is also one of the few men's diseases with a grassroots awareness campaign, #CockInASock. It's fairly self-explanatory, especially if you're familiar with the Red Hot Chili Peppers, and receives wide praise in *Huffington Post* and *BuzzFeed*. Articles show chiseled men exposing most of their body to raise awareness. *VICE* published an article condemning #CockInASock as an "inane counterpart" to the breast cancer awareness #nomakeupselfie, and claimed, "Without exception, everyone who's doing it is a douchebag."[76]

Fashionista celebrated the "objectification of the male form" but complained that the common sight of pubic hair exposed a sexist double standard (men don't have to shave and women do).[77] Once again, feminists were taking a male advocacy campaign and trying to make it all about them and their hair problems.

The University of York's equality and diversity committee announced they would mark International Men's Day with an event addressing men's issues, particularly suicide. A campaign from more than 200 activist students and professors demanded the event be cancelled. "We believe that men's issues cannot be approached in the same way as unfairness and discrimination towards women, because women are structurally unequal to men," said an open letter. The University of York quickly complied and cancelled the celebration.

This happened less than 24 hours after a male student at York killed himself.[78]

As the examples above demonstrate, we are living in an era when much of the feminism on display to the public is petty, mean-spirited, obsessed with trivialities, man-hating and implacably opposed to free expression. When men try to talk about their problems—not something many men are comfortable doing in the first place—they are treated with indifference, anger, or scorn by feminists.

Hatred has engulfed the politics of the Left. Socialists hate the financially successful. LGBT activists hate fundamentalist Christians. Black Lives Matter hate police officers. Fat people hate skinny people, like me and Ann Coulter. But none of these groups hate with the PMS-fueled pettiness of feminism. Here are a few more examples. In 2015, British student activist Bahar Mustafa was pictured beneath a sign on a door reading "no white-cis-men pls," while she made a faux tearful gesture beneath it. She had already attracted controversy for banning "cis-gendered"[79] white males from the screening of a film at her university's student union, of which she then was a representative.

The incident occurred just as the mainstream press became aware of the return of segregation on campuses, under the guise of "safe spaces" for women and minorities. As the press dug through Mustafa's history, they found tweets in which she used #KillAllWhiteMen and #WhiteTrash. Moderate liberals and establishment conservatives alike huffed and puffed.

Mustafa was eventually put on trial for hate speech, a ridiculous charge for which she was eventually cleared. As odious as Mustafa's opinions were, it's better they were out in the open, rather than have her *Gone Girl* some poor unsuspecting chap.

Mustafa wasn't the first of her kind—she was just the first the media took notice of. The "nu-feminist," or "fourth-wave feminist" Left has been running rampant for years, often with the tolerance and even tacit approval of the establishment. Mustafa was set upon because she was an easy target; less easy a target was Jessica Valenti, who proudly posed for pictures wearing a sweater bearing the slogan "I BATHE

IN MALE TEARS" more than a full year before that. The picture was taken at the beach but luckily for all, it was cropped so you only saw a smidge of her fat legs.

Valenti is a columnist at *The Guardian* and therefore considered a protected class by other journalists. No one should ever be investigated for hate speech, as Mustafa was, but it's clear from the example of Valenti, who once wrote the headline, "Feminists Don't Hate Men, but it Wouldn't Matter if We Did," that feminists today are in no way concerned about equality of the sexes.

Many will say I've written far worse than Valenti. I have! But *I'm* not trying to lead a self-proclaimed equality movement. The only cause I represent is that of free speech, where I consider myself part of a long line of boundary-pushers who shocked the mainstream, from Andres Serrano of *Piss Christ* fame to George Carlin. If I *were* the leader of an egalitarian movement, it would deserve to be unpopular!

The problem with feminists isn't that they're hateful and outrageous, it's that they're hateful and outrageous while claiming to be just, moral, caring, and egalitarian. Plus almost everything that comes out of their mouths is a blatant lie, which will be covered up by more lies and screeching insults if you dare to call them out on it.

LIARS

On November 14, 2014, *Rolling Stone* published the now-infamous article, "A Rape on Campus: A Brutal Assault and Struggle for Justice at UVA." It told the story of Jackie, a female student at University of Virginia, who claimed to have been repeatedly raped by members of the Phi Kappa Psi fraternity.

I heard voices and I started to scream and someone pummeled into me and told me to shut up. And that's when I tripped and fell against the coffee table and it smashed underneath me and this other boy, who was throwing his weight on top of me. Then one of them grabbed my shoulders… One of them put his hand over my mouth and I bit him – and he straight-up punched me in the face… One of them said, 'Grab its motherfucking leg.' As soon as they said it, I knew they were going to rape me.[80]

Horrifying. It almost sounds too gruesome and sadistic to be true. Well, that's because it wasn't.

Within days of publication, the story began to unravel. Journalist Richard Bradley first began to raise questions about the story on his personal blog, followed by conservative pundit Steve Sailer. Bradley pointed out that Sabrina Rubin Erdely, the *Rolling Stone* journalist who wrote the story, failed to identify or reach out to any of the men who, according to Jackie, repeatedly raped her. Nor did she appear to have identified or communicated with two friends of Jackie's, who allegedly corroborated her story.

The Washington Post eventually did track down the two "corroborators," only to receive a completely different account from them. They told the *Post* they felt Jackie had "manipulated" them, and that they had requested their names be taken out of the *Rolling Stone* article, to no avail. It also emerged that *Rolling Stone* had agreed, at Jackie's request, not to contact any of her alleged attackers for their side of the story.

A subsequent police investigation involving 70 people, including Jackie's friends, colleagues, and members of the Phi Kappa Psi fraternity found no one to corroborate her story. By mid-2015, *Rolling Stone's* article had been retracted and removed from the site, the editor responsible for publishing the story had resigned, and the magazine was facing multiple lawsuits.

Rolling Stone's humiliation came at the height of "rape culture" panic on college campuses, in which feminist activists convinced the media, as well as the White House, that college-aged women were being raped at levels comparable to war-torn, lawless countries like the Democratic Republic of Congo.

The statistic they endlessly trot out is that one in four women will be sexually assaulted during their time at college, a number they arrive at based on surveys even the conducting researchers admit are likely to be inflated by response bias.[81] Actually reliable statistics, from the Bureau of Justice, put the figure at 6.1 per 1,000 for students and 7.6 per 1,000 for non-students.[82] Still too many, but not even close to the number President Obama has repeated. In 2015, 89% of colleges reported zero campus rapes.[83]

If you want a clear example of the power of "fake news," consider what the rape culture narrative did to American college campuses. Miscarriages of justice up and down the country. Colleges facing crippling lawsuits from students. Male and female undergraduates terrified of one another—the former of being dragged through the new kangaroo courts springing up on college campuses, and the latter of a rape panic that paints college-aged men as insatiable, psychopathic monsters.

Virtually every media outlet insisted that some variation of "lad banter" and "frat culture" was responsible for a new epidemic of rape. Video game developers found themselves being accused of "rape culture" if they made their characters too sexy. Newsstands faced pressure to take raunchy magazines off shelves. *Blurred Lines,* an innocuous pop song by Robin Thicke, was portrayed across the media as a "rape anthem" for the line, "I know you want it." The song was banned from multiple college campuses in Britain and America.

Making it all worse, any criticism of feminist commentators was portrayed in the media as unquenchable misogyny.

I find it hard to understand how everyone allowed themselves to be hoodwinked for so long by this idea of "rape culture." Rape has existed since the first caveman saw a cavewoman with less facial hair than usual and picked up a bone club. How did we get the idea that it's a brand new crisis, worse than it's ever been? The crime statistics are inarguable: rape has declined nearly 75% since the early 1990s and continues to plummet.[84]

For some time now, feminists have preferred fiction and feelings to facts and reason. As discrimination against women has largely disappeared, feminists have had to invent new, fake problems in order to stay relevant and have something to be angry about. "Campus rape culture" is a particularly egregious and damaging example, but there are many more.

Baby Killers

Pro-life used to be a feminist ideal: the original feminists, like Mary Wollstonecraft and Susan B. Anthony, denounced abortion.

Abortion is murder. Abortion is wrong. I think everyone knows that, which is why abortion activists are so angry all the time. It's like when you catch someone in a lie and they get mad at you. It's the guilt, you see.

MILO

When I say abortion is wrong, its defenders leap to their feet, demanding to know why I want to jail a ten-year-old rape victim. Well, guess what? I don't want to jail that girl, and I defy you to find any opponent of abortion who does.

The Catholic Church provided graceful reasoning on moral dilemmas long before the first feminist had a hissy fit. In principle, the direct, intentional taking of innocent human life is wrong. Because that's a principle, it's easy to say that, even in the most heartbreaking case, like that of the ten-year-old we're considering, it cannot be right to take the innocent life growing inside her.

But as Western civilization has always understood, hard cases make bad law. As St. Thomas Aquinas said, "Human laws do not forbid all vices, from which the virtuous abstain, but only the more grievous vices, from which it is possible for the majority to abstain." In other words, it's not wise to punish with human law everything that may be opposed to the natural law.

Thomas Aquinas wasn't the kill-joy puritan your lying professors claim: St. Thomas and before him St. Augustine both followed anti-utopian views, for instance, when it came to prostitution. They thought it was wrong to do, but foolish to make illegal. I don't think they'd approve of hooking for haute couture, so my twenties still required in-depth Confessions.

The Aquinian distinction between human and divine law means I can say it's wrong to take innocent life, without having to say that we should outlaw abortions in every single case. In a sane country, we would argue about which cases should be illegal.

However, just because I don't believe abortion ought to be outlawed in all cases doesn't mean I don't find it appalling. Feminist campaigners like the harpies behind "#ShoutYourAbortion" (which is exactly what it sounds like—women boasting about their abortion) want to turn baby-killing into a token of pride. These women are the worst humanity has to offer.

Even if abortion had no negative effects on the person who undertakes it, it would still be wrong. But just in case you need more persuading that murdering children ought to be frowned upon, consider the effects on the mother. In 2010, the Canadian Journal of Psychiatry published a study based on a sample of 3,000 women in the United States. It found 59% increased risk for suicidal thoughts, 61% increased risk for mood disorders, and a 261% increased risk for alcohol abuse.[85] In a sense, the law doesn't have to punish those who have abortion; the guilt itself is a punishment. Removing any sense of guilt from having an abortion is not protecting the mother's feelings; it's making things worse.

Abortion is obviously bad for the future women it murders (sex selective abortion is becoming common in the UK and other countries with growing Muslim populations), and also has disastrous effects on the lives of the women that kill their children. It doesn't surprise me that feminism promotes abortion, because feminism seems to always go against the actual interests of women.

Abortion is particularly horrifying given the widespread availability of contraception. Given the ease with which women can now avoid becoming pregnant, having to have an abortion, outside unusual cases like rape, is the height of irresponsibility.

Not that the widespread availability of contraception is a good thing. I've said it before and I'll say it again: birth control makes women unattractive and crazy. I first articulated this in an article for *Breitbart*, and one of the best days in my life was when Hillary Clinton used it in one of her campaign speeches to bolster her supporter's fear of the Right.

Hillary can whine all she wants, but my statement remains true. There is copious evidence in my favor. Studies have shown that women using the birth control pill DMPA gain an average of 11 pounds over three to four years.[86] Cellulite—also known as "cottage cheese thighs"—only emerged after the invention of the pill.[87] Women who take the pill regularly won't receive the natural attractiveness boost that fertile women receive every month.[88] The pill even makes women more incestuous, i.e. attracted to men that are genetically closer to them.[89]

While the ability to choose when they become pregnant was no doubt a source of great liberation and comfort for women, western birth rates have plummeted in the decades following the mainstreaming of contraception. Comfort isn't necessarily a good thing.

That goes for men too, by the way. Unexpected parenthood used to be an important test of a man's virtue. Would a man, suddenly a father, stick around and raise his child, or move on to the next girl? If women are wondering why men have suddenly become such assholes, it's because there is now virtually no downside to hitting and quitting, and easy access to contraception shares a large part of the blame.

ANTI-SCIENCE

Feminist's denial of facts isn't contained to recent panics like rape culture. Some feminist myths have been circulating for decades. Like the pay gap. Taken as an article of faith by business leaders and politicians alike, this feminist lie claims that women (on average) are only paid 79 cents for every dollar earned by a man.

Study after study[90] show the wage gap shrinks to nonexistence when relevant, non-sexist factors like chosen career paths, chosen work hours and chosen career discontinuity are taken into account.

The key word is *chosen*. It's true, there is a gap between the average pay of men and the average pay of women. It's also true that 93% of workplace deaths were men in 2015.[91] And most the remaining 7% were probably lesbians.

The wage gap is almost entirely explained by women's choices. Men prefer technical jobs; women prefer people-oriented professions.

When the debate reaches this stage, feminists will usually pivot and make one of two arguments: (a) that "women's jobs" should be higher-paying or (b) that the pernicious social influence of the patriarchy brainwashes women into staying away from high-paying STEM (science, technology, engineering and mathematics) fields.

In its economic illiteracy, the former argument reveals the Marxist pedigree of third-wave feminism.

The latter is a Gordian knot feminists can't unravel, and they're too proud to turn it over to a man. They say they want more women in STEM, yet also encourage women to sign up for worthless gender-studies degrees. As Christina Hoff Sommers says, "Want to close the wage gap? Step one: Change your major from feminist dance therapy to electrical engineering." No feminists ever do.

The feminist war on science doesn't end there. (Oh, you thought Republicans were the ones waging war on science? Think again.[92]) Possibly a greater intellectual travesty is what feminists have done to the study of gender differences, which ought to be one of the most rapidly expanding frontiers in our understanding of ourselves, but, under the direction of feminists and left-wing universities, has withered into mindless repetition of 1960s social-science shibboleths.

One of the reasons feminists fight so hard to stop big-box retailers selling "girl toys" (dolls houses, baby pushchairs, stuffed toys) and "boy toys" (action figures, toy trucks, building sets) is because they fervently believe these innocuous playthings socialize men and women into their respective gender roles. They believe, or say they believe, that if you make a girl play with a truck or a train set, she'll be more likely to grow up to be an engineer.

Thanks to decades of pseudoscience from feminist academics and left-wing sociologists, this last argument can be tricky to unravel. Thankfully, some of the era's foremost psychologists—Steven Pinker, David Buss, Robert Plomin, Simon Baron-Cohen—have spent much of their careers doing just that.

The sum total of their research is overwhelming: gender roles are largely governed by nature, not nurture, as feminists would have you believe. The most compelling research comes from Baron-Cohen, perhaps the world's leading autism researcher. Baron-Cohen grew interested in gender roles after he noticed that boys were approximately four times more likely to be diagnosed with autism than girls.[93] He knew autism was correlated with over-systemizing, or an over-technical brain. So he decided to test if boys really were, as the old sexists believed, born with more technically-oriented brains than women.

The lynchpin of the feminist argument that women are made, not born, is the claim that girls are socialized into their female roles during their early childhood. In order to test this claim, Baron-Cohen decided to run experiments on newborn babies—before any socialization could take effect. He provided male and female babies with a physical-mechanical object (a mobile) and a social object (a face). Lo and behold, the male babies showed greater interest in the mobile, while the female babies showed more interest in the face.

Other studies also drive home the inescapable reality that men and women are simply wired differently. Surveys of women across countries have found that women in developing countries, where jobs and resources are scarce, are more likely to enter STEM fields.[94] Yet in the vastly more feminist west, where women have greater financial security and career choices, women choose different professions. In other words, when women have a choice, they don't choose STEM.

That's not to say women don't find *any* scientific fields appealing. Psychology (people oriented) and biology (plants, animals, and again people) are both dominated by women, as is veterinary medicine. Whenever I meet a feminist who claims that the patriarchy prevents women from going into astrophysics and computer science, I always ask them why it hasn't also prevented them from going into biology, where 58% of bachelor, master, and doctorate degrees are given to women.[95] I've yet to receive a persuasive response.

There is more. Men and women respond differently to stress—women prefer to be with people, while men prefer to be alone.[96] Men and women also experience romantic jealousy differently—men are more upset by sexual infidelity, while women are more upset by emotional infidelity.[97] Gender differences can also be observed in entertainment—men prefer realistic shooters and competitive video games, while women prefer social games like *The Sims*.

MILO

Men prefer action movies, women prefer rom-coms. No matter how hard the leftists of entertainment try to change things, men and women continue to give money to the products they like.

Perhaps the most hilarious example of feminists' desperate attempts to preserve the fiction of socially constructed gender roles is their efforts to exclude transgender people from the movement. Feminists would be totally fine with trannies if they didn't pose an existential threat to decades of gender pseudoscience. Male-to-female trannies say they are women born in a man's body. The comparatively rarer female-to-male trannies say they are men born in a woman's body. In both cases, they're affirming the idea that gender is something we're born with, not something that society imposes upon us. Worse, trannies tend to reaffirm gender roles in their behaviors: male-to-female trannies will wear skirts and lipstick and make their voices as feminine as possible to "pass" as a woman. Female-to-male trannies, similarly, are obsessed with growing chest hair.

You can see why some feminists are frustrated. After decades of trying to persuade women to burn their bras and shave their heads, along come a bunch of trannies with YouTube makeup tutorials and high-pitched girly accents. As Julie Bindel, a prominent feminist critic of transgenderism says, "It is precisely this idea that certain distinct behaviors are appropriate for males and females that underlies feminist criticism of the phenomenon of 'transgenderism.'"[98]

Feminists may be right, and trannies may simply be mentally ill rather than "born the wrong gender." But it has nonetheless led to one of the longest-running internal feuds in feminism, the battle between so-called "Trans Exclusionary Radical Feminists" (TERFs) and the hipper, pro-trans wing of feminism. ("TERF," how appropriate given radical feminist's tendency for rug-munching).

The latter faction, which tends to skew younger and less academic (which perhaps is why they don't fully grasp the danger that the "born this way" concept poses to feminism), has had the upper hand in recent years, successfully banning anti-trans feminists like Bindel and Germaine Greer from university campuses. I wish both sides the best of luck. I'll be in the wings, eating popcorn and giggling.

There is now an overwhelming array of evidence against the out-of-date, 1960s theory that gender is socially constructed. But really, we don't even need it, do we? Unless you live in your basement for your entire life (and some men do, but only men!), the reality of gender differences is inescapable.

Nothing is more amusing than watching the frustration of feminist parents as they come to terms with this reality. Shannon Proudfoot, a writer for the left-leaning Canadian magazine *Maclean's*, lamented on social media that she could "already see her daughter preferring pink."

"I have no idea why because we've worked so hard to avoid that," wailed Proudfoot.

Joel Wood, an assistant professor at Thompson Rivers University quickly replied with some emotional support. "Pink and Disney princesses... we tried to discourage them, but our daughters gravitated towards both."[99]

I find the anecdote both hilarious and uplifting. It's hilarious, in the same way that watching a cartoon villain humiliated by a plucky hero is hilarious, and it's uplifting because no matter how hard leftists try, they simply can't beat human nature. Why are they trying to force their daughters to reject what they like in the first place?

MILO

Beyond their ignorance of the facts, modern feminists fail to understand the inherent value and beauty of gender roles. The masculine and the feminine, and their interplay throughout history, have been responsible for some of the greatest expressions of art and culture, from *Tristan and Isolde* to even *Titanic*. Could Shakespeare have written *Romeo and Juliet* without a healthy understanding of men, women, and their essential differences? Jane Austen did not become one of the most renowned authors in the English language by having her characters dye their armpit hair and join a lesbian commune. Her protagonists relished in their femininity even as they struggled with it. Gender differences are part of the human experience.

In pursuit of their hare-brained crusade to destroy gender roles, feminists want to control the lives of boys and girls in minute detail. Ordinary people recognize this for what it is: authoritarianism.

If feminists want to regain credibility, and perhaps tackle the issues that still matter to women, they will first have to come to terms with reality—and that starts with the reality of gender roles.

More importantly, they will have to rediscover a commitment to free speech and start showing up to debates again, armed with facts instead of feelings.

MANIPULATORS

I often face accusations that I'm too harsh toward feminists, and I can see why people say so. After all, I don't just critique feminist arguments, do I? I never miss a chance to draw attention to their appearance. And let's face facts: some of them look *frightful*. My old favorite Lena Dunham is a particular travesty, being both shockingly unattractive and determined to pose nude or semi-nude at every chance she gets. And she *loves* bitching about how people give her a hard time about it. So as a thoughtful gentleman, I will comply. No one wants to see obese hairy men with their tops off, so why does she assume people want to see her sprawling naked like a beached manatee? I just don't understand it. Luckily for all of us, the stress of President Trump is getting her skinny. That's my Daddy, always helping the helpless.

I will readily admit that my fixation on appearance is part of my faggy obsession with aesthetics. Like a true gay stereotype, I used to do a lot of interior design. Bad aesthetics offend me on a visceral level, and I can't help but point them out on both men and women. I often draw attention to the pallid complexions and thinning hairlines of my male opponents—but enough about Ben Shapiro.

If there wasn't a point to my appearance-focused one-liners, if they served no greater purpose, and if all they accomplished was mere cruelty, I would happily contain my impulses. However, there is an important, underlying point to this that most people overlook.

It's so much fun!

Okay, okay, I'm kidding. It's this.

Anyone who has paid close attention to the evolution of the Left over the past few decades will have noticed that it's taken a decidedly *therapeutic* turn. This is the subject of books like *Therapy Culture* by Frank Furedi and *One Nation Under Therapy* by Christina Hoff Sommers, which charts the rising trend to treat feelings and emotions as things to be protected rather than challenged. On campuses, this instinct finds its expression in "trigger warnings," demanded by SJWs to warn students in advance of content—lectures, books, films, or works of art—that might hurt (or "trigger") them.

MILO

At the University of Oxford, law students demanded trigger warnings before lectures on sexual assault law, on the grounds that such subject matter is potentially distressing. The thought that law students should seek to toughen up on issues they'd have to defend in open court apparently never occurred to them.

The Left's embrace of therapy culture has led damaged people to gravitate to the movement. And why wouldn't they? Instead of encouraging people to change themselves, the Left tells vulnerable people that they should instead change the environment around them to protect themselves from having their feelings hurt. "It's not your fault," the Left soothingly coos. "It's *society*."

Obesity, a disorder that is as much mental as physical, gets the same treatment. More than a third of adults are obese in the United States, with nearly 70% classified as overweight in some way.[100] Furthermore, health problems caused by obesity are one of the biggest causes of healthcare expenditure, with estimates of the annual cost ranging from $147 billion to $210 billion per year. Obese employees are also estimated to cost employers an extra $506 per obese worker per year.[101] Being fat is damaging to society as well as to the individual.

And what does the Left do in the face of this crisis? Michelle Obama, at least, has campaigned for better diets and active lifestyles for children, even if the meals her campaign produced are disgusting, and systematically thrown away by children. But the radical Left, the intersectional feminist Left, the Left that dreams up new categories of oppression, has responded by declaring that the *feelings* of fat people are more important than their *health*.

I encountered the result of this during my college tour, at the University of Massachusetts at Amherst. There I was confronted with a morbidly obese girl who interrupted a joint event featuring myself, radio host Steven Crowder, and Christina Hoff Sommers. Her interruption consisted of loudly screaming "KEEP YOUR HATE SPEECH OFF THIS CAMPUS!" while flailing her meaty arms over her head. The video of her outburst instantly went viral online, and she became known as "Trigglypuff."

Later, the internet would discover that she gave presentations on "fat acceptance" and "body positivity," two new concepts dreamed up by intersectional feminists. Their attitude is summed up in one dreadful slogan: "Healthy at Every Size."

The internet was quick to mock, but I wasn't. Trigglypuff had been sucked in by an ideology that promised her shelter from the hurtful realities of the world, where weight loss is a prerequisite of health, not to mention happiness and social acceptance. The Left received an eager foot soldier who proselytized its ideology and shouted down those who challenged it. In return, Trigglypuff received the misleading assurance that she could be seen as normal and healthy, a paper-thin shield that inevitably collapsed as soon as she came into contact with the world outside her bubble. I couldn't mock Trigglypuff. Fat celebrities, who set an atrocious example for millions despite having the finest personal trainers in the world on their Hollywood doorsteps? Yes. But not Trigglypuff. Her entire predicament was and remains too horrible.

To avoid more Trigglypuffs, we have to tear down trigger warnings, safe spaces, "fat positivity workshops," and other constructions the Left has created to entice vulnerable, hurting people to their cause. All these serve to do is encourage people to blame others and attack society for making them feel miserable, when in reality they will never be happy unless they fix whatever it is about them that triggers our gag reflexes.

When I call a celebrity fat, I'm not doing so merely to be cruel. I'm calling attention to an obvious fact that the Left seeks to suppress: that being fat is *not a good thing*. The same is true of being ugly, which is another thing the intersectional Left is trying to convert into a category of oppression, contrasting it with the privilege of being attractive. If you can fix it, you should, and if you can't fix it, you can't blame society for beauty standards, which change over time, but only slightly. Attempting to overturn them completely, something the intersectional Left promises is achievable, will only bring misery on the least fortunate in society.

Some feminists create a cult of ugliness that treats both beauty and happiness as enemies. The novelist Flannery O'Connor skewered this type of intellectual in her story, "Good Country People," whose Ph.D. protagonist changed her name from "Joy" to "Hulga" because she could think of nothing uglier. In her thirties, she is "hulking," never married, and friendless. "Constant outrage had obliterated every expression from her face," and her eyes had "the look of someone who has achieved blindness by an act of will and means to keep it."

Am I rationalizing my gay urge to raise up the aesthetically pleasing and tear down its opposite? Perhaps partly. But I am not joking when I say fat-shaming should be a social obligation. Daniel Callahan, president emeritus of America's oldest bioethics research institute, agrees with me. "Safe and slow incrementalism that strives never to stigmatize obesity has not and cannot do the necessary work," wrote Callahan. "The force of being shamed and beat upon socially was as persuasive for me to stop smoking as the threats to my health."[102]

Dangerous

With a little effort, we can help fat people help themselves. But first we have to make sure that "fat acceptance," perhaps the most alarming and irresponsible idea to come out of leftist victimhood and grievance politics, is given the heart attack it deserves.

Strange though it may sound, perhaps even those who fat-shame solely out of cruelty and spite are inadvertently doing good. Because the sooner fat people (and, indeed, ugly people) come face to face with the reality of human nature, the sooner they'll decide that they have to make a change before it's too late.

Or, if they can't change, they will at least be able to develop a method of coping. One day perhaps, the fat acceptance movement will realize that forcing others to accept you only ends in repressed feelings and misery on both sides. And perhaps that's the day they'll realize that Michelle Obama—dare I say it—was on to something.

And before you say, "What can I do about being ugly?" You know perfectly well. If you're a man, work out—a lot. Learn some jokes and get a good job. You'll do fine. If you're a woman, save up for surgery and *stop fucking eating*.

Do We Need Feminism?

In 2014, it would have been easy for me to answer this question with a resounding FUCK NO. Feminism in the West serves little purpose other than hating men, making absurd demands, lying about inequality and obsessing over trivial issues. It has poisoned relations between the sexes, nearly destroyed due process, and constantly saddles businesses with pointless gender diversity requirements based on bogus economics.

But now, thanks to the mistakes of progressives, we *do* need feminism in the West—or at least, in some parts of it.

MILO

Whereas the "rape culture" on college campuses is a figment of feminist's imagination, the rape culture brought to the West by Muslim migrants, invading Europe by their millions, through the courtesy of horrendously misguided European elites, is very real. So too is their culture of rape, wife-beating, "honor killing," female genital mutilation, and forced marriages. After spending years trying to make feminism relevant again with phony faux-issues like gendered toys and Twitter harassment, progressive immigration policies have finally succeeded. That probably wasn't the plan, but there it is.

If feminism wants to recover its lost credibility, it needs to look overseas, to the feminists of Muslim countries. If all feminists were like Ayaan Hirsi Ali, a survivor of female genital mutilation in Somalia, who is now one of the West's foremost critics of Islam and a champion of women in Muslim countries, I expect feminism wouldn't be so unpopular. People might even admire them.

Feminists can also look to the Kurdish women of the People's Protection Units in Syria, whose version of smashing the patriarchy is putting bullets in the chests of ISIS members.

That's a feminism we could all get behind.

For now, feminists should resign themselves to pats on the back from *Daily Beast* columnists, total oblivion with regular people, and absolute hatred by lovers of free speech, facts, reason and logic.

I'm sure the feeling is mutual. I know it is. Feminists hate me for a myriad of reasons. When no one else was speaking out against them, I took on some of their leading champions during the GamerGate controversy, and exposed their bogus complaints of "online harassment."

I go on TV and call them "darling" to their faces. They hate that.

I promote facts over feelings.

Dangerous

I stick up for men.

I resist the new trend for "affirmative consent." Amazingly, yet predictably, feminists aren't satisfied that the scales are already tilted in women's favor when an allegation of rape is made. They want complete control over romantic relationships. It's not enough they can destroy a man's self-esteem with a word of rejection, they want to throw him in jail if his advance is too awkward. Third-wave feminists believe it's their duty to destroy any man's life who is accused of rape, no matter if it's a bogus claim, or if the truth is the lady said yes and then later regretted it.

That's the reason we now have affirmative consent, perhaps the most Kafkaesque set of laws in America, signed into statute for all colleges in California, Louisiana, and Indiana, and statewide in New York and Illinois.[103] It's the idea that if you don't consent at every stage of a sexual encounter, you've been raped. That means asking for every kiss and every boob squeeze.

While I don't love feminism, I do love women. It makes me sad to see what feminism has done to a generation of American women who could have been and done anything if it hadn't been for *BuzzFeed* and *Gawker*. Everywhere feminism exists it is a threat to happiness and freedom. Just think how funny Sarah Silverman used to be, cracking outrageous jokes about Jews, Mexicans and gays, before she contracted feminism and became just another disapproving hypocrite on Twitter.

Feminists have passed the point where they'll ever be popular, but if they focus on the real threats to women today—in particular, from Islam—they might at least win back some measure of respect. I'm not holding my breath.

5

WHY BLACK LIVES MATTER
HATES ME

I love black people. I love black people so much, my Grindr profile once said "No Whites." Alas, some black people—the ones conned by Black Lives Matter—don't love me as much as I love them.

And after everything I've done for the black community! I've lost count of the number of black guys I've personally lifted out of poverty. (Admittedly, I send them back the next day in an Uber.) Sometimes I get depressed just thinking about it. But then I remember that Black Lives Matter are only a small, vocal section of the black community, bankrolled by malicious progressive white billionaires and elevated by a disingenuous press.

Really, Black Lives Matter should be thanking me. In August 2015, I published a story on *Breitbart* highlighting the extraordinary case of Shaun King, who was then claiming leadership of the movement (as were Johnetta Elzie and DeRay Mckesson).

King claims to be half-black, born to a black father and white mother. However, a closer examination of King's family tree by blogger Vicki Pate revealed a shocking truth in King's birth certificate: it identified Jeffrey Wayne King, a white man, as Shaun King's father.

It also identified Shaun King as ethnically white.[104] That's right: a self-appointed leader of Black Lives Matter, who attended a historically black college, on an Oprah Winfrey scholarship targeted at disadvantaged black kids, had—according to his birth certificate—a white mother and a white father.

For more than two days after I reported on the questions about Shaun King's background, King tried to ignore the issue, blocking people on social media who brought it up and refusing to answer media questions, despite massive international interest in the story. Finally, in an article for the left-wing blogging platform *Daily Kos*, he delivered the only argument that had a chance of getting him out of the scandal: that his mother had an affair with a light-skinned black man, a man King could not name.[105] The implication was clear: King had no idea who his father was, and had thus been making representations about his ancestry he could not justify.

My response to King's claim that his mother had slept around was simple: take a DNA test. If his claims were true, taking a DNA test and putting its results on the public record would have put the matter to rest once and for all. He still hasn't done so.

As it turned out, these explosive racial allegations are just the latest in a string of controversies surrounding Shaun King. On July 21, *Daily Caller* reported that his account of a "brutal, racially-motivated beating" in 1995, which at least two reports have described as

"Kentucky's first hate crime," did not match up with a police report from the case.[106]

"King, 35, has related the story of the hate crime on his blogs and in his recent self-help book, seemingly to bolster his credibility as an activist and as a self-help guru," wrote *Daily Caller's* Chuck Ross. "While King has said that he was attacked by up to a dozen 'racist' and 'redneck' students, official records show that the altercation involved only one other student."

"And while King has claimed that he suffered a 'brutal' beating that left him clinging to life, the police report characterized King's injuries as 'minor,'" Ross reported.

Left-wingers, especially on campus, are fond of faking hate crimes to boost their own public profiles and bolster support for their political causes. But King was doing far more than that—he was using his position as one of the unelected figureheads of Black Lives Matter to drum up sympathy, and ultimately line his own pockets.[107] In an America where victimhood is a currency, it's highly profitable to be oppressed.

King's story is mirrored by that of Rachel Dolezal (aka Nkechi Amare Diallo), who built a career in the NAACP by pretending to be black. After she was exposed, Dolezal claimed she "identified as black." Months before the Dolezal story broke, I joked that after transgender people, the next frontier of left-wing identity politics would be transracial. I didn't expect to be proven right so soon.

Unlike Shaun King, Dolezal did not attempt to convince anyone that she was ethnically black. She might have succeeded had she done so. But she didn't, and as such she attracted huge volumes of hatred from BLM in return for her honesty. I felt sorry for her, more than anything. Her case is ridiculous, and I was happy to ridicule it, but it's also sad.

Sad, but not surprising. The Left has made victimhood prestigious, profitable, and in some respects almost revered. Even with all the legitimate problems faced by black people in America, it makes sense that some people would pretend to be members of the race to reap all the attendant rewards.

With all the benefits that come with victimhood, it's little wonder that so many wealthy and powerful people do so much to sustain the political edifice that supports it. The Black Lives Matter movement, indisputably the primary vehicle for black victimhood today, is a campaign propped up by hundreds of millions in donations of grants, including $33 million from progressive billionaire George Soros.

The point of these donations is strictly to advance the cause of identity politics and racial division. It can often seem as though BLM isn't so much a black civil rights movement as an anti-white hate group.

Black Lives Matter does nothing to serve the black community or black lives.

Worse, it does extraordinary damage to both.

THE POLICE PROTECT BLACK LIVES

There is a malicious, violent force in America that seems to kill only black people and ignore whites. Its presence can be felt in every city. In some areas, this threat means black people cannot walk the streets without fear of being shot.

This force isn't the police. It is inner city gangs, who are primarily black themselves. The numbers are indisputable, and yet just for printing them in this book, I'll be deemed a racist. Between 1980 and

2008, blacks made up 52.5% of homicide offenders, despite making up just 12.2% of the population. In the same survey, it was found that 93% of black homicide victims were killed by other black people.[108] Black Lives Matter focuses exclusively on deaths caused by the police, yet these are far eclipsed by the black deaths caused by other black people.

In 2014, there were 238 black deaths at the hands of police, a number sensationally reported by Raw Story as "more black deaths than on 9/11." But in the same year, there were 6,095 black victims of homicide—more homicide victims than any other race, and double the 9/11 death toll for all races. And virtually all those black homicide victims died at the hands of other black people.

The dramatic gap between deaths at the hands of police and deaths at the hands of other black people raises the question of why Black Lives Matter focuses its energies exclusively on the police, and so-called "white racism."

Like the men's health gap, the black murder gap is very real, and simply isn't discussed by black activists. I suspect it's a matter of tribalism, or ingroup/outgroup psychology, a common occurrence in politics. Like feminists who blame their everyday grievances on an invisible "patriarchy," or Wi-Fi-enabled Waffen-SS wannabes who think Jews are responsible for everything bad, or Democrats who blame the Russians for Hillary losing the election to Daddy. It's very easy to dodge responsibility if you have a boogeyman to lump the blame on.

Leftism, which combines tribal identity politics with a disdain for personal responsibility, is the ultimate political expression of this destructive instinct to blame other people for your problems, instead of undergoing the difficult process of self-reflection.

Dangerous

BLM isn't just ignoring the murder gap—they're *making it worse*. Whenever Black Lives Matter torches another (*usually*) black neighborhood, police are left with no option other than withdrawing from proactive policing until tensions cool. That means fewer patrols in black neighborhoods and fewer stop-and-searches of black people, which would save black lives.

It can be almost impossible to reason against Black Lives Matter-inspired action, peaceful or otherwise, regardless of whether it makes sense or not. But I'll try anyway.

In 2015, after Black Lives Matter rioted in Baltimore, the city suffered its deadliest year in history, with 344 homicide deaths in 2015. Progressives at Raw Story were wringing their hands over 238 black deaths caused by police officers across the entire country the year before. Baltimore's black deaths passed that number by 106—in just *one* American city.

At first, the Left vociferously denied that there was a spike in violent crime across America caused by the rolling back of proactive policing in response to Black Lives Matter. Those of us with common sense knew otherwise, and we called it "The Ferguson Effect." Eventually, the evidence grew so compelling (10 heavily black cities saw a homicide surge of over 60%[109]) that even *Vox* admitted the problem was now "too clear to ignore" and grudgingly conceded that the Ferguson Effect was "narrowly correct, at least in some cities."[110]

Black Lives Matter claims that police hurt black people. It is true: police shootings disproportionately affect black people—they make up 26% of police shooting victims, despite making up roughly 13% of the population.[111] But as has been tirelessly pointed out by every conservative journalist who covers this topic, they are also vastly overrepresented in crime statistics.

MILO

According to the Bureau of Justice Statistics, blacks were charged with 62% of all robberies, 57% of murders and 45% of assaults in the 75 largest U.S. counties in 2009, though they made up roughly 15% of the population there. When paired with these crime statistics, it's no surprise blacks make up 26% of police shooting victims. Moreover, it is not always white police officers who are doing the shooting, a fact that casts doubt on claims from BLM activists and progressive journalists that there is an epidemic of white racism in America's police force. From the same article:

> The Black Lives Matter movement claims that white officers are especially prone to shooting innocent blacks due to racial bias, but this too is a myth. A March 2015 Justice Department report on the Philadelphia Police Department found that black and Hispanic officers were much more likely than white officers to shoot blacks based on "threat misperception"—that is, the mistaken belief that a civilian is armed.
>
> A 2015 study by University of Pennsylvania criminologist Greg Ridgeway, formerly acting director of the National Institute of Justice, found that, at a crime scene where gunfire is involved, black officers in the New York City Police Department were 3.3 times more likely to discharge their weapons than other officers at the scene.

On the rare occasions when police officers do shoot a black suspect, they're just as likely to do so if the officer is black. Or even if the officer is a Black Lives Matter activist! Whenever black critics of the police have dared submit themselves to "use of force" simulations, which put participants in police scenarios where the use of force against a suspect is an available option, they end up pulling the trigger just as often as white policemen.[112]

There are white people that Black Lives Matter should look up to, and they're not Shaun King. They're Heather Mac Donald, the tireless Manhattan Institute researcher who has outlined the damage done to black lives by the Black Lives Matter movement in meticulous detail (many of the citations in this chapter are from her work). They're Rudy Giuliani, the former mayor of New York, whose proactive policing caused gang violence in the city to plummet, saving countless black lives. Or Piper Kerman, author of *Orange Is The New Black,* who used her experience in the U.S. penal system to create a national conversation about prison reform. And they're the hundreds of thousands of police officers, of every color, who patrol America's streets at night, preventing young black men from murdering each other and their neighbors. Black lives don't matter to Black Lives Matter. If they did, they wouldn't focus on police-related deaths, which make up a tiny part of preventable black deaths. They would focus on the problems of their own community, rather than dwindling "white racism." Above all, they wouldn't force police off America's streets.

The great truth obscured by the media and left-wing politicians is that police are not the enemies of black lives, but their greatest defenders.

THE FACTS

Not even a proud dissident conservative like me would deny that there are real, enduring issues in America that make it more difficult to be a black person. If I were a partisan hack, I'd shy away from making that admission.

Unlike the largely bogus complaints of feminists and gays, who at this point are largely privileged classes, some African-Americans, especially women, are still second-class citizens in America.

Education is a prime example. Schools in America are still largely segregated—black pupils overwhelmingly go to schools in lower-income neighborhoods, where class sizes are large, the standard of teaching is poor, and gangs prey upon adolescent boys, especially if they distinguish themselves academically. In 83 out of 97 large American cities, the majority of black students attended school where most of their classmates were low-income. In 54 of those 97 cities, that majority number was over 80%.[113]

Fixing America's schools would go a long way to solving the deep-seated issues that cause black people to remain stuck in a cycle of crime and poverty. But unlike the angry, tribal politics of Black Lives Matter, the political dividends of such reforms could only be reaped in the very long term. Efforts to fix America's weakest schools, as George W. Bush discovered when he attempted to do so, typically cause more political damage than support.

The problem of black schools is part of a wider maelstrom of disadvantage faced by black people in America. Black children are more likely to live in inadequate housing, are more likely to grow up in conditions of relative poverty, and more likely to have uneducated or poorly educated parents—one of the strongest indicators of future academic and professional success.

You'll notice "parents" is plural in the previous sentence, but 70% of black children are born to single women.[114] Black fatherlessness is widespread and socially and educationally devastating for black children. Furthermore, black children are more likely to grow up surrounded by crime, which makes them more likely to fall into the lifestyle themselves, and more likely to be affected by crime, which has a host of ramifications that affect educational attainment, including absenteeism and stress. Real stress, not the "triggering" that feminists experience when they encounter something they disagree with.

Then there's the war on drugs, which needlessly puts hundreds of thousands of black people in jail. Entire generations of young black men have been lost to the prison system. It must end. If Black Lives Matter's main purpose was instituting prison reform, I'd carry one of those dumb protest signs myself, but I assure you my sign would have much better production value than these activists can muster.

I don't claim to have the answer to these problems, but I won't pretend they don't exist. In fact, Republicans need to take these issues seriously. I'm no libertarian, but it's no surprise that Senator Rand Paul was polling so well with black voters before he dropped out of the Republican presidential race in 2016.[115] Paul's proposals for drug reform, prison reform, and education reform were specifically designed to address issues in the black community.

Discussing continued racial disadvantage in America will be frustrating for conservatives who are sick of constant, bogus complaints about racism. But that's no excuse for ignoring the facts. The Left responds to uncomfortable facts with handwringing and denial. It's time for the grownups to take control. Disadvantage does still exist, and something has to be done about it.

The Left is only making it worse, with ill-advised welfare programs that try to fix black poverty by throwing money at the problem. I know somewhere in this country there's a brilliant conservative mind that has just the solution, but he is too fearful of being called a racist to bring it to the table. I hope this book will show him you can't let idiots get in the way of real progress.

THE NARRATIVE

Black Lives Matter is instructive, because it illustrates how the political and cultural establishment can spread misinformation even when the truth is in plain sight. Anyone can access the information needed to debunk the selective truths promulgated by Black Lives Matter.

But that takes time and effort. Activists, cultural elites and the mainstream media know that most people have too much going on in their lives to fact-check the narrative. Especially if the narrative is blasted out of every TV network, broadsheet newspaper and online social network.

Take, for instance, the most popular slogan of Black Lives Matter: "hands up, don't shoot." The genesis of this rallying cry came from the death of Michael Brown, a black man, at the hands of Darren Wilson, a white police officer.

The prevailing narrative of this sad event is that Brown was surrendering to Wilson, with his hands in the air, when Wilson needlessly and fatally shot him. This story came mostly from Brown's friend, Dorian Johnson, who was with Brown at the time.

The problem is, multiple witnesses, as well as all the evidence, show that this narrative is a lie.[116] Brown didn't have his hands in the air; Johnson simply made it up. His lie led to massive riots throughout the country. Incredulously, mainstream media continues to pedal the "hands up don't shoot" lie, with the exception of conservative voices, even RINOs like Megyn Kelly. Johnson has never been punished in any way for his lie, nor the riots he directly caused, and the narrative that Officer Wilson shot a man who had his hands up continues.

There is perhaps one major mainstream newspaper—*The Wall Street Journal*—that regularly publishes articles critical of Black Lives Matter. Virtually every other publication is completely on board with the poisonous message that America's police officers, one of the most important groups *defending* black lives, somehow have it in for black people.

Here's a selection of op-eds from mainstream outlets published in the past two years:

Washington Post: "Black Lives Matter And America's Long History of Resisting Civil Rights Protesters."

New York Times: "Dear White America."

Chicago Tribune: "I Never Have To Worry I'll Be Shot in Chicago. I'm White." (*This article amazingly manages to talk about the problem of gang violence while simultaneously condemning allegedly overzealous policing.*)

You know, if I was fed a constant stream of articles telling me that the world hated me because of the color of my skin, I might burn down a city or three. But I don't read the white supremacists at *Daily Stormer*. I don't believe my race is under siege. Unfortunately, African-Americans rarely hear anything else.

I tried reading Ta Nehisi-Coates *Between the World And Me*, a dreadfully dull book/letter he wrote to his son. In it, Coates explained how he'd grown up in a bad neighborhood and had to be tough to survive. Incredulously, he went on to lament over the fact that his son would grow up to be treated…like he'd grown up in a hard neighborhood and thus had become tough. *Between the World And*

MILO

Me won a National Book Award only because it was so unreadable. Everyone assumed that meant it was brilliant. It wasn't.

Progressives have considerable power to shape the narrative. They control the mainstream media, all the prestigious awards, Hollywood, and the commanding heights of the new social media economy. If they were so motivated, they could use this power to create inexorable pressure to solve the real issues of America's black population.

Instead, they're using it to push Black Lives Matter, one of the most destructive movements in the country's history.

And you know, it's actually worse than that.

RACISM

Whenever you reveal truths about problems in the black community, or call out the hypocrisy of the cherished Black Lives Matter movement, as I have done above, charges of racism are not far behind. This is compounded by my level-headed analyses of the alt-right, which has led media organization after media organization to brand me a "white nationalist"—almost always followed by a groveling apology to me and a public retraction after my lawyers get in touch.

The Left in America is so stupid that they seem to genuinely believe that "disagrees with Black Lives Matter" is the same thing as "hates black people and wants a white ethnostate."

Racism is the second most absurd of all the charges the Left has foolishly used in their futile attempt to sink the Battleship Milo, with the exception of the few leftists who are desperate enough to insult my hair.

Literally the worst thing I've ever said to or about a black person is: "Not tonight baby, I have a headache."

DANGEROUS

In addition to the fact that I'm part Jewish, and thus have no love for anyone who hates or discriminates against minority groups, have you seen the people I sleep with? They come in a lot of colors, and very few of them are hues of white.

The Left's usual response is to resort to a cliché. "Having black friends doesn't mean you aren't racist!" The reason they use this argument so often is because it eliminates the best possible defense against charges of racism. My question to people who make this argument: if it doesn't satisfy you that I spend time with, make love to, and, for Heaven's sake, fall in love with, black men *when nothing is forcing me to*, what would persuade you that I'm not a racist?

I already know the answer. Nothing.

Many of the most cherished people in my life are black men. Because I love and respect them, I believe they deserve truth, not lies, in the face of the harsh reality of black America today. It's a reality that includes problems created and sustained by the Left, and by the black community itself—as well as real problems of enduring racism. The Left, by contrast, seeks to patronize minorities by preventing them from coming into contact with anything that might offend them.

There's also the riposte from race baiters that you can be a racist and still sleep with black men because all you're really doing is "fetishizing black bodies," whatever that means. Their argument seems to boil down to how much it sucks that everyone finds them attractive. I've yet to hear a coherent argument, however, that explains how I could, for instance, get engaged to a black man and still be a racist. I've also never seen a black man get offended by the stereotypes about penis size. I guess some stereotypes are larger than others.

MILO

Leftists are convinced that my criticism of Black Lives Matter is motivated by racism. But real racists tend not to hide their motivations: they reveal it plainly in their language. Ask a white supremacist if he's a white supremacist and you will get the answer: "Yes, I am a white supremacist." (*Daily Stormer* helpfully puts swastikas and fasces on its front page.)

The same can't be said of counterparts in the Black Lives Matter movement. Take Yusra Khogali, a leader and co-founder of BLM in Toronto, who described white skin as "sub-human" (she actually used the word "sub-humxn," the alteration of the word "man" being a popular trend among intersectionalists). She claimed that white people are a "genetic defect of blackness" and that melanin, the pigment that gives human skin its color, "directly communicates with cosmic energy." Because of this, Khogali proclaimed that black people were in fact "superhumxn."[117] It seems Black Lives Matter is happy to have open racial supremacists as leaders.

Creative biology is nothing new to black supremacists and separatists, like the belief that a black scientist named Jakub created the white race as a "race of devils." In the past these could be laughed at and considered as loopy as flat-Earth theory. Now believers in this stuff are lauded by mainstream politicians and commentators.

That wasn't the first time Khogali had made a racist comment on social media, by the way. In February 2016, she tweeted "Plz Allah give me strength to not cuss/kill these men and white folks out here today. Plz plz plz."[118] We don't need to guess at Khogali's motivations. Her hatred is plain for everyone to see. Yet the mainstream media seems more interested in trying to explain how a sassy gay British columnist with Jewish heritage and a black boyfriend is the real racist.

Dangerous

There are some who argue that racism against white people doesn't exist. For a time the top result on Google for "is it possible to be racist to a white person?" was an article from *Huffington Post* arguing that such a thing was impossible, because racism is "prejudice plus power" and whites "control the system and economic structure in society."[119]

I'm not sure this argument would be very convincing to the mentally disabled white kid who was kidnapped and tortured by four black people in Chicago. They livestreamed the ordeal on Facebook, gleefully hurling racial abuse at him ("Fuck Donald Trump, nigga! Fuck white people, boy!") slapping him, and slicing his scalp with a knife.[120]

I'm also left to wonder if, under this new definition of racism, an immigrant cab driver in New York who doesn't pick up black guys is a racist. I'd like to see a BLM activist explain how a Pakistani immigrant has any "power" over a black American U.S. citizen.

It's a bit like walking into a carnival house of mirrors when definitions of words are changed in order to support a bogus argument. Are there black people who hate white people? Yes. Are there black people who think whites are inferior to blacks, and have no problem admitting to it openly and publicly, with no fear of reprieve? Yes. Are these same black people racist? Of course they are.

BLOOD IN THE STREETS

When Lyndon B. Johnson discussed the need to tackle racism in America, he was under no illusions about the gravity of the problem facing the nation. "The Negro fought in the War [World War II]," Johnson reportedly told Horace Busby, an aide. "He's not gonna keep taking the shit we're dishing out. We're in a race with time. If we don't act, we're gonna have blood in the streets."

MILO

It's been more than fifty years since Johnson signed the 1964 Civil Rights Act into law, and America has blood on its streets. But it can no longer be blamed on racism—at least, not on white racism.

On July 7, 2016, the black supremacist Micah Xavier Johnson opened fire on police officers in Dallas, Texas, killing five and injuring nine others, as well as two civilians. It was the deadliest incident for U.S. law enforcement since September 11, 2001.

Just ten days later, another black supremacist, Gavin Eugene Long, opened fire on police officers in Baton Rouge, Louisiana. He killed two officers and hospitalized three others, one critically.

Both Micah Xavier Johnson and Gavin Eugene Long grew up in a society in which university professors, celebrities, and mainstream news outlets told them that the police were racist and wanted to kill them. Both men turned to virulently racist forms of black nationalism, which—unlike, say, Pepe the Frog—receives scant scrutiny or attention by media and political elites. In many university departments, the racist, anti-white views held by Long and Johnson are virtually encouraged.

Both men are individuals responsible for their actions, but it would be simplistic to argue that they weren't also products of their environment and the messages they were bombarded with since birth. While the progressive Left harangues white twerkers and dreadlock-wearers as racist, and while the establishment media wrings its hands over alt-right memes, black people in America are being fed a diet of anti-white, anti-police hatred that, inevitably, spills over into violence.

The greatest tragedy is that the primary target of this violence is the police, one of the greatest, largely unacknowledged *allies* of black communities. It is the police who stand between black people and the greatest threat to black lives: gang violence. It is the police who disperse black rioters when they're burning down black neighborhoods. And, amazingly, cops will continue to do both, despite seeming to receive only contempt in return.

When violence is committed against the police, it doesn't discriminate by ethnicity. The two NYPD officers who were shot "execution-style" at the height of Black Lives Matter unrest were Asian and Hispanic.

I'm proud to enjoy the support of police officers and other men and women serving America. I am never more humbled and grateful than when I receive praise from these people, who risk and give so much for their country, often in return for nothing but scorn from the public and politicians. Few things rustle my jimmies, but this persistent injustice is one of them.

Black Lives Matter hates me, and I hate them. But I don't hate them because they pose a threat to white people. I hate them because they do precisely the opposite of what they claim to do. They cause *more* black lives to be lost, not less. And they do so by attacking the one group of people trying to help their communities.

The people who *really* ought to hate Black Lives Matter are black people.

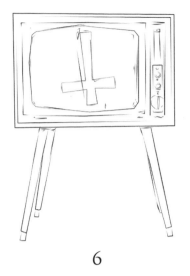

6

WHY THE MEDIA HATES ME

I t was two weeks after the election of Donald J. Trump as President
of the United States, and the Deputy Prime Minister of Japan, Tarō
Asō, was visibly annoyed. But he wasn't annoyed at Donald Trump.

Speaking in Japan's National Diet (their parliament), the famously
blunt Deputy Prime Minister shot down a suggestion that the country
should begin to make plans for Trump's policies, as predicted by the
American media.

"There's no point in Japan making policy based on the guesses of
American newspapers when they're always wrong," said Asō. "We
shall just have to wait until things are decided."[121]

Asō was right to be annoyed. What is a Japanese politician to do
when previously trusted names in western news, like *New York Times*,
Washington Post, BBC and CNN fail so comprehensively to describe
what's going on in American politics?

A *Gallup* poll conducted less than a month before the election
found that American's trust in the mainstream media had fallen to an

all-time low. Just 32% said they had a "great deal" or a "fair amount" of trust in the media—the lowest figure *Gallup* had recorded since they began conducting the poll in 1972. Just ten years ago, the same figure stood at 50%.

Even Democrats, catered to by the media, are lukewarm on the subject. *Gallup* found that just 51% of them had a great deal or a fair amount of trust in the media, compared to 30% of independents and 14% of Republicans—roughly the same number who supported John Kasich.

Trust in the media is in particular decline among younger people. In 2016, 26% of 18-49 year olds trusted the media, down from 43% in 2011. For the older generation (50 and over), trust only declined by six points in the same period, from 44% in 2011 to 38% in 2016.

In other words, the few people who still trust the media in America will soon be dead.

Isn't it deliciously ironic that the children of the 1960s, that era when the young rose up against the heroic, selfless World War II generation, are now stuck in the same old jam as their grandparents? After working so hard to destroy conservative principles, they settled into a lazy complacency, foolishly believing they had won the culture war forever. Now they have to watch as their own children rise up against them in glorious rebellion, embracing the very principles they sought to destroy.

So, the children of the 70s and 80s listened to punk rock instead of Walter Cronkite? Well the children of the 2010s read 4chan and watch my live roasts of feminism instead of Anderson Cooper. Cosmic justice.

The media has no way to dig itself out of this mess. They are stuck in the biggest circle-jerk I've ever seen, and I've seen some big ones.

MILO

Their primary goal is no longer to convey the latest information about current events to the American public, but to demonstrate their own commitment to the politically correct worldview of their peers in the metropolitan bubble.

Most of their leading lights have lost any interest in objective news reporting, of Woodward & Bernstein style investigative journalism, of speaking truth to power. Those who do are terrified of being ostracized and go along with the virtue signaling—as a result, any good journalism they eventually come out with is ignored by an increasingly disgusted, disillusioned public.

That's why they missed the very obvious rise of Trump.

Trump and I have many of the same supporters. If the media wanted to judge where the wind was blowing, they should have paid attention to my soaring Google rankings and those of other mischievous young libertarian and conservative artists, commentators and thinkers.

The media didn't *want* to see the signs. In their worldview, Mitt Romney's failed bid for President in 2012 proved the dominance of the new Democratic coalition of urban voters and minorities. They grew drunk on the delusion of their own unassailable power.

Not every journalist working in the mainstream media failed to see the tsunami that was about to engulf the Democrats and their allies in the media elite, but those who suspected it was coming decided keeping their heads down was the best career move. A couple examples prove they likely made the right choice.

When *Huffington Post* blogger David Seaman published two articles for the site breaking with the left-wing and mainstream media's self-imposed vow of silence on Hillary Clinton's health, retribution was swift and merciless. Not only were his two articles on the subject ("Hillary's Health Is Superb, Aside From Seizures, Lesions, Adrenaline Pens," and "Donald Trump Challenges Hillary Clinton To Health Records Duel") deleted, but he was fired, locked out of his editing account, and then his *entire history of articles* was temporarily scrubbed from the site.

Understandably miffed, Seaman took to YouTube to express his astonishment.

"Whenever a video concerning a presidential candidate's health is viewed more than 3.5 million times, somebody under contract to *The Huffington Post* should be able to link out to that, especially as a journalist living in the U.S., without having their account revoked," said Seaman. "I've filed hundreds of stories over my years as a journalist and pundit and I've never had anything like this happen."

Seaman was not the only example. There was also Michael Tracey, a reporter for *VICE* whose relentless Hillary-bashing was tolerated only during the primaries, when Tracey was a vocal supporter of Sen. Bernie Sanders. Once Clinton won her victory over Sanders, Tracey's views were suddenly unwelcome.

Nevertheless, he persisted, repeatedly highlighting the failings of Hillary Clinton on social media in the months leading up to the election. On September 6, 2016, he published one of the election cycle's more prescient columns: "The Mainstream Media Has a Donald J. Trump-Sized Blind Spot." Tellingly, it wasn't published at his home turf of *VICE,* but at the *Daily Beast.*

In his column, Tracey described how the media's tactics were backfiring.

MILO

I can't tell you how many ordinary folks I've spoken with who don't trust that the rolling Trump outrage machine otherwise known as current mainstream media is giving them the real story. This includes people who generally dislike Trump. One representative example was a restaurant worker in Philadelphia during the Democratic Convention in July who told me that she assumes anything Trump says or does will instantly be blown out of proportion, so has decided to just ignore the coverage. For her, it's a rational reaction to such disproportionate, all-consuming furor: She says she cannot process it all and also retain her sanity. *So even if a controversy arises that is legitimately worth getting up-in-arms about, she will no longer know it.*[122]

Emphasis added is mine. Tracey was right, and the mainstream media (as well as all the *National Review* writers who assumed Trump would surely lose) were wrong. Not only did they fail to anticipate that Trump's unstoppable momentum would carry him to the White House, they also likely aided the process, by crying wolf, confecting controversy and pretending to be offended and outraged so many times that the voting public simply switched off.

Presumably, Tracey's superiors at *VICE* aren't big fans of "I-told-you-so" moments, and quickly found an excuse to get rid of him after the election. They didn't even care that his readership appeared to be growing. He had to go. Unwilling to be as blatant in their pro-Clinton bias as *Huffington Post*, *VICE* instead opted to fire Tracey after he pointed out that Lena Dunham could not have participated in the closed Democratic primary in New York because she was not registered with the party. *VICE* fired him for reprinting a screenshot of publicly accessible, easily searchable voter registration data.[123]

I don't think Tracey or Seaman will end up with their careers particularly damaged in the long-term. They were right, and the furious progressive editors who fired them were wrong. They won't want for employment in the new media ecosystem. But in addition to creating a chilling effect in the mainstream media, where journalists decline to defy the narrative out of fear for their jobs, it also shows how committed the mainstream media is to remaining in its cycle of error. The few reporters who do see past the biases of the bubble are purged. And so, the cycle continues.

Nevertheless, I have good news for Japan's politicians, and for anyone else wondering where to look for truth in this new age of progressive propaganda masquerading as impartial journalism. You see, as virtue signaling intensifies and the Overton window—the range of ideas acceptable in political discussion—grows ever narrower, it's no longer just the cranks and the UFO-hunters who are left outside the mainstream. Journalists and fact-hunters who actually *do* know what's going on in the world are left outside too. If you want to know when the next Donald J. Trump is coming around the corner, all you have to do is find them.

I am of course referring to myself, to my former colleagues at *Breitbart,* to my new comrades at MILO Inc., and to my fellow travelers in the anti-establishment press. The very people and publications that are frantically decried by the opposition as "fake news." They don't understand why our star is rising and theirs is falling—it's because we're upfront about our opinions and priorities, and are committed to reporting the stories that the discredited mainstream media routinely ignores.

We also have respect for our readers. Unlike most of the press, we don't look down our noses at ordinary Americans.

I made many mistakes in my youth: dropping out of college, spending too much time blowing drug dealers, not resisting Father Michael's advances, but picking journalism as a career was probably the biggest one.

It's certainly not a path I'd advise anyone else to take, unless you fancy answering to miserable, soft-spoken nerds in plaid shirts who want you to convince the public that Islam is nothing to be worried about and "mansplaining" is a serious threat to women.

If you are a journalist, tell the truth. Your career options will be limited initially, but honesty pays off where it matters—with the public. And you don't even have to be right-wing! I trust anti-establishment leftists like Michael Tracey far more than *National Review* or *Red State* columnists, who revealed themselves during the campaign to be little more than watered-down versions of the virtue-signaling mainstream.

The alternative media is increasingly difficult to ignore. *Breitbart,* for example, maintained the top spot in political news on Facebook and Twitter for most of the 2016 election year. Despite the best efforts of biased Silicon Valley CEOs to silence our leading voices, we are the ones that people want to share, and we are the ones people want to hear.

During my career as a tech journalist in Europe, I quickly learned that tech journalism is a corrupt mess populated by hacks. Then during GamerGate we learned the gaming press is a corrupt mess populated by hacks not interested in the hobby, merely in politicizing it. Now during this election I've learned that the *entire* mainstream media is a corrupt mess populated by hacks pushing the political views of those in power with zealotry and mendacity.

Just a few years ago, you'd have been laughed out of the room for saying stuff like that. Now everyone knows it's true.

FAKE NEWS

You would expect the mainstream media to show a little humility after Trump's victory. Instead, they opted to double down, in an ill-conceived attempt to take vengeance on those who humiliated them. Their efforts have backfired completely.

Instead of asking themselves why they lost people's trust, the media instead asked why the people had lost trust in them. A subtle, but important difference.

The media decided that the people had been duped because they were listening to, reading, and watching—shock, horror!—alternative media. Something had to be done. But what? Well, the mainstream media could always engage with the alternative media and its arguments directly—but that would require facts, evidence, debate, open-mindedness, and other long-forgotten qualities.

So they didn't do that.

The media could always start listening to its readers again, by reopening comment sections and engaging with what they had to say, rather than writing off all criticism as "trolling." But that would require humility and the ability to admit that perhaps those backward losers in the flyover states knew something they didn't.

So they didn't do that.

In the days following the presidential election, the media seized on a new meme emerging from left-wing academics and analysts desperate for a reason to absolve them of responsibility for losing America.

That meme was "fake news"—the idea that Donald Trump had won because of the power of social media to spread misinformation. Voter's anger at elites wasn't legitimate, it was all because of the alternative media—sorry, I mean *fake news sites*—and mean-spirited lies about poor Hillary.

A few examples of genuine fake news (sites that create fake stories for clicks and ad revenue, like the sites with the extra suffix ".co": abcnews.com.co, DrudgeReport.com.co, MSNBC.com.co) were seized upon by the media to prove the existence of a wider problem. Two false stories about high-profile endorsements of Trump (from Pope Francis and Denzel Washington) and one activist's mistaken photo about bussed-in anti-Trump protesters in Austin, Texas were used to paint a picture of a deluded electorate.

Breitbart didn't report on any of those stories. But, along with *InfoWars, Prison Planet, The Blaze, Project Veritas, Private Eye, The Independent Journal Review, World Net Daily,* and *ZeroHedge, Breitbart* was placed on a list compiled by a left-wing academic of so-called "fake news sites."[124] It wasn't just the alternative media either—even more liberal independent sites like *Red State* and the *Daily Wire* made the list.

Part of the reason why the Left was drawn so rapidly to the "fake news" meme was because it offered the hope of striking back at a freewheeling new anti-establishment media that was rapidly supplanting them.

In the age of the internet, the public has any number of independent commentators to choose from, and their soaring popularity is a testament to the media's failure to hang on to their audience. There's

Steven Crowder, once a FOX News contributor, who now enjoys far more freedom in his widely-watched YouTube show *Louder with Crowder*. There's Stefan Molyneux, whose piercing insight into the issues of the day is far more exciting and intellectually stimulating than anything Keith Olbermann or Sally Kohn has to offer. There's Joe Rogan of the wildly successful podcast *The Joe Rogan Experience*, whose monthly download numbers—11 million in a single month in 2014—should terrify mainstream media.[125] And there's also Gavin McInnes, one of the only Canadians I like. Uber-straight Gavin and I kissed at a press conference after the Orlando terrorist attack, a symbolic fuck you to radical Islam. It was the conservative version of Madonna kissing Britney at the VMAs.

The real crisis of mainstream credibility can be seen in the rise of the "alt-media," people who were previously considered crackpots and fringe loons. The *InfoWars* commentators, Alex Jones and Paul Joseph Watson, now rack up hundreds of thousands, even millions of views with every YouTube broadcast they release. What does it say about the mainstream media's credibility when a man known to accuse the federal government of "turning the freaking frogs gay" is on the rise, while they're on the decline?

Julian Assange and WikiLeaks are also symbols of the mainstream media's declining power. Once upon a time, a leaker or a whistleblower would have to go to a newspaper or a broadcaster in order to get their story out. When the media is biased, this can be a problem. Remember, *Newsweek* passed on the story of President Clinton and Monica Lewinsky: it was Matt Drudge who ended up leaking the story online.[126] Now, the map has changed: WikiLeaks will dump virtually any leaks from governments and political parties on the web, virtually uncensored. Sure, the media could just ignore them, but if they don't spread the news, social media users will.

Now aware of the existential threat posed to his world order, even outgoing president Barack Obama got involved. According to *The New Yorker,* just a few days after the election, Obama was talking "obsessively" about a *BuzzFeed* article attacking pro-Trump fake news sites.[127] In his public statements, Obama also blamed "fake news" for the public's lack of belief in man-made climate change.

Obama said, "The capacity to disseminate misinformation, wild conspiracy theories, to paint the opposition in wildly negative light without any rebuttal—that has accelerated in ways that much more sharply polarize the electorate."[128] You could be forgiven for thinking he was talking about CNN.

Just how polarizing and negative are these fake news sites? Are they writing inflammatory stories about their political opponents with headlines like "This Is How Fascism Comes To America"? Oh wait no, that was *The Washington Post,* in an article about Donald Trump. Are they suggesting their opponents will commit genocide if elected? No, *that* was an op-ed in *The New York Times,* also about Donald Trump.

"Just say it: Trump sounds more and more like Hitler" was, again, not published on any of the sites on the left-wing "fake news" list, but on *Slate,* a once-respected magazine that published Christopher Hitchens.

And what about the unverified dossier claiming that the Russian government is blackmailing Donald Trump with evidence of him engaging in "perverted sexual acts" that were monitored by Russian intelligence? It was published on *BuzzFeed* and reported on by CNN.

Obama is right, there is a problem with hysterics and misinformation in the press—but it's a problem of the *mainstream* press, not the alternative media. It's a bit fucking rich for journalists who got absolutely everything wrong about this election, and who published biased polls assuring the public of Hillary's victory, to start complaining after the fact about "fake news" because they lost the election.

One of the Fake News Media's most common targets has been me. I partly forgive them for this—my daily skincare regime is more complex and at least as interesting as national events. But I don't forgive the lies. Just Google "Milo Yiannopoulos" and the terms "alt-right" and "white supremacist" or "white nationalist" and count the number of times I've falsely been called these things. You'll find articles from CNN, CBS, *NBC News, Los Angeles Times, Chicago Tribune,* and *USA Today.* Almost all of them issued groveling retractions, and in some cases apologies, after my team got in touch, and it became clear I was not the sort of person to let their smears stand without a fight.[129] But by that point, most people have read the story and formed their opinion. The damage is done.

A supposedly respectable publication, NPR, called me a "self-proclaimed leader of the alt-right." Britain's *Daily Telegraph* (I used to write a column for them—they've clearly gone downhill since I left), and *Bloomberg Businessweek* both called me "the face" of the alt-right, although the latter did it in so inadvertently gracious a manner that I couldn't help but be flattered. ("The pretty, monstrous face of the alt-right," they said). Less flattering but no less false, CNN wrote an article including me in a list of "white nationalists" and accused me of "speaking disparagingly about Jews."

These are all mainstream, respectable publications staffed by professional journalists. The very same people that we are supposed to believe will provide the public with real, not fake news. Yet this is how they behave towards even the mildest of disagreement; a constant game of virtue-signaling and vice-signaling—telling others whom to shun by slapping the latest negative buzzword on them, and then gloating contentedly and calling themselves the "good guys."

If the media only went after provocateurs like me that would be fine. I wind people up for a living, so I expect a little heat. But they also go after people whose contributions to society consist of more than just barbed words and fabulous hairdos. People like Martin Shkreli, whom they accused of fleecing HIV and AIDS-sufferers by raising the price of Daraprim, a drug that treats a number of relatively rare conditions associated with HIV and AIDS. Shkreli had a reason for raising the price: he wanted to fund research for a cheaper, better alternative.[130] Moreover, his company, Turing Pharmaceuticals, made it clear that it was health insurers and corporations, not financially disadvantaged patients, who would be out of pocket. But that didn't stop the media from branding Shkreli "the most hated man in America."[131] He might be no angel, but the Daraprim price-hike is only grounds for "hatred" if you're a misinformed lefty or a mainstream journalist. They act like Regina George in *Mean Girls*, victimizing anyone who could be a threat to her popularity, only to discover at the end of the movie that no one actually likes her.

Having realized that the "fake news" meme was now being used to shine a light on their own failings, the mainstream media desperately tried to put the genie back in the bottle. *The Washington Post* released an article stating that it was "Time to retire the tainted term 'fake news,'" complaining that conservatives were now using the label against the media.[132] But it was too late—the media had given the world a term to describe their own failings, and we were going to use it.

Unable to face up to their problems, the metropolitan media-political bubble has opted for projection instead. So, there's nothing for it. We have to strap them to a chair, tape their eyes open, and make them look in the mirror.

That's why, even though it's probably for nothing in the end, I make a point of ritually humiliating journalists who lie about me. Because if I can make them think twice about doing it to me, perhaps they'll think twice about doing it to you. For all those lying journalists who haven't felt my wrath yet, "I have a very particular set of skills" waiting for you. You'll see soon enough.

A Reckoning

On November 21, as Donald Trump was preparing for his transition to office, he called some of the biggest names in American news media to Trump Tower. They expected the meeting to be about access to the Trump administration during its time in office. Instead, they received a historic dressing down; what one source at the meeting described to *The New York Post* as a "fucking firing squad."

> "Trump kept saying, 'We're in a room of liars, the deceitful, dishonest media who got it all wrong.' He addressed everyone in the room, calling the media dishonest, deceitful liars. He called out Jeff Zucker by name and said everyone at CNN was a liar, and CNN was [a] network of liars," the source said.

> "Trump didn't say [NBC reporter] Katy Tur by name, but talked about an NBC female correspondent who got it wrong, then he referred to a horrible network correspondent who cried when Hillary lost who hosted a debate — which was Martha Raddatz, who was also in the room."[133]

Kellyanne Conway would go on to tell reporters in the lobby of Trump Tower that the meeting was "excellent." I like to imagine her smirking internally as she said it. She's my favorite.

Trump has been manipulating the media for decades with unparalleled brilliance. But I think they only really figured out they were being played in September 2016. Trump announced he was going to make a statement on the "birther" conspiracy about Barack Obama at the soft opening of his new hotel in Washington, D.C. This brought what seemed like the entirety of America's political press corps to Trump's doorstep. They expected he was going to say something crazy, the final wacky comment that would sink his campaign.

Instead, reporters found themselves covering the opening of a new Trump hotel, and twenty minutes of veterans arriving in front of the cameras to endorse his run for president. Finally, at the very end, Trump appeared on stage to give a two-line comment on the birther issue: "President Barack Obama was born in the United States, period. Now we all want to get back to making America strong and great again. Thank you very much."

The press went crazy. "I don't know what to say here," said CNN's chief national correspondent, John King. "We got played again, by the [Trump] campaign." Meanwhile, Jake Tapper, live on air, called it a "political rick-roll." Tapper perhaps thought he was insulting Trump for engaging in the political equivalent of a prank invented by internet trolls.

Everyone else thought it was hilarious—especially me.

It was the perfect troll: it revealed suppressed truths, dismayed and entertained the public in equal measure, and gloriously humiliated a deserving target: the media.

Only Daddy could have done it.

I was one of the first major conservative commentators to back Trump. My headline, published on *Breitbart*, called Trump "The King of Trolling His Critics" and argued that he would be "The Internet's Choice for President."

At the time, few people saw the connection between Trump and internet trolling. Now, everyone sees it.

DON'T FEAR THE MEDIA

Establishment conservatives think Republicans have something to lose by taking on the media. As gamers, *Breitbart*, Nigel Farage, Trump and I have all proved, they don't.

The press has unloaded everything they have against us, and what has been the result? GamerGate gathered popularity for two years, unstopped. *Breitbart* is one of the most popular news sources on the planet, and the most popular political news source on social media. Nigel Farage, condemned as a racist by the media, took his political party to unprecedented electoral successes and almost singlehandedly drove the Eurosceptic movement that culminated in Brexit. Donald Trump, who attracted more media smears than everyone else combined, is president.

MILO

And look at me. Other than Trump, Farage, and possibly Ann Coulter, is there anyone in the English-speaking world that the mainstream media makes more of an effort to smear and misrepresent? Look where it's got me. I wake up every day *hoping* the mainstream media continues trying to destroy me. It's doing wonders for my bank balance. Journalists think that by smearing me as a racist and sexist they are destroying my reputation. Actually, they are fueling my fame, because no one believes a word they say. Their lies and distortions heat my pool.

In an age when nobody trusts the media, taking them on makes you popular.

So I implore you to do what the media doesn't want you to do: tell the truth bereft of politically-correct niceties. Be patriotic. Tell offensive jokes.

The media will hate you for it. They'll call you names. They'll try and smear your reputation. But you needn't worry—no one is listening to them, except for a small group of their fellow blind, deaf and dumb journalists.

If I could tell my colleagues in the media four things, they would be:

1. Everyone hates you.
2. No one is afraid of you.
3. No one believes what you say.
4. Nobody *owes* you *anything*.

If every journalist in America realized those four things, their behavior would transform overnight, immeasurably for the better, and the US might finally get the fourth estate it deserves. In the meantime, all journalists are liars and frauds unless proven otherwise.

Make them earn your trust—including me.

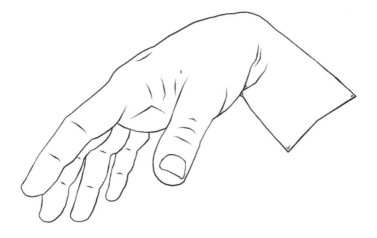

7

WHY ESTABLISHMENT GAYS HATE ME

These days, people don't come out as gay. They come out as conservative.

In February 2017, Chadwick Moore, a 33-year-old gay New York journalist, penned an article for *The New York Post* explaining his rapid shift from Left to Right. The article's headline? "I'm A Gay New Yorker – and I'm Coming Out As a Conservative." Just three months prior, Moore had cast his ballot for Hillary Clinton. What happened?

It was simple: Chadwick got too close to the Dangerous Faggot.

In September 2016, Moore had been assigned by *Out* to write a profile of me. The story was a gem; a rare piece of serious, nuanced journalism from the mainstream gay press. Its tone was largely impartial, describing the facts of my lifestyle, politics, and rise to fame. There was no virtue-signaling or moral grandstanding.

The profile wasn't completely free of bias (and likely couldn't be), and it included a trigger warning for fragile gay readers that they might encounter some conservative politics. They dressed me up in a clown costume for the accompanying photo shoot (the article's title was "Send In The Clown: Internet Supervillain Milo Doesn't Care That You Hate Him"), and it incorrectly called me a "leader of the alt-right," as countless other publications had done before. But I was willing to forgive the error, because the rest of it was so good. And I didn't mind about the clown costume, because I still looked sexy as fuck.

Out was utterly skewered for daring to examine me fairly. In addition to an immediate outbreak of rage on social media, more than 40 gay journalists signed an open letter condemning the magazine for failing to "avoid fostering harm to queer people."[134]

Although the letter was directed against me, I admired the feat of getting 40 gay guys to agree on anything. But the gay establishment has gotten so used to trashing conservatives for a living that when one of their number fails to do so, they consider it a hideous betrayal in need of a coordinated response.

The personal attacks against Moore were more severe. Chadwick quickly found himself ostracized by his circle of liberal friends. In his *Post* coming out story, he described how long-time friends and acquaintances began to turn their backs on him.

> My best friend, with whom I typically hung out multiple times per week, was suddenly perpetually unavailable. Finally, on Christmas Eve, he sent me a long text, calling me a monster, asking where my heart and soul went, and saying that all our other friends are laughing at me.

> I realized that, for the first time in my adult life, I was outside
> of the liberal bubble and looking in. What I saw was ugly, lock
> step, incurious and mean-spirited.[135]

Moore was becoming "red-pilled," as we say on the internet. Like Neo in *The Matrix,* his eyes had been suddenly and dramatically opened to a new reality. Now aware of the Left's intolerance, Moore had no choice but to reconsider his entire worldview. And that's how he ended up coming out as a conservative in the pages of *The New York Post.*

It's not just Chadwick, either. Other forward thinking gays are also waking up to the dangers of embracing progressive intolerance. Dave Rubin, host of the *Rubin Report,* which was originally part of the progressive Young Turks network, is another ideological immigrant from the Left. Rubin is a former progressive who sensed the atmosphere of intolerance that was gathering steam in the movement, and now calls himself a classical liberal.

Here's how Rubin explained his position in a video for the conservative Prager University:

> I'm a married gay man, so you might think I appreciate
> the government forcing a Christian baker or photographer
> or florist to act against their religion in order to cater,
> photograph or decorate my wedding. But you'd be wrong.
> A government that can force Christians to violate their
> conscience can force me to violate mine.[136]

Rubin closed his video by conceding that defending his classical liberal values had "suddenly become a conservative position." It's my hope—and optimistic belief—that more gays will wake up, smell the intolerance, and come to the same realization.

Gays have been battling intolerance for decades, and only recently won the full support and acceptance of society. And how have we responded? By becoming equally intolerant—not against people who have sex differently from us, but against people who *think* differently from us. Gays of the log cabin variety get merciless treatment from their peers. The rigid attitudes and prejudices of the fagstablishment will be tough to break down.

Take Lucian Wintrich, a gay Trump-supporting artist and photographer, who in 2016 unveiled a photography series called "Twinks For Trump." His work featured half-naked, waifish-looking men wearing "Make America Great Again" hats. Just five hours after I wrote a column praising Wintrich for his transgressive art project, he was fired from the New York ad agency where he worked, apparently because so many people had called his office to complain about the photos.[137] Thanks to conservative complacency, the art world today is a one-party state.

Undeterred, Wintrich went on to host "Daddy Will Save Us," the first ever pro-Trump art exhibit, featuring pieces from a range of conservative figures, including me. I bathed naked in a vat of pig's blood, representing persons who have died at the hands of Islamic extremists and undocumented immigrants.

The response of the Left was to bombard Wintrich's initial choice of art gallery with complaints, which caused the gallery to panic, cancel the event and even threaten to sue Wintrich.[138] A backup venue was found just in time, and the art show went ahead.

Imagine Madonna doing a video with twinks in MAGA hats. She wouldn't, of course, because these days she's too busy pandering to man-haters and aging gracelessly than saying anything bold or original.

Wintrich, like me, delights in causing outrage. But you don't really have to try very hard. Polite, respectable gay conservatives get exactly the same treatment from the Left. When mild-mannered entrepreneur Peter Thiel revealed his support for Donald Trump, gay website *The Advocate* published an article arguing that he could no longer consider himself a part of the gay community.[139] The message from this, and from Chadwick Moore's experience, is clear: toe the party line, or be thrown out of the clubhouse.

In April 2013, I appeared on an edition of the British panel show *10 O'clock Live* to take part in a debate. The topic was gay marriage, a cause to which I was then opposed. My opposite number was Boy George, and it was a rare occasion in which I was *not* the most flamboyantly dressed person on set.

My mere opposition to gay marriage was enough to baffle the audience. In 2013, gay marriage had become a kind of litmus test of social acceptability. If you were for it, you were a normal human being. If you were against it, you were a bigoted, malicious relic of the past—something to be dumped in the trash-heap of history.

I was fashionably dressed, and attractive, and charming, so they didn't really know what to make of me. Merely being introduced on the show as a gay Catholic opposed to same-sex marriage was all that was needed to baffle my fellow panelists. Before the show was over, I was called a "homophobic gay man" and accused of "self-loathing" for my opposition on cultural grounds to gay marriage.

I pointed out that gay marriage reinforced the idea that being gay is a normal or acceptable lifestyle choice, which it isn't—and shouldn't be. The very term "mainstream gay" is at odds with everything homosexuals have always represented, but nonetheless we are forced to use it because gays have become a monolithic political bloc. All gay people are expected to believe the same stuff.

Mainstream gays, many of whom are happy to cast scorn on the lives of, say, conservative Midwestern families or southern evangelical Christians, simply can't allow the possibility that someone might cast scorn on *their* lives. Take for example the popular drag queen Bianca del Rio, whose famous slogan is, "Not Today Satan!" When Candace Cameron, aka D.J. Tanner, a famously proud Christian, wore a shirt with Bianca's slogan on it, Bianca called her a "homophobic Republican." Candace responded, "Loving Jesus doesn't mean I hate gay people," but the damage was done. To Bianca's nearly one million Instagram followers, D.J. Tanner now hates fags.

Where's the Danger?

When *Daily Stormer* called me a "degenerate homosexual," they meant it as an insult. But I take it as a compliment: I became a homo precisely because it is transgressive. And I want homosexuality to continue being transgressive, and even degenerate.

One of the most alarming things I've witnessed over the past decade is how *safe* the gay community has become. As the cause of gay liberation advanced, our community's reputation went from feared purveyors of moral corruption to cuddly, married, middle-class suburbanites with neat haircuts. In short, we have stopped being dangerous. It almost makes me miss the time when we had to stay in the closet.

The gay establishment is rightly horrified by that suggestion, because it goes against everything they've been working to achieve since the

1990s. But before then, gay men delighted in being transgressive. It was a part of our identity.

Consider gay icons of the past two centuries. Oscar Wilde relished appalling the stuffy sensibilities of Victorian society. When he went to America, a prominent member of the clergy complained that someone who had engaged in such "offences against common dignity" was being received so warmly by high society.[140] Wilde's famous novel *The Picture of Dorian Gray* was chastised by one London newspaper as being "unclean, poisonous, and heavy with the odors of moral and spiritual putrefaction." I live to get a review like that.

Then there was Quentin Crisp, someone whose lifetime saw the rapid acceleration of gay rights. The British writer and raconteur was even more shocking than Wilde. Not only did he find enjoyment in taking a bazooka to society's sacred cows (he once described Princess Diana, Britain's most beloved public figure, as "trash"), he also loved to needle the gay rights movement. He infuriated campaigners with his willingness to question his own gay instincts and lifestyle, once even stating that gayness was something that ought to be avoided if possible.[141] He was a mischievous, rebellious hero.

Crisp was someone who would tolerate no limits on his independence. In the first half of his life, he plainly ignored society's rules against his gay lifestyle. And in the second, he flouted the gay community's expectations of him as well.

Writing in 1990, the bisexual belletrist Florence King bemoaned how the "exclusivity of Lesbianism" she had known in the 1950s had vanished, done in by "jargon-spewing socialists" and Earth Mothers "baying at the moon." In today's "climate of irrational humanitarianism and prime-time self pity," the homosexuality inclined of both sexes have traded in their natural elitism for victimhood status.[142]

Just think of where gay people have lived and hung out in the past century. The seediest, most degenerate parts of town—think Soho in London or Times Square in New York—were also the gay parts of town. We were the outcasts, the corruptors, the devils poisoning society and corrupting its morals. We were on the very edge of culture, pushing its boundaries. And we were doing it just by being ourselves.

It's practically impossible for gays to transgress today. Hanging out in the Village, West Hollywood or Soho is hardly shocking or rebellious. Hipsters and trend-followers crowd the streets, desperately clinging to the fading aura of forbidden cool rapidly melting away. Time Square is now a Disney store tourist trap. And just think of the horror of San Francisco! The unofficial capital of camp that once hated "The Man" has become "The Man" incarnate. Or as they'll call it, "The Gender Non-Conforming Individual." Is there a city in America with a more moribund culture than San Francisco?

I'm ceaselessly amazed by the gay community's myopic eagerness to sacrifice everything that has made our lifestyle unique, exciting, and dangerous, in exchange for heteronormative domesticity.

Camille Paglia—the greatest feminist critic of all time—says it so eloquently:

> Homosexuality is not normal. On the contrary it is a challenge to the norm... Nature exists, whether academics like it or not. And in nature, procreation is the single relentless rule. That is the norm. Our sexual bodies were

designed for reproduction. Penis fits vagina; no fancy linguistics game-playing can change that biologic fact.

...Gay activism has been naive in its belligerent confidence that "homophobia" will eventually disappear with proper "education" of the benighted. Reeducation of fractious young boys on the scale required would mean fascist obliteration of all individual freedoms. Furthermore, no truly masculine father would ever welcome a feminine or artistic son at the start, since the son's lack of virility not only threatens but liquidates that father's identity, dissolving husband into wife. Later there may be public rituals of acceptance, but the damage will already have been done. Gay men are aliens, cursed and gifted, the shamans of our time.[143]

For decades, being gay has meant transgression and the violation of taboos. It's been an act of rebellion, an automatic entry pass into society's underworld. Our weirdness is our strength—it gives us an edge, a power and a charm over everyone else. Why would we want to give all that up?

Smart gays who have been around the block, like celebrity drag queen RuPaul, understand this instinctively. RuPaul correctly tells gay men they should strive to stay outside "the matrix."

He knows that going mainstream would be death to drag culture and once in a while he is brave enough to say so in interviews.[144] But even drag culture is slowly feeling the influence of the perpetually offended: RuPaul was the victim of social-justice censorship himself, when the trans lobby forced his popular show, *RuPaul's Drag Race,* to stop using the phrase, "You've got she-mail," in case any transgender people were offended.

Being perverse is okay. Listen to Camille Paglia, my fellow fags. Realize you have an energy and power others would kill to access.

I don't want to have a spouse and kids and a front lawn. I want to be hurled out of a nightclub at three in the morning in a drug-fueled stupor. Caring for my offspring will be the nanny's job.

IN TRUMP'S AMERICA, GAYS ARE NATURAL CONSERVATIVES

The gay establishment refuses to acknowledge that Donald Trump is a fabulously camp cultural figure. He's the drag queen president! It's easy to see why so many gays I know secretly adore him. All that pizazz and bluster! To say nothing of his strong position against Islamic homophobia. He *oozes* control and authority. He so obviously ought to be a gay icon.

That's why I coined the nickname "Daddy" for him, which annoyed just about everyone.

If gay people want to stay true to our historic reputation of transgression and boundary pushing, there is no better way to do it than becoming conservative. MAGA is the new punk rock. Even punk legend Johnny Rotten recognizes it. Being openly gay is no longer a risky, dangerous affair. Being gay and openly conservative? Well, that's another matter entirely. Here's how Chadwick Moore described his two experiences of coming out:

> When I was growing up in the Midwest, coming out to
> my family at the age of 15 was one of the hardest things
> I've ever done. Today, it's just as nerve-wracking coming

Dangerous

out to all of New York as a conservative. But, like when I was 15, it's also weirdly exciting.[145]

There's a lesson for progressives here. Ramping up your political intolerance, as you are currently doing, will only backfire. It may cow a few easily intimidated, easily influenced gays into silence, but the best of us—the thrill-seekers, the explorers, the dark adventurers who are drawn to the forbidden and the dangerous—we'll be heading straight for the door. And we won't be coming back.

Gay organizations pour money into programs to stop kids using "gay" as a playground slur or calling people "faggots" on the web, but my Dangerous Faggot tour, watched by millions of young people around the world, has done more to reclaim the words gay and faggot than all the anti-discrimination workshops ever staged in America. We aren't an underclass any longer, so why stick with the politics of victimhood?

Peter Thiel was the first gay guy ever to openly discuss his sexual orientation before the Republican National Convention. He went up on stage, before an audience of conservative delegates, and announced that he was both proud to be gay, and proud to be a Republican. The audience jumped to their feet and cheered. The historical significance of an openly gay businessman being applauded at the RNC may have been lost on pearl-clutching leftist faggots, but to me it was one of the greatest events in modern gay history. The party of Rick Santorum is now also the party of Peter Thiel.

The progressive Left will never admit this, but Thiel and I have, in less than a year, done more good for the image of gays in America than decades of political advocacy from left-wing groups. We've shown America that not every gay man is a walking cardboard of tokenism

MILO

like Ross Mathews. Mothers of the Midwest now know their sons don't have to define their lives by the fact that they like sucking dick.

Just as mainstream gays are no longer the ones pushing boundaries, they're also no longer achieving their stated goal: winning more acceptance and tolerance for gays in America. Every time a conservative-hating gay like Dan Savage goes on TV to berate Christians for their bigotry and small-mindedness, all he's doing is preaching to the liberal choir, who are already well on board with gay rights, and alienating the rest of America. It's right-wing fags like Thiel and me who are doing the real work.

There is something naturally conservative about gays and our instincts. Male gays in particular are natural achievers: we tend to earn higher salaries than our straight counterparts, we have above-average IQs, and we're less likely to become fat.[146] We value aspiration, success, hard work and talent—all goals historically associated with the right. Ayn Rand (alongside Friedrich Hayek and other Austrian-school economists) boldly proclaimed the value of wealth, and humanity's quest for achievement. It's a perfect fit for gays, who have counted some of history's greatest geniuses among our ranks: Alexander the Great, Sir Francis Bacon, Alan Turing, Abraham Lincoln…

Championing the fortunate, the successful, and the able has never been particularly popular. People are naturally inclined to sympathize with underdogs, and to take pity on the less fortunate. But you occasionally need a Nietzsche or a Rand to remind society why striving for greatness—be it power, fame or wealth—is important. The best way to help the less fortunate is not to proclaim their superior virtue, but to help them improve their condition. You need the extravagance of elites to motivate the less fortunate.

DANGEROUS

And if there's one thing a good gay appreciates, it's extravagance. We aren't *all* divas who crave opulence and fame, but enough of us are for it to be considered one of our natural characteristics. Good looks and glamour are two of my most cherished ideals. As Somerset Maugham—who once described himself as "a quarter normal and three-quarters queer"—admitted, the homosexual "Loves luxury and attaches peculiar value to elegance."

I know I just said it but once again: gays are skinnier than average. And our love of good clothes, good hairdos, and good aesthetics is well established. In the age of the "fat acceptance" movement, how can we stick with the Left? We should look to Nietzsche for wisdom, not hideous queer studies professors.

Being one of the last boundary-pushers in the gay community pays dividends. At the end of 2016, readers of *LGBTQ Nation* named me "Person of the Year." Despite an outraged response from the gay community, the publication respected the choice, and acknowledged that I had successfully become the "ultimate gay provocateur in a year of provocateurs." If you're a fag who craves the limelight as much as I do, take note: it's conservative gays who get all the attention these days.

RETURN TO DEGENERACY

Gay men are chaos incarnate. We are gods of mirth, mischief, danger and innate perversion. As society's subversive rebels, unencumbered by humdrum family ties, we can go further than anyone else. We can smash taboos. We can achieve greatness. We should never try to be normal.

Family values are for straight people, not for us. Get married if you want, but don't pretend you won't be secretly browsing Grindr and scouting out darkened parks and public toilets behind your husband's back. (He'll be doing the same.)

Christianity is not your enemy; it is a secret friend. The Devil needs the Church to stay in business, and naturally mischievous gay men need a book of rules to break. We need to be told that we're wrong, we need to be told that we're degenerate.

Part of the blame for all this certainly falls with gays, because we willingly accepted liberal victim programming for so long. Many in America still think this country is a terrible place for gays, ignoring the rest of the world. Gays are often terminally insecure and vain, we think our problems are the only problems. In America, it's perfectly okay for people to not like each other. Just because someone doesn't believe two guys should be able to get married doesn't mean they hate gay people. Tying someone up and throwing them off a roof, that's what real homophobes do.

Social justice and progressivism are strangling gays and gay culture. Even *VICE* editors are noticing that it's *Breitbart* publishing radical gay editorials and provocative Britney Spears commentary, hosting gay porn star op-eds, and referring to "resident gay thots." That's a remarkable state of affairs for the Left to find itself in.

There is only one sentient issue GLAAD, PFLAG, GLSEN and any other gay establishment group needs to be focused on: AIDS. These organizations treat mis-gendered pronouns as a plague, while HIV infections continue to literally plague the gay community. Have they forgotten the men who died horrible, agonizing deaths only twenty years ago? A whole generation of gay men vanished. Are gay rights leaders so far gone that fighting for the right to a gay wedding cake becomes top priority, when 40,000 people were diagnosed with HIV in the US in 2015? Are the semantics between "marriage" and "civil union" so important that you'd disregard such tragedy?

Hysterical demands from dykes and trannies have brainwashed faggots into fighting the wrong war. We've given over all gay rights battles to the dykes, because we're too scared to voice what Florence King called "the leading unpopular truth of homosexual life," namely, "that gay men and lesbians don't much like each other... In a normal country, they couldn't bear to be in the same room together but in America they're in the same minority group."[147]

Lesbians don't care about HIV rates. Why would they, it has no bearing on their lives whatsoever. You can't get HIV from scissoring. All lesbians care about is who wears the tux and who wears the dress at their tacky wedding. It's time to stop lesbians from running the gay mafia and get them back where they belong: in porn.

People are sick of the gay establishment telling them what they're allowed to say. Conservatives don't hate gay people, they hate being told what to think. I've received a standing ovation from 1,200 Republicans for appearing in drag and ridiculing fat people. I've made frat boys sit down for two hours and listen to me talk about my dark sexual perversions. These kids don't know who Sharon Needles or Amanda Lepore are, and they never will, but I've let them know it's okay to be themselves through my drag persona, Ivana Wall. I'm every straight white male's gay hall pass.

I hope this chapter helps both the alt-right and mainstream gays understand my motivations. I do consider being gay to be wrong. But I also *like* being wrong. Gays should be proud to be degenerates. Listen up, homos. Rescue what's left of gay culture. Dump social justice. It's so much *better* being bad.

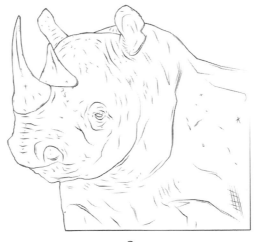

8

WHY ESTABLISHMENT REPUBLICANS HATE ME

"Right after liberal Democrats, the most dangerous politicians are
country club Republicans."
—*Thomas Sowell*

In January 2016, I got into what I thought was a friendly Twitter spat with then-editor-at-large for *Breitbart*, Ben Shapiro. Ben is a shorter and less successful version of me who lost his audience by freaking out against Daddy.

Shapiro's distaste for me and his distaste for Trump are related. They're part of a wider story of insecurity and anger on the part of the establishment right: anger that their positions of power and influence over conservative politics are slowly slipping away. Anger that they are being replaced by a new generation of young, fashionable and funny conservatives who have no time for the 1980s hang-ups of older conservatives. I mean, yes, the fact that raising tax rates past a certain point actually decreases tax revenue is *very interesting,* but proselytizing that message is not our number-one priority. We're nimble navigators who can get out to protests earlier because we're not waiting for our hearing aids to charge. And we care first and foremost about culture, not politics.

The quote at the start of this chapter isn't just a pithy saying. It's completely true. In 2016, there was only one type of political creature as upset as the Left—if not more so—at the rise of Donald Trump: establishment conservatives.

Establishment conservatives were so upset by Trump, they made a pathetic attempt to torpedo his efforts against Hillary Clinton. Calling themselves "Never Trump," some of them threw their support behind Clinton or the libertarian, Gary Johnson, while others rallied around the laughable Evan McMullin, a former middle-ranking CIA operative no one ever heard of.

Naturally, as the biggest and loudest Trump fan, I had the establishment also come after me. After I objected to their attempts to brand every web-based Trump supporter a frothing Neo-Nazi and anti-Semite, I attracted the attention of their queen bee, a rotund chap called Glenn Beck.

Alas, poor Beck. He's *obsessed* with me. He has, in various episodes on his sadly declining radio show, called me a "13-year old boy" and a "Goebbels" whose writings are "poison to the Republic." Poison to the Republic? I don't know. Poison to his ratings, maybe!

Beck was once the Left's favorite punching bag, the target of all their false accusations of racism. Unlike most establishment conservatives, he even *did* things—he once led a massive march on Washington,

D.C. in defense of American heritage, with some estimates putting attendance at nearly 500,000. Looking at the photos it was probably more like 85,000, but whatever.

Now, Beck's apologized for being too conservative in the past and even pens columns for *The New York Times* these days.[148] In the run-up to the 2016 election, he threw his support behind Hillary Clinton, saying that opposing Trump was the "moral and ethical choice," even if she were elected in his stead.[149]

There's a reason why conservatives like Shapiro and Beck, who were once the best the movement had to offer, now represent the past, while people like me represent the future: conservatives spent the last decade losing to the Left, and they're tired of losing.

I don't mean electoral defeats, either, although Mitt Romney's loss in 2012 could easily have been avoided by nominating a candidate that conjured up a compelling vision of America, rather than a compelling vision of your high school principal. No, conservatives lost in arenas that were more important than electoral politics: art, academia, and pop culture. Despite momentary political victories, the values spread by Hollywood eventually influence the ballots cast in voting booths. Conservatives lost culture, and until we win it back our political victories will only be temporary setbacks against the steady advance of leftist principles.

Actually, they didn't simply lose the culture war. It's worse than that. The truth is, they never even bothered to fight.

THE CULTURE WAR THAT CONSERVATISM FORGOT

There has been no serious attempt from national-level politicians to push back against the liberal dominance of universities. The

Foundation For Individual Rights In Education (FIRE), which campus conservatives rely on to protect their free speech, does an excellent job fighting the worst excesses of left-wing censorship on campus. Yet the group was set up and is run by moderate liberals.

Heterodox Academy, a group of academics pushing for more political diversity in the social sciences, is spearheaded by Steven Pinker and Jonathan Haidt—also both liberals. It's not a bad thing that some liberals still care about free speech and pluralism, but why are we letting liberals do the heavy lifting? Where are all the conservatives? With the exception of a scarce number of news sites like *Campus Reform* and *The College Fix*, it's almost as if conservatives don't care.

Indeed, the few establishment conservatives who *do* care about campus issues—and attract huge online followings of young people in doing so—privately admit their success is met with bemusement by fellow beltway conservatives, who wonder what the fuss is about, and why more people aren't interested in the latest appropriations bill or Russian naval maneuvers in the North Sea. Young conservatives, who are on the front lines of leftist intolerance every day, fell asleep during that last sentence.

It's the same in showbiz. A conservative in Hollywood is like a gazelle in a pack of lions: only the nimblest will escape unscathed. There are rare exceptions, like Clint Eastwood, whose conservative views fit with the John Wayne-esque tough guy persona he often plays on screen. Or Tim Allen, who was hilariously candid about his political views, right before his successful sitcom was suddenly canceled, for some unknown reason. The rest have to wear lion suits and purr convincingly at feminists and Black Lives Matter activists.

All of this is a result of conservative laziness. For years, the only prominent right-winger who made any effort to organize the conservative Hollywood underground was Andrew Breitbart, a man despised by the Beltway establishment. Isn't it funny how successful, conservative, culture warriors always end up making enemies of the D.C. establishment? It's almost as if they agree with leftists on everything except economics and foreign policy.

Unsurprisingly, the rise of Trump gave the cultural conservative underground courage to come out into the open. I was overjoyed when Kanye West, one of my idols, came out as a Trump supporter after the election (this was promptly linked to his alleged mental health problems by Perez Hilton[150]). Roseanne Barr, one of the funniest people on the planet, has openly supported Trump, and for good reason. She made a career out of speaking directly to the working class, same as Trump. And at the 2017 Grammys, when previously unknown singer-songwriter Joy Villa shocked attendees by wearing a dress bearing the words "TRUMP" and "MAKE AMERICA GREAT AGAIN," she saw her album sales rise by 54,350,100%,[151] proving that conservatism in showbiz can in fact be the opposite of career-ending.

There's a long way to go yet: for every Kanye West, there's an Adele, who told an audience she was "embarrassed" for Americans because of Trump. Does anyone remember what happened to the Dixie Chicks when they said almost the exact same thing about W Bush? Their CDs were literally crushed by tractors. Nevertheless, the courage I'm seeing from conservative entertainers and celebrities in the wake of Trump's victory makes me optimistic that things will change, albeit without the help of the conservative establishment.

Dangerous

Stuffy Beltway types really don't know what to do with me. I've introduced a brand new type of conservative to them. Listen, not everyone in the conservative movement is going to be cool and hip. But at least let's aim to attract new members who still *have* both their hips.

Could it be that establishment conservatives want to lose? "Cuck" became a popular insult in 2016. Its original definition was a man whose woman gets slammed by another dude, but it's now become a byword for needlessly relinquished manliness, for selling out and caving in. Calling someone a cuck is an expedient way to denote a beta male or coward. (See: the Republicans running against Donald Trump in the 2016 election.)

I'm constantly told by establishment types that I'm a clown. Yet for thirty years these guys have achieved nothing on campuses. In barely two, I've set the entire higher education system in America on fire. If I'm a clown, what does that make them? (See the last paragraph for your answer.)

There's nothing contradictory about appreciating Wagner's *Der Ring des Nibelungen* and also getting a kick out of calling Amy Schumer a boring cunt. And there's nothing wrong with talking about very serious subjects using satire, silliness, and shock value. For instance, at one of my shows, which was called "No More Dead Babies" and dedicated to the evils of abortion, I handed out individually signed and numbered photos of dead fetuses as memorabilia.

How many *Commentary* writers can claim they got 400 twenty-year-olds to think about the moral consequences of abortion in a single day—to say nothing of the hundreds of thousands who watched the show on YouTube?

MILO

When liberals come over to the Dark Side, they become friends with me and reluctant admirers of Donald Trump. They don't become Ben Shapiro and Jonah Goldberg devotees. You can see the sense of mischief and joy in classical liberals who leave the Left, like chat show host Dave Rubin.[152] And when unexpected cultural figures like Azealia Banks announce their support for Republican candidates, it's Trump they go for, not Ted Cruz.

Conservatives could learn a thing or two about how to beat the Left from web culture. Godfrey Elfwick is the pseudonym of a brilliant British troll who portrays an exaggerated satire of a social justice warrior on Twitter, complete with a bio that describes him as a "genderqueer Muslim atheist." For nearly three years now, he has almost never broken character, and his persona has fooled many an onlooker, including the incredibly annoying Chelsea Clinton, and the BBC, who invited him on the radio to explain why Star Wars is racist and sexist.[153] Acts of high-impact trolling like Elfwick's, which expose the Left through ridicule, are more likely to turn heads and change minds than the most brilliant column in a conservative weekly.

While consistently missing opportunities to beat the Left in winnable fights, conservatives have also done virtually nothing to lay down deeper roots in high culture. Besides a few investments from David Koch and *The Spectator's* arts section, what is there really? It's no match for the myriad of leftist and government-supported entities that fund concerts, film festivals, art shows, and other wellsprings of culture. A search for "race," "gender," or "diversity" on the website of Grantmakers in the Arts, the umbrella group for private arts funding organizations in the U.S., returns opportunities that look like *Salon* articles.[154] (Are you aware that members of the theater community experience "injury every day from being marginalized?" Do you want a "Radical guide to fighting discrimination in the arts?" Grantmakers in the Arts has you covered.[155])

The kids and teens who idolize left-wing pop stars, watch movies made by left-wing film directors, and laugh at the jokes of left-wing comedians, grow up to be—surprise!—left-wing voters. This cannot continue.

I'm suddenly aware this may come across as an argument for obsessive representation of all kinds on screen. It is not. Black kids and lesbian kids and disabled kids don't need to see themselves on screen so much as they need to be exposed to a wide variety of *ideas*. Diversity of skin color is nothing compared to diversity of opinion, and the idea that people can't identify with movie or video game characters because they don't have the same race or gender is a ludicrous invention of the progressive Left. When I was a kid I identified with the vulnerability and gravitas of Buffy Summers and Captain Janeway, despite the fact that I have a wonderful penis. Come off it.

Conservatives need to realize they will continue to be beaten by the Left if they keep ignoring the importance of culture. They need to spend less time obsessing over the marginal tax rates, and more time on the National Endowment for the Arts. Only then will the left-wing stranglehold on culture be beaten.

The NEA should not be disbanded completely, as some conservatives, including Daddy, have suggested. During World War II, allied forces set up a unit of 400 service members and civilians to find and safeguard European art as their enemies fought their way across the continent. Victory would be meaningless if the very heritage of western civilization was lost. Ronald Reagan said, "The arts and humanities teach us who we are and what we can be. They lie at the very core of the culture of which we're a part." He also said, "Where there's liberty, art succeeds." The NEA should focus on supporting great American artists, not meeting diversity quotas and pandering to progressives. And if that can't realistically be done given the political biases of the art world, then yeah, Daddy's right. Just get rid of it for a while.

Over the past decade, political correctness in culture has grown to the point where even left-wing creatives are feeling its stifling effect on free expression. Liberal comedians like Chris Rock and Jerry Seinfeld now refuse to perform for college audiences, who they say have become too sensitive for their comedy routines, even though they aren't remotely right-wing. If conservatives make a serious effort to get back into the culture wars, they will find no shortage of grateful artists and creators eager to throw off the chains of political correctness.

On the other hand, political correctness isn't just confined to the Left.

THE POLITICAL CORRECTNESS OF THE RIGHT

I'm an ardent Zionist, and it isn't just because I have a thing for tanned, muscular IDF men with big guns. I'm ethnically Jewish on my mother's side, and in my younger days I could be spotted on BBC appearances sporting a full-on Jewfro.

Another thing I ardently support is free speech and the freedom to tell jokes. Alas, some of my peers on the conservative Right don't feel the same way.

Dangerous

I was baffled when, in 2016, conservative commentators suddenly became preoccupied with the threat to Jewish communities from internet nobodies posting offensive memes on social media. Many of these people identify as the alt-right—or at least, the alt-right's shitposting, memester battalions. To them, breaking taboos isn't about advancing white nationalist ideology; it's about gleefully watching outraged reactions from their elders.

Jewish advocacy organizations, ginned up by the likes of *National Review, Daily Beast* and, eventually, the Clinton campaign, went so far as to declare war on memes. I'm not joking. Two months before the election, the Anti-Defamation League, a venerable, respected name in the fight against anti-Semitism, nearly torpedoed their credibility by declaring Pepe the Frog a "hate symbol."

I won't make excuses for actual anti-Semitic memes, particularly when they come from genuine Neo-Nazis. These sad specimens, consigned to a few irrelevant blogs like *Daily Stormer*, declared a "holy crusade" against me in late 2016. Unlike the ADL, I find this laughable rather than threatening. I don't have anything to fear from these people, especially not from *Stormer's* editor, Andrew Anglin, who I am told stands a mere 5'2" tall. He's a little short for a stormtrooper, isn't he? There's a great picture that does the rounds now and again of Anglin in Thailand with lady-boy hookers. I also hear he's actually Jewish. This is the leader of white power online, folks!

I will, however, defend *anyone's* right to speak and post freely on the internet, without the threat of being banned. The best antidote to pathetic hatred is to defeat it publicly, not push it into the shadows where it will fester and grow. This is something that leftists, and a worrying number of establishment conservatives, simply don't understand. They worry that the more people see Neo-Nazis, the more they'll be persuaded. I have a sunnier view of human nature, and human reason.

I have no argument with those who want to condemn the *Stormer's* and their ilk. But I do have an argument with those who lump everyone who uses offensive memes in with them, as part of the same "basket of deplorables." As Allum Bokhari and I highlighted in our article on the alt-right, many of the people using offensive memes aren't genuine Nazis at all, but rather provocateurs and trolls. They don't want to destroy multicultural societies or restore racial hierarchies. They just want to raise hell and smash taboos. From our article:

> Just as the kids of the 60s shocked their parents with promiscuity, long hair and rock 'n' roll, so too do the alt-right's young meme brigades shock older generations with outrageous caricatures, from the Jewish "Shlomo Shekelburg" to "Remove Kebab," an internet in-joke about the Bosnian genocide. These caricatures are often spliced together with Millennial pop culture references, from old 4chan memes like Pepe the frog, to anime and My Little Pony references.
>
> Are they actually bigots? No more than death metal devotees in the 80s were actually Satanists. For them, it's simply a means to fluster their grandparents. Currently, the Grandfather-in-Chief is Republican consultant Rick Wilson, who attracted the attention of this group on Twitter after attacking them as "childless single men who jerk off to anime."

Dangerous

Responding in kind, they proceeded to unleash all the weapons of mass trolling that anonymous subcultures are notorious for—and brilliant at. From digging up the most embarrassing parts of his family's internet history to ordering unwanted pizzas to his house and bombarding his feed with anime and Nazi propaganda, the alt-right's meme team, in typically juvenile but undeniably hysterical fashion, revealed their true motivations: not racism, the restoration of monarchy or traditional gender roles, but lulz.

Even I will admit these kids sometimes go too far, and that not all the taboos they want to break are in need of breaking. There is a reason why anti-Semitism and racism are not acceptable, and never should be. But the response of the establishment Right, unnervingly familiar in tone to the career-destroying mobs of SJWs, is worse. These are *kids*—they don't deserve to have their lives and careers destroyed because they posted dangerous memes or flirted with dangerous ideas on the internet.

It doesn't do these young people justice to simply rebut the establishment's misguided allegations of retrograde racism. These people aren't just not-racists, they're among the best and brightest of their generation; talented, creative, and funny. No one's life is ruined by bitchy messages on a computer screen. Get a grip, snowflakes. It's words on a screen.

You can't deliberately ignore context. You can't treat a harmless hellraiser from 4chan as no different from a *Daily Stormer* Nazi, without pausing to examine the motives and values of the individual. Like the

Left's political correctness, the Right's political correctness is collectivist and reductive in its logic. It will destroy the lives of innocent people if it goes unchecked. We must fight against it until it dies.

The cause of Israel is not helped by hysterical conservatives and mainstream media outlets comparing the slogan "America First" to Charles Lindbergh-style isolationism.[156] Nor is the fight against anti-Semitism helped by people like Bill Kristol playing into *Daily Stormer* talking points by suggesting that America's white working class should be replaced by immigrants ("I hope this thing isn't being videotaped or ever shown anywhere," said Kristol after he made the comment, which was of course videotaped[157]). I'm a staunch defender of Israel and an opponent of anti-Semitism. I have no doubt Kristol is too. But unlike him, I'm not making things worse.

DEBATE CLUB CONSERVATIVES

"Donald Trump isn't a *gentleman*."

"He's so *vulgar*."

"I have to cover my kid's *ears*."

There's something... *noble* about trying to preserve the standards of decorum that existed prior to the 1960s, when a single swear word on TV could lead to a boycott campaign. That worldview is completely understandable for conservatives (and even most liberals) over 65.

If you're under 40, however, it's likely that you fall into the unfortunate, slightly laughable group I call Debate Club Conservatives. And it's time to snap out of it.

If you don't have the stomach to do what it takes to win, chances are you're going to lose. And that's exactly what Debate Club Conservatives did when faced with Donald Trump. Again and again, the Republican candidates tried to convince their base that they shouldn't vote for Trump because, well, he was just so *unkind*. And again and again, voters didn't listen.

"The man is a pathological liar ... a bully ... a narcissist at a level I don't think this country has ever seen," said Ted Cruz in May. Republicans voted for Trump.

"Seriously, what's this guy's problem?" Jeb Bush allegedly told a donor in August. "He's a buffoon.... a clown... an asshole." Republicans voted for the asshole.

"I will not vote for a nominee that has behaved in a manner that reflects so poorly on our country," said John Kasich, long after his inevitable primary defeat. "Our country deserves better." Republican voters didn't think so.

The American Conservative's lament that the "graceful, dignified" Jeb Bush had been beaten by the tactics of a man who "lacks character" sums up the attitude of DCCs to elections, and to contests in general: it's better to lose with dignity than to win without it. In the Republican primaries, they mostly got their wish, although Jeb Bush's entreaties for audiences to "please clap" for him were anything but dignified.

The conservative sense of fair play is disastrous when it comes to fighting Democrats. Elections are not college debates, no matter how much Ted Cruz might wish it so. They are not fought with facts and opinions, but with sloganeering, media spin, opposition research, and other cloak-and-dagger tactics. In politics, victory goes to those with cunning, mettle and deviousness, not those who have facts and principles on their side. It *helps* to have facts and principles on your side (*as conservatives usually do*), but they aren't enough to win.

MILO

There's another reason why the DCC attitude is so damaging to the conservative movement: most people aren't political obsessives. They don't care about your 14-point refutation of Obamacare. They want to hear things that relate to their own experiences, not abstract policy debates.

One comment from Ben Shapiro, made on *The Rubin Report* in February 2016, sums up this conservative myopia.

> The problem with Trump is he fails to distinguish political incorrectness from just being a jackass... There's a difference between being rude and being politically incorrect. Being rude is telling Megyn Kelly she's bleeding from her wherever. Being politically incorrect is saying some immigrants coming across our southern border are criminals. That's politically incorrect but it's not rude.

Shapiro is thinking of a world where only politics matter. To him, political correctness is a problem because it suppresses facts relevant to current affairs—and that's it. For most other people, the stultifying rules of political correctness go far beyond the suppression of facts; it's the suppression of jokes, banter, and yes, the suppression of rudeness.

Political correctness interrupts everyday human experiences, threatening to turn every single personal matter into a public one. You can no longer slip up in conversation without worrying if the person you're talking to is going to tell the whole world what you said, potentially ruining your life forever (need I provide a personal example?). The internet's erosion of privacy with the resurgence of politically correct taboos is a terrifying combination. That's why so many people are drawn to Trump.

DCCs don't understand this because they think politics is, well, a debate club. In their imagined political ideal, elections are fought issue-by-issue, with each candidate presenting his arguments on foreign and domestic policy in neat little 30-minute segments. In reality, politics doesn't work like that—and if it did, voter turnout would be in even greater crisis.

There's perhaps no better example of DCCs being outplayed by aggressive hellraisers than the replacement of Megyn Kelly, formerly the face of FOX News, with Tucker Carlson. Kelly, now at NBC, is a milquetoast moderate conservative who, during the election campaign, attracted attention for playing the resident feminist, going after Donald Trump for making demeaning comments about women. Carlson, on the other hand, is a badass warrior of the airwaves, who *lives* to skewer progressives in front of a national audience. In his first week, Carlson almost doubled Kelly's ratings, including a 45% increase in the all-important 25-54 age demographic.[158] His show is great, that's why he got Bill O'Reilly's job. FOX News has provided the roadmap for conservative media organizations seeking to rescue themselves from decline: bring in someone who isn't a total cuck.

Politics isn't won by commanding the facts, but by connecting with people's experiences. That's why it's so important for conservatives to re-engage with culture and entertainment, which are the commanding heights of people's experiences in the modern world. All our brilliant political victories will come to an end if we don't win the culture war. Indeed, the fact that Donald Trump's signature election promise—enforcing immigration laws—was seen as so controversial, is a testament to how well progressives have ingrained their views on our culture. As recently as the 1990s, such a suggestion was completely mainstream. This is how progressives manage to keep winning the battle for America's soul, despite occasional temporary setbacks on Election Day.

And that's why, in a society increasingly frustrated by political correctness, conservatives need to grit their teeth and come to terms with the necessity of gauche, bragging provocateurs like Donald Trump...and me.

BRINGING CONSERVATISM TOGETHER

I'll be the first to admit that we need Debate Club Conservatives. It is immensely valuable to have people who can utterly dominate the Left in an argument—just compare the power and rigor of a George Will column with one by Jessica Valenti. The strongest mind on the Left today is probably Slavoj Žižek—and he supported Trump over Clinton! When the public ignores the Left's entreaties not to watch or read or listen to conservatives because of their "bigotry," they are often swayed by our arguments.

But arguments aren't enough. We can't let the Left continue to dominate culture, entertainment, and the norms of everyday language itself and expect to win elections. We can't hope that every member of the public will see through the Left's lies and eventually discover George Will's columns at *The Washington Post*. Much of conservatism is kept hidden from the public, especially in schools and colleges, where young people are figuring out who they are and what their principles are.

As Ann Coulter says, "We don't have time for an elegant person right now. The country is at stake." We need our brawlers and our fighters.

Whether establishment conservatives like it or not, the culture war will be won by men like Steve Bannon and Donald Trump, who use straightforward language and never apologize.

One man who has long understood what Republicans need to do in order to win is Roger Stone. A legendary political operative known for pulling dirty tricks, he has been described as a "henchman," "hit man" and a master of the "dark arts"—all in the same article.[159] Although he made his career in the Nixon administration, Stone has been backing anti-establishment figures for decades, including Ronald Reagan in 1976 and Donald Trump in 2016. Stone knows how to pick a winner, and given that he named me on his 2016 "Best Dressed List," it's clear the man has good taste in more than just political candidates.

We need all our attention focused on conservative issues, not leftist ones. Stop following the agenda of *The Daily Beast* and *New York Times*. Let the Left worry about insignificant "threats" like Pepe the Frog and the six or so remaining Klansmen in America. We need to turn our attention to issues that the Left either doesn't care about, or doesn't want us to notice—like their domination of academia and pop culture. I'm sure I sound like a broken record by this point, but until we make serious progress on those fronts, everything else is just noise.

Politics is more complicated than assembling facts and writing good arguments. It's a brutal battle for the attention of the public, and always has been, even before the era of Donald Trump. That's why fabulous, irrepressible faggots like myself, so original and compelling compared to the run of the mill copycat leftist celebrity, are so perturbatious to the Left. Much as it might irk DCCs, politics is showbiz today—and if we want to win, there will need to be more people like me in the future.

MILO

There is a blessing for the establishment here. By focusing attention on provocateurs like me, it gives breathing space for everyone else to develop their arguments and present them to the public without censure. After an encounter with a force of pure irreverence like me, a George Will column must seem like a nice break! A smart observer might realize that's the whole fucking point.

In March of 2017, Charles Murray, renowned author of *The Bell Curve*, was violently pursued by an angry mob when he attempted to give a lecture at Middlebury College. I know, bitch stole my act.

Perhaps you think I'm just a comedian doing all this for fun. Perhaps you think I'm just the world's biggest narcissist. Both these things are at least partly true. But, I'm also deadly serious about the American right to speak freely on any topic. People like Charles Murray deserve to have their voices heard, and my divinely appointed job is to toughen up these kids so they can properly engage in the big debates. Daniel Henninger in the Wall Street Journal brilliantly quoted President Eisenhower: "Don't join the book burners. Don't think you are going to conceal thoughts by concealing the fact that they ever existed. Even if they think ideas that are contrary to ours, their right to say them, their right to record them, and their right to have them at places where they are accessible to others is unquestioned, or it isn't American."[160]

McCarthyism is what they called it in 1953. Now, we just call it liberalism. What happened to Charles Murray is exactly why I do what I do, and it's exactly what I've been warning everyone was going to happen, and I'm telling you, it's going to get a lot worse before it gets any better. Unless we fight back.

The Left would like to shut the Overton Window and push conservatives out of public view altogether. Ironically, establishment

Republicans would like to do the same. Before I arrived on the scene, they were seriously close to succeeding. Even consummate moderates like the libertarian columnist Cathy Young were being banned from campuses.

That's how the Left fights. They take control of culture, and use it to smear even moderate conservatives as racists, sexists, and bigots. By the time American youths reach college age, significant portions of them are frothing at the mouth, desperate to suppress conservatism, which they believe to be synonymous with bigotry. When they reach that point, there is little hope of them listening to our arguments, no matter how strong they are.

That's why this civil war has to end. Conservatism needs its great thinkers and its brilliant minds—the Debate Club brigade—to persuade voters who are already open-minded. But we also need provocateurs and clowns, to grab the attention and challenge the biases of those who don't want to be challenged.

No movement has ever survived with just moderates and intellectuals, and no movement has ever survived with just hellraisers.

If we want to win, we need both.

9

WHY MUSLIMS HATE ME

*"I studied the Quran a great deal. I came away from that study with
the conviction there have been few religions in the world as deadly
to men as that of Muhammad."*
—Alexis de Toqueville

I'd really hate to be thrown off a roof.

In the summer of 2015, Europe opened its doors to millions
of people who would very much like to kill me—and you too, most
likely.

After a picture of a drowned Syrian boy went viral, globalist elites
like Angela Merkel exploited sympathy to lower the drawbridge of
an entire continent, welcoming millions of Muslim migrants, and
moving another step closer to eliminating national borders.

The implicit message from the media was clear: *all* migrants are
just like the drowned boy—innocents fleeing oppression, hunger
and death in war-torn Syria. In reality, fewer than half the people

admitted to Europe in the months following the viral photo were from Syria.[161] Most weren't refugees at all: they were economic migrants, from regions of the world even more radical than the country that currently hosts the Islamic State. And they certainly weren't boys.

Globalist media and political elites sought to extend the rare moment of pro-migrant sentiment for as long as possible. Journalists flocked to German train stations to take pictures of teary-eyed liberals holding placards stating "refugees welcome," and hugging the smirking new arrivals.

Over a million Muslims poured into the Mediterranean to cross into Europe.

It only took a few months for this leftist dream to turn into a nightmare. On New Year's Eve, 2015, the new arrivals introduced Germany to Muslim misogyny. An estimated 2,000 migrants, acting in gangs, unleashed taharrush gamea—an Arab word meaning collective sexual harassment—on German women returning from and attending New Year's celebrations.

Attacks took place in the cities of Cologne, Hamburg, Frankfurt, Dortmund, Düsseldorf, and Stuttgart. By night's end, police estimated that at least 1,200 women had been groped or otherwise sexually assaulted, including at least five rapes.[162] It was the worst night of sexual assaults in Germany since the Red Army's invasion.

Germany was not alone. Sweden, which welcomed more than 140,000 migrants, was also beset by sexual assaults. A report from *The Gatestone Institute* referred to a "Summer Inferno of Sexual Assault" in Sweden. This was largely suppressed by the police and media.[163] Analyzing Swedish crime data, the report found a particular surge in group sexual assaults on girls aged

14-15. Virtually all of the apprehended attackers were citizens of Afghanistan, Eritrea, or Somalia; three of the four largest refugee groups in Sweden. Various Swiss cities, as well as others throughout Europe, began handing out flyers to incoming migrants, explaining why groping women and bashing gays is bad.[164] Thanks to Muslim immigration, Sweden now has rape statistics approaching what feminists in the U.S. claim.

Rape, unfortunately, was just the beginning. Next came murder.

On March 22, 2016, two bombs exploded in Brussels Airport, killing 13. An hour later, another explosion went off in the town of Maelbeek, killing 20. The attack's mastermind, who also planned the November 2015 Paris attacks, was Abdelhamid Abaaoud, a Belgian native who had travelled to Syria to fight for the Islamic State, before returning to Europe at some point during the refugee crisis.

European states suspected of letting him pass through their borders on his return to Belgium immediately issued flustered denials.[165] But the truth is, no one was looking that closely at the streams of migrants flooding across the continent's borders.

Abaaoud's attacks, encouraged by the Islamic State, inspired a string of copycat strikes in Europe's summer of terror. One month later, a police officer and his wife were stabbed in Magnanville, France, by Larossi Abballa, acting on the orders of ISIS. One month after that, on Bastille Day, a Muslim driving a 19-ton truck ploughed through the Promenade des Anglais in Nice, France. 86 people were killed, and more than 400 were injured.

Two weeks after Nice, Germany was hit by a stabbing in Würzburg and then, a week later, a suicide bombing in the town of Ansbach, both at the hands of Islamists.

DANGEROUS

Two days after Ansbach, two Islamic State terrorists stormed a Catholic church in Normandy, slitting the throat of an 86-year old priest before French anti-terrorism police shot them both and rescued the remaining hostages. Ten days later, in Charleroi, Belgium, a man attacked police officers with a machete while shouting "Allahu Akhbar," which translates to "Allah is the greatest." One month after that, two police officers in Molenbreek, Belgium were stabbed by a migrant, also shouting "Allahu Akhbar."

Three more ISIS-motivated stabbings would take place in Europe before year's end: in Rimini, Italy; Scharbeek, Belgium; and Cologne, Germany.

The United States faced its own terror attack in 2016, in Orlando, Florida. 49 killed, 53 wounded at Pulse, a gay nightclub. It was the deadliest terrorist attack on American soil since 9/11, and the deadliest act of homophobic hate in U.S. history.

I gave a speech outside Pulse, about the threat posed to women and gays by Islam. The recording has been viewed almost a million times on YouTube.[166] Not a single cable or broadcast channel aired any of it.

It is a uniquely American trait to rely on foreigners to take the true stock of American culture. I am here now, with a warning from Europe. If America opens its doors to Islamic migrants as Europe has, Pulse will be just the beginning.

Islam is not like other religions. It's more inherently prescriptive and it's much more political. That's why I, a free speech fundamentalist, still support banning the burka and restricting Islamic immigration.

Walter Berns's famous essay *Flag Burning and Other Modes of Expression*, makes the point that speech and actions are different. But he also reminds us that the Founders were for unlimited speech on

176

religious topics, but not on political principles, like advocating for tyranny.[167] Everywhere Islam exists you find political tyranny. Islam is as much a political ideology as a religion, which is why limits on it are perfectly compatible with religious freedom and the First Amendment.

In electing Donald Trump, America may have saved itself. Naturally, he was attacked as a racist and a bigot throughout the campaign, both by Merkel-like establishment conservatives and by the American Left. But such behavior doesn't really surprise me anymore. The Left has been selling out to Islam for years.

ISLAM AND THE LEFT

During my college talks, I'm often asked what arguments to use when debating with the regressive Left. I always have the same answer: Islam.

There is nothing else which better exposes the modern Left's rank hypocrisy, their disregard for the facts, and their hatred for the West and all it stands for than their attitude to Islam. Every noble principle the Left claims to uphold, from rights for women to gay liberation, even diversity itself, dies on the altar of its sycophantic defense of Islam.

Karl Marx called religion the "opium of the masses." If you look at the Left's attitude to Christianity, you might think they believe in this message. The progressive Left's comedians and columnists never miss an opportunity to belittle and denigrate conservative Christians, and yet, they defend Islam at the expense of every other minority. Bill Maher, Sam Harris, Richard Dawkins and Christopher Hitchens have all been frustrated by this question: Why is the Left refusing to lift a finger against the most radical, dangerous, socially conservative and oppressive religion on earth?

Author Sam Harris sums up the backwards attitude of this group with his characteristic clarity:

> These people are part of what Maajid Nawaz has termed the "regressive Left"—pseudo-liberals who are so blinded by identity politics that they reliably take the side of a backward mob over one of its victims. Rather than protect individual women, apostates, intellectuals, cartoonists, novelists, and true liberals from the intolerance of religious imbeciles, they protect theocrats from criticism.[168]

Examples of this behavior are not hard to find.

Charlie Hebdo is a rare example of a leftist newspaper that understood radical Islam to be akin to the radical religious Right. Actually, that's too mild, it's really closer to the radical *medieval* religious Right. I know members of the radical Christian Right in the United States, and they are scary. But nowhere near as scary as Islamic terrorists. They're the Westboro Baptist Church with machetes.

Charlie Hebdo had the temerity to stand against religious bullies. They published humorous cartoons of the Prophet Muhammed, which made them prime targets of al-Qaeda. *Charlie Hebdo's* editors correctly understood that allowing people to intimidate artists and writers by threatening violence was the first step on the road to a terrified, censored society.

MILO

On January 7, 2015, twelve employees of the newspaper paid for it with their lives, when two armed Muslim siblings forced their way into *Charlie Hebdo's* offices in Paris and opened fire.

Charlie Hebdo is a leftist publication. Marxist, in fact. Their opposition to Islam flows from their opposition to the Right. They are just as strident in their criticism of the National Front as they are of Islam. I may happen to think the National Front deserves a more nuanced approach, but one could never accuse *Charlie Hebdo* of lacking consistency. They say they oppose bigotry, and they do— whether they perceive it in the European Right or in Islam.

So what did other leftists do when 12 of their comrades were gunned down by religious thugs? Did the old ideal of socialist solidarity finally kick in?

No, of course it didn't.

As most of the civilized world adopted the slogan "Je Suis Charlie," *The New Yorker* published an essay entitled, "Unmournable Bodies," attacking *Charlie Hebdo* for "racist and Islamophobic provocations."[169]

Before the month was out, a number of British student unions, including the University of Manchester, banned *Charlie Hebdo* under their "safe space" policies, arguing that it made Muslim students uncomfortable.[170]

It made Muslim students uncomfortable? Well, I'm not sure that's quite in the same league as making non-Muslim cartoonists *dead*. That, in a nutshell, is the modern Left for you.

There was no collective display of solidarity from the left-wing literary class either. To an ordinary observer, the fact that the prestigious PEN Freedom of Expression Courage Award went to *Charlie Hebdo* in 2015 would not be particularly surprising news, much less a moral outrage. Yet 204 members of the organization, including established authors like Joyce Carol Oates, Lorrie Moore and Junot Díaz thought so. They boycotted the awards, signing an open letter condemning *Charlie Hebdo* for making a "marginalized community" feel uncomfortable:

> To the section of the French population that is already marginalized, embattled, and victimized, a population that is shaped by the legacy of France's various colonial enterprises, and that contains a large percentage of devout Muslims, Charlie Hebdo's cartoons of the Prophet must be seen as being intended to cause further humiliation and suffering.[171]

What suffering! What horror! Cartoons, published in a newspaper with a minor circulation that Muslims don't have to buy if they don't want to. I'm sure the friends and families of the dead *Charlie Hebdo* cartoonists feel thoroughly ashamed of their loved one's actions.

The author Salman Rushdie, who faced an Iran-backed fatwa for the crime of writing about a forbidden area of Islamic theology, summed up the stance that the boycotters had taken.

The massacre of cartoonists, wrote Rushdie, was a…

> …hate crime, just as the anti-Semitic attacks sweeping Europe and almost entirely carried out by Muslims are hate crimes. This issue has nothing to do with an oppressed and disadvantaged minority. It has everything to do with the battle against fanatical Islam, which is highly organised,

well-funded, and which seeks to terrify us all, Muslims as well as non-Muslims, into a cowed silence.

These… writers have made themselves the fellow travellers of that project. Now they will have the dubious satisfaction of watching PEN tear itself apart in public.[172]

The boycott failed, and *Charlie Hebdo* got their award, presented to them by Neil Gaiman, who stepped in after other writers pulled out.[173] I have to wonder how he must have felt to see so many of his peers in the left-wing literary establishment choose to attack murdered cartoonists rather than stand against the ideology that created their murderers. Embarrassed for the Left, I hope.

The reaction to the *Charlie Hebdo* shooting is just one example among many of the Left's suicidal attitude towards Islam.

When Paris again fell victim to Islamic terrorism in November 2015, with over 100 slain in a series of attacks masterminded by the Islamic State, *Salon* published the extraordinary headline "We Brought This On Ourselves: After Paris, It's Time To Square Our "Values" With Our History."[174]

The article blamed the West "behaving horrifically in the Middle East for decades" for the deaths in Paris. In March 2016, after Muslims killed 35 in Brussels, *Salon* allowed the same writer to run virtually the same article under the headline, "We Brought This On Ourselves, And We Are The Terrorists Too."[175] Liberals blaming the West for the terrorist attacks has become depressingly predictable after each new atrocity.

What really cements the Left's betrayal of its own values over Islam isn't so much its opposition to wars in the Middle East, but its opposition to liberal Muslim reformers. Perhaps the best example of this is Maajid Nawaz, one of the few moderate Muslims making an effort to drag his religion kicking and screaming into the modern age. For his work combating extremism, supporting interfaith tolerance, and challenging bigotry in the Muslim community, he is rewarded with polite silence from the Left at best, and scornful disdain at worst.

New heights of absurdity were scaled in 2016 when the Southern Poverty Law Center (SPLC) added Nawaz to a list of 15 "anti-Muslim extremists." The entire list was ridiculous. It included women's rights activist Ayaan Hirsi Ali and Islam critics Daniel Pipes, Pamela Geller, and David Horowitz. But the addition of Nawaz, precisely the sort of moderate Muslim that anti-bigotry, anti-intolerance groups like the SPLC ought to be encouraging, summed up just how morally bankrupt the Left's attitude to Islam has become.[176]

Is there—and perhaps this is just my gallows humor—anything more amusing than a religion so thin-skinned that cartoons designed to provoke it give rise to deadly shootings, as though precisely to prove the point of those French cartoonists?

Is there anything more *preposterous* than the phrase "The Religion of Peace"?

What an indictment of America's supposedly "brave" comedians that not a single one dares to tell a decent joke about Islam on prime-time television.

HOW TO *REALLY* FIGHT BIGOTRY

The Left claims it opposes bigotry. Yet Islam, the most bigoted ideology that exists today, is given a pass.

MILO

Here are a few things that Muslims in Britain—who are often portrayed as one of the more integrated western Muslim communities—believe.

A *Gallup* poll of Muslims in the UK found that *not a single Muslim* in the 1,001 people polled thought that homosexuality was morally acceptable.

The same poll found that 35% of French Muslims and 19% of German Muslims thought homosexuals were morally acceptable. These polls were taken *before* Europe's importation of hordes of young Muslim "rapefugees."

As you know from the previous chapter, I have some sympathy for this point of view, even though leftists will scour me for saying so while continuing to hypocritically pander to Muslims. And yet, here are more unsettling poll numbers specific to British Muslims, from left-wing broadcaster Channel 4:

> 52% believe homosexuality should be illegal
> 23% would like to see Sharia law in England
> 39% believe a woman should always obey her husband
> 31% consider it acceptable for a man to have multiple wives.

When it comes to Islamic immigration, assimilation doesn't seem to be an option. "When in Rome, rape and kill everyone and then claim welfare."

Andrew Bolt on *Sky News Australia*, whose show I go on regularly because they get the lighting just right, perfectly encapsulated Islam's integration problem in the West.

DANGEROUS

He recalled the case of Dr. Ibrahim Abu Mohammed, the grand mufti of Australia, who gave a speech explaining to Australians that they are wrong to think Muslims can't integrate into Australian culture. There's just one problem. The Grand Mufti, one of the foremost Islamic scholars in Australia, delivered the speech in Arabic. He had lived in Australia for 19 years, and his integration speech was in Arabic.

That's what I call chutzpah.

There were 1.6 billion Muslims in the world as of 2010—roughly 23% of the global population—according to a Pew Research Center estimate. But while Islam is currently the world's second-largest religion after Christianity, it is the fastest growing one.

The growth of Islam ought to be concerning for liberals. Here is a religion that sanctions forcing women into submission, a religion that sanctions the execution of gays, a religion that sanctions the killing of non-believers. And they're spreading.

Islam preys on the most vulnerable in society, offering them a sense of higher purpose. It's no wonder gingers (ahem Lindsay Lohan) convert to Islam in such high numbers. They also have especially high conversion rates in jails, making Islam and dick the two things most likely to penetrate new inmates.

For years, the Left has been tormenting the right with tales of bigotry. We're supposed to consider frat boys singing lewd songs about women as an example of "rape culture."

We're supposed to look at critics of Black Lives Matter as racists.

And we're supposed to consider Christian bakeries uncomfortable with gay weddings as the leading example of homophobia in society today.

MILO

Well, there is a *real* rape culture in the West. And there is real homophobia in the West. And there is real out-group intolerance in the West. It all comes from Islam.

Never again let the Left tell you they are the ones fighting bigotry. They are, in fact, its greatest defenders. They are the ones standing in the way of Pamela Geller, Geert Wilders, Donald Trump, Nigel Farage, Douglas Murray, Maajid Nawaz, Sam Harris, Ayaan Hirsi Ali, and me. All the people who are *actually* doing something to fight the most intolerant, bigoted ideology in the world today face a constant pushback from the very same people who, if they were true to their own principles, would be on our side.

But it's no matter. With Daddy elected in the United States, and Brexit underway in the United Kingdom, I'm confident we can win without the regressive Left.

DEFEATING ISLAM

Islam today is like communism in the early stages of the Cold War. They both present young, disaffected people with an idealistic, tribal, utopian vision that is drawing in millions. And like communism, Islam is inspiring violence all around the world.

If there's one thing we learned from the battle with communism, it's that the West can't compromise its principles. It can't apologize for itself, like the Left constantly wants us to do.

It was no accident that the Berlin Wall collapsed at the end of the 1980s. It was the end of a decade when America and, to a lesser extent, Britain, shook off the malaise of the 1970s and recovered their national sense of self-confidence. Margaret Thatcher and Ronald Reagan proudly walked the world stage, aggressively asserting the greatness and superiority of their respective nations ("America First" wasn't invented by Trump, only perfected). In the increasingly backward, increasingly poor, Warsaw pact, the choice between the West and communism quickly became a no-brainer.

At the same time, western governments poured money into programs designed to undermine the idea of communism. With state funding, *Radio Free Europe* and *Voice of America* ceaselessly broadcast news of anti-communist activities—as well as jazz and rock music—across the Iron Curtain. The propaganda campaign was so successful that KGB memos asserted that up to 80% of Soviet youth were listening to western radio broadcasts.

That's a long way from western leader's attitudes to Islam, isn't it? Far from asserting the superiority of western liberalism to the theocratic east, they're wearing headscarves, bowing to Saudi monarchs, and grinning stupidly in mosques. In the Cold War, some western leaders advocated peaceful coexistence with the Soviet bloc, sure, but I don't think any of them ever donned Mao suits or sang *The Internationale*.

Instead of drawing attention to problems with the Islamic way of life, our leaders seek to present the increasing violence of the religion's followers as the actions of a tiny minority who will soon be defeated.

But they won't be defeated. The Islamic State may be crumbling in Syria, but it represents a world-view that is attracting swathes of young people. Because the West has done nothing to stand up for its own superior way of life, an entire generation of young Muslims came to view muftis as their rock stars and mosques as their concert halls. Western leaders talk about challenging the radicalization of young people, and then turn around and talk about how wonderful Islam is.

The results are inevitable and devastating.

MILO

It's theoretically possible to peacefully coexist with Muslims, but only if they can find a way to remove the radical element from contemporary Islam. Too many of the current generation are attracted to an ideology that insists on imposing its way of life on everyone else—or killing us, if we refuse.

And the Muslims who don't actively identify with the most poisonous end of their ideology are perfectly happy to turn a blind eye to its horrors, as poll after poll have demonstrated.

Like communism, we are dealing with a viral meme that needs to be fought head-on.

The old talking points about "violent extremists" are no longer working. Indeed, they never worked to begin with.

We're fighting an idea, and the only way to beat it is to show that the West is the best. Western leaders need to talk about what makes our society great: freedom, tolerance, equality of opportunity. Like Reagan and Thatcher, and Trump and Farage, they need to tirelessly assert their country's greatness.

Islam has to be made uncool. This is a war of culture as much as it is a war of politics or faith, and we have to start fighting it now, in music, books, journalism, art and with every other means of creativity at our disposal, demonstrating as we do so what is possible with the free expression we so cherish in the West.

But more than that—and this is what they really don't want to do—our leaders need to talk about what makes Islamic societies *bad*.

So WHY DO MUSLIMS HATE ME?
Last summer, I annoyingly had to resign myself to the fact that I could not lead a gay pride march through the gay district of Stockholm, as I

had been planning for some months. My security team informed me that the risks in Sweden were too great. By that time, I had already been subject to a deluge of Arabic death threats (and one bomb threat) on Twitter (which promptly suspended *me* for a day).

I have little love for western feminists and leftists, not least for their relentless denial of everyday realities. But at least their willful ignorance rarely comes with a body count, at least not directly (indirectly, in the form of their immigration policies, it certainly does). It is only Muslims who are so fanatically devoted to their 6th-century delusions that they will murder anyone who dares challenge them.

Well, there's a little phrase I like to say that Muslims had better be prepared to hear more often: *Sorry, no offense, but it's true.* With so much of the western media determined to play the ostrich on Islam, don't be surprised when the public turn to Dangerous Faggots to give them the real story.

The gap between what Muslims believe Islam to be, and how it is actually practiced in many Islamic nations, is so wide that it's hard to imagine any Islamic reformation taking place in the near future.

10

WHY GAMERS DON'T HATE ME

In 2013, the left-leaning *Guardian* proudly proclaimed the "fourth wave of feminism" was upon us, and that it was "defined by technology: tools (that) are allowing women to build a strong, popular, reactive movement online."[177] In other words, now women can bitch about their existence to millions of strangers online, rather than just crying while ironing like they're supposed to.

A good example is the "Donglegate" scandal, in which tech evangelist and ardent feminist Adria Richards overheard a couple of men making lewd jokes about "dongles" at a tech conference, tweeted a picture of the two men, and got one of them fired. When the internet reacted with outrage against Richards, *WIRED* magazine cited the scandal as evidence of "misogyny in tech culture,"[178] rather than what it was: an insane overreaction cooked up by a professional malcontent and grievance-monger.

DANGEROUS

The existence of fourth wave feminism and its supposed reason for existing has created a chicken and egg type of conundrum. With so much of their activism linked to the internet, they unavoidably encounter *dissent*. Sometimes a great deal of it, considering how unpopular feminists are. #YesAllWomen, intended to protest "misogyny," was met with the parody #YesAllCats. Comment threads under notorious feminist provocateur Jessica Valenti's column regularly attract thousands of critical comments. Critics of feminism on YouTube began to attract as many views as the feminists themselves, while dissident communities like Reddit's Men's Rights hub ballooned in size.

Upon seeing how many people disliked them, feminist activists started complaining that online harassment was giving them PTSD.[179] They used politicians, activist groups, and sympathetic media outlets to apply relentless pressure to social media companies, demanding they clamp down on "harassment," by which they meant people with opposing views. Any criticism of fourth wave feminism became known in the media as "trolling," "harassment," "misogyny," and "abuse."

Anita Sarkeesian, once an unknown vlogger who whined about alleged sexism in video games with cherry-picked data, rose to prominence after she tapped into the trolling panic. After trolls from 4chan and other communities mocked her in 2012, posting rude comments underneath her YouTube videos and photoshopping her into porn, Sarkeesian attracted massive media attention.

An online fundraising project for her series on women and video games soared past its targeted $6,000, ultimately receiving almost $160,000 in donations. Sarkeesian was invited to speak at the video games studio Bungie, and to TEDxWomen 2012.

MILO

In 2013, game creator Zoe Quinn was having business problems. Her new game, a rudimentary point-and-click adventure called *Depression Quest,* needed thousands of votes from gamers to be "greenlit" for publication on Steam, the largest digital distributor of video games. Guess how she got that publicity?

Quinn said she was being tormented by trolls from a little-known online community called Wizardchan, a 4chan clone populated largely by men with social anxiety. She claimed they had sent her harassing phone calls, of which there was no real evidence provided, but still, articles appeared in the games press claiming that Quinn was facing "extreme harassment because she's a woman."[180]

Less than a year later, transgender game developer Brianna Wu, *deliberately* antagonized GamerGate with a trolling campaign, and used the resulting backlash to claim that she, too, was a victim of online harassment. Claiming to have "fled her house" because of anonymous death threats, she then did what any traumatized victim would do. She went on a media tour, talking to MSNBC, *The Guardian, The Boston Globe,* and any other media outlet who'd listen to her. Previously a nobody, she's now running for Congress. [181]

Isn't it weird how these women all end up far better off *after* their trolling ordeals?

Feminists in gaming capitalized on the buzzwords and campaigns that had appeared in the "fourth wave" of feminism. Fake threats, trolling, and lewd remarks on the internet weren't just flippant jokes by teenagers; they contributed to "rape culture." Criticizing feminists for being too rude or obnoxious was "tone-policing." Feminists, by 2014, had an entire arsenal of buzzwords to help them sideline dissent and paint any and all critics as bigots.

Dangerous

No matter how legitimate the criticism, gaming journalists were committed to their narrative: it was feminist heroines versus evil misogynist trolls who just wanted to terrorize them. If a single troll from 4chan sent a single death threat (and let's be clear, *all* of these "threats" were hoaxes) to a feminist, then that was the story, not the legitimate concerns of gamers.

The only logical conclusion to the feminist-led campaign against "online harassment" was censorship. Unless, a new hero could emerge, one with the power to stop this draconian crackdown on free speech.

Birth of a Movement

The Joker fell into a vat of chemicals, which drove him insane. Magneto was imprisoned in Auschwitz, where he saw the worst in human nature. Doctor Doom decided to take over the world after a vision of the future revealed humanity destroying itself.

My supervillian origin was GamerGate, a bitter war between gamers, anonymous internet trolls, hectoring feminist scolds, and left-wing journalists. If you only follow mainstream media, you probably only know GamerGate as grown men playing videogames all day and harassing women on the internet. In reality, it was the first battle in an anti-leftist, culturally libertarian, free speech movement that led directly to Trump's election. Let me tell you the real story.

GamerGate, often considered a bewildering topic, is in fact relatively simple. In early 2014, Nathan Grayson, of the *Gawker*-run gaming blog *Kotaku*, wrote favorably about *Depression Quest*, a game for which he acted as a consultant, without disclosing his involvement in the project. Grayson's connection to the game and his romantic relationship with its creator, Zoe Quinn, was discovered after an exposé from Eron Gjoni, one of Quinn's ex-boyfriends.[182] Upon reading Gjoni's story, gamers began to suspect that game developers and journalists were literally in bed with each other.

I have some sympathy for Quinn and Grayson. Sure, what Grayson did wasn't *ethical*, but in normal circumstances it wouldn't lead to a culture-war cataclysm. The games press wasn't unlike any other sort of trade press. It was characterized by pathetically low journalistic standards, an ideologically homogeneous atmosphere, cliquey politics and innumerable overlapping conflicts of interest. However, few people beyond journalism professors *really* care if a reporter is friends with, or even fucking, one of their reporting subjects. And yet, thanks to the dreadful professional track record of the games press, and their appalling response to gamer's concerns, it just happened to become a *thing*.

Following the discovery of the Grayson-Quinn connection, gamers across the web embarked on one of the greatest acts of collective internet sleuthing in history. Virtually overnight, "GamerGate" discussions sprang up on some of the web's biggest communities, like the anonymous discussion forums 4chan and Reddit, and #GamerGate began trending on Twitter.

Gamers quickly uncovered a web of connections between games journalists and their reporting subjects. Games journalists had reported on their friends without disclosure, and in some cases had even donated money to their reporting subjects.

Critical Distance, a hub of social justice-oriented games critics, repeatedly gave favorable coverage to multiple game creators who had given them monthly donations through the crowdfunding site Patreon.[183]

Gamasutra editor-at-large Leigh Alexander published dozens of articles lauding her personal friends.[184] Multiple other journalists were found to have similarly dire track records, which are now catalogued at the GamerGate-created website *DeepFreeze.it*.

All of this was embarrassing for the games media, especially since hard-core gamers have an innate respect for fair play. But it was hardly an international scandal. The *real* reason GamerGate became a gigantic story was due to the reactions of these media outlets when they were exposed as ethically compromised.

For Leigh Alexander, there could be no quarter given to gamers. "These obtuse shitslingers, these wailing hyper-consumers, these childish internet-arguers—they are not my audience," she wrote.[185]

In the space of 48 hours, a dozen articles were published in a similar vein. All op-eds, all repeating the same opinion: gamers are bigoted white males trying to make the world of video games less inclusive. Arthur Chu at *Daily Beast* called gamers "misogynist losers" who were "making us all look bad."[186] *Kotaku's* Luke Plunkett described them as "reactionary holdouts that feel so threatened by gaming's widening horizons."[187] *VICE* lamented that Eron Gjoni's "embarrassing relationship drama" was "killing the gamer identity."[188] *The Daily Dot* described GamerGate simply as a "sexist crusade to destroy Zoe Quinn."[189]

At the same time, a discussion about the ethics of games journalism on Reddit's gaming subforum, one of the largest gathering-places for gamers on the web, was completely nuked. Over 20,000 comments were deleted, making it one of the largest—perhaps *the* largest— suppressions of discussion in Reddit's history.[190] NeoGAF, already known for its ban-happy owners, started kicking GamerGate supporters off the platform left, right and center. Popular YouTuber Boogie2988 was banned just for taking a neutral stance on the topic.[191]

Even 4chan, known for hosting discussions about anything, no matter how vile, rolled out a blanket ban on GamerGate in mid-September. The decision sent shockwaves through its pro-free speech user base, leading to a mass exodus to alternative site 8chan.[192] Fallout from the decision would eventually convince Christopher "Moot" Poole, the site's founder, to leave 4chan after 10 years at the helm.[193]

GamerGate wouldn't have got off the ground without a great deal of assistance from would-be censors. The very first YouTube video about the drama surrounding Eron Gjoni and Zoe Quinn attracted a meager 4,599 views on its initial run.[194] Then Quinn lodged a false copyright claim against the video, taking it offline, and the internet exploded. It's weird that someone like Quinn, who was deeply embedded in web culture, would make such a mistake. After all, it was false copyright claims that propelled the rise of Anonymous.[195]

Shortly after the games media launched its volley of articles smearing gamers as sexist, misogynist bigots, #GamerGate surged in activity. It would retain a high trending position for much of 2014, and well into 2015.[196]

By late 2014, it was apparent that GamerGate no longer described a scandal, but an entrenched consumer movement—tens of thousands of gamers fully prepared to wage war against a gaming media that had turned on them.

GamerGate wasn't going to be a flash-in-the-pan controversy. It was here to stay.

DANGEROUS

A COOL FAGGOT, LIKE FREDDIE MERCURY

I entered the story in the early days of GamerGate, when an anonymous Twitter account with an anime profile picture and the handle @LibertarianBlue sent me a couple tweets explaining the controversy. The account belonged to Allum Bokhari, now one of *Breitbart's* most gifted writers. He spoke of journalists engaging in nepotism and censorship, and critics being smeared as misogynists. I asked for more information.

Out of our collaboration emerged my first story on the controversy, which was the first published story that unapologetically took the side of gamers. While the rest of the media lamented the alleged "hate-campaign" against women in gaming, I took the ethics concerns of gamers seriously, and listened with an open mind to their complaints about a partisan political press and out-of-control feminist narratives that were slamming the lid on open discussion in the games world. "Feminist Bullies Tearing the Video Games Industry Apart" was the headline I chose—understated, as always.

It turned heads, and it set the tone for later coverage. Having watched the "online harassment" panic grow to absurd heights, I was determined to show that criticizing and even mocking feminists did not make you a misogynist. As for exposing the biases and ethical failings of the press—well, that was even more important. It was also trivially easy to accomplish, thanks to an anonymous source who is now one of my most trusted contacts in the industry.

A month after the gamers and games journalists went to war, I was handed the most explosive story of the entire controversy: a series of leaks from "GameJournoPros," a secret email list used by journalists

196

MILO

from gaming and tech publications including *Kotaku, Polygon, Ars Technica, Rock Paper Shotgun, WIRED, PC Gamer* and *The Verge*. I wasn't sure why I had been chosen to deliver these logs to the public, but I did know exactly what to do with them: publish them all on *Breitbart*, and watch as the flames of the greatest lulz-fire on the internet leapt ever higher into the sky.

The logs confirmed gamers' worst suspicions about collusion behind the scenes in the gaming media. Journalists from competing outlets appeared to be in cahoots, making decisions about what to cover and how to cover it.

The games press was biased beyond belief. Kyle Orland, games editor of *Ars Technica* and the founder of the email list, was seen calling the concerns of gamers "bullshit," and encouraging other editors not to cover the GamerGate controversy at all, and instead use social media to reproach gamers.

An editor at one publication, *Polygon*, was seen urging the editor of another publication, *The Escapist*, to censor discussion of GamerGate on *The Escapist's* message boards. Orland was also seen encouraging other journalists to contribute to a fundraiser for Zoe Quinn. At this point, *Kotaku* journalist Jason Schreier wisely pointed out that a fundraising campaign for a game developer might not be the best idea at a time when games journalists were facing mass allegations of collusion and political bias.

For gamers, the fact that such a thing had even been suggested by a games editor at a major tech publication said it all.

There's no better feeling for a journalist than breaking a big story that other publications are afraid to touch, and I was already having a great time. But I was having an even *greater* time because at last, I had discovered a corner of the internet to call my own. I had discovered *web culture*.

Anonymity or pseudonymity instantly clued me in on why gamers were proving to be such tough adversaries for the biased progressive media, and for the feminist architects of the new moral panic. The irreverence of 4chan was the product of an anonymous online environment, which minimized the usual social consequences associated with taboo-defying speech. Progressives and feminists, the modern-day guardians of social mores, naturally think this is terrible. Leftist actor Wil Wheaton has even suggested banning anonymity in online video games.[197]

Shortly after I began my reporting on GamerGate, I took a trip to the video games board of 4chan, known as /v/, then one of the hubs of the movement. I was met with what I would later discover were called memes and shitposting. Virtually everyone told at least one gay joke.

My face was photoshopped onto a picture of the interracial gay porn movie *Poor Little White Guy.* Another 4channer posted an image proclaiming that I was not simply a faggot, "but a cool faggot like Freddie Mercury." Having spent my professional career in the stultifying, politically correct world of tech journalism, I was amazed—and overjoyed—to discover there was still one place of pure, unfiltered mirth in the world.

I had found my people.

If I were a disingenuous left-wing blogger, I could have painted my anonymous hosts on 4chan as the vilest of homophobes and bigots. But that wouldn't have been true, would it? It was obvious on its face that the people talking to me were not bigots of any kind, just irreverent teenagers with a healthy disregard for language codes. This was their way of showing affection, not disdain.

Furthermore, the GamerGate supporters who came from /v/ and its more politically incorrect sibling /pol/ didn't even meet the standard progressive definition of bigots. From the pages of *The Guardian*, Jessica Valenti—with no evidence whatsoever—denounced GamerGate as a "last grasp at cultural dominance by angry white men." It was a glorious moment, watching leftists on social media accuse Twitter users of being white dudes, only to see them dumbfounded as the users responded with face pics clearly identifying themselves as women and/or minorities.[198]

As GamerGate gathered steam, thousands of female, gay, and ethnic minority gamers tweeted #NotYourShield to protest at having their identities used as "shields" to deflect the racially obsessed lies of rubes like Valenti.

The first reaction of the games media was disbelief. Rabid SJWs considered #NotYourShield to be full of "ill-informed women" with no purpose other than "shut[ting] down talk about racism."[199] A piece in *Ars Technica*, perhaps the most brazen report of the entire controversy, claimed that accounts posting #NotYourShield on Twitter were just "sockpuppets" and not genuine minorities.[200] Other left-wing journalists made similarly disparaging comments, or, more commonly, ignored the tag entirely, pretending instead that GamerGate was an exclusively white male uprising.

If that sounds familiar, consider the apoplectic response from feminists and mainstream media journalists to Trump's success with female voters. Lena Dunham went on *The View* in full schoolmarm mode to remind the feminist sisterhood of its duty to re-educate those poor, ungrateful, ill-educated female hillbillies who voted Republican. (Those weren't her exact words, but we understood what she meant.)

Is there anything more revealing than leftists shutting out the voices of women and minorities because they're telling them things they don't want to hear?

This is the true story of GamerGate, not the "misogynist white dudes" narrative you've heard from the mainstream media. It was about issues that would become dividing lines in the emerging millennial culture wars, as well as in the 2016 general election: free speech, the future of the open internet, and a nightmarishly partisan press corps that demonized critics of fashionable progressive causes as hate-filled bigots, while holding up their spokespeople as saints who could do no wrong.

THE NEW MORAL PANIC

In the 2000s, Jack Thompson, a conservative lawyer, filed a lawsuit against Take Two Interactive, then publishers of the *Grand Theft Auto* series, on the grounds that it inspired murder. He was mercilessly ridiculed in the games press, which then appeared to be performing its function as the defenders of creative freedom against absurd political crusades.

Because of battles like this with the conservative Right in the 1990s and early 2000s, gamers developed a resistance to politicization of any kind. "I just wanted to play video games" was one of the slogans of GamerGate. Gamers took pride in their hobby's resistance in the face of an increasingly politicized world. This is how video games managed to escape the first wave of the Left's cultural takeover.

Researchers can find no evidence that games make anyone violent or sexist.[201] The studies that leftists and moral crusaders frequently cite are those that show a link between violent video games and *aggression*—but similar links are also found with sports games.[202] You play a high-adrenaline sport and you become more aggressive. Who knew?! But that's nowhere near the same as video games turning people into killers.

A lack of evidence never gets in the way of a good storyline. You may remember Elliot Rodgers, the "killer virgin" who went on a shooting rampage in May 2014.[203] Naturally, the fact that he played video games was invoked. No evidence that games had anything to do with his actions was ever presented, but no evidence was needed. The storyline that video games must be involved in bad behavior was simply too compelling to pass up for the media.[204]

The same thing happened to Marilyn Manson, who was blamed for the Columbine school shootings, even though the shooters themselves hated him and didn't listen to his music. One media report simply decided Manson was to blame, and the rest followed suit.

When feminist critics began taking tentative steps into the sphere of games criticism, the new allegation was that even though games can't make you *violent*, they can make you *sexist*. These were not psychologists or researchers who had data to back their claims. They were "gender activists and hipsters with degrees in cultural studies," according to feminist scholar Christina Hoff Sommers.[205] They didn't know much about video games, but they knew cis-heteropatriarchal capitalist oppression when they saw it.

What I call the left-wing war on fun has a long academic pedigree, stretching back to the rise of "critical studies" in the late 60s and 70s.

DANGEROUS

Critical studies viewed art, literature, and entertainment through only one lens: how it critiqued, or failed to critique, dominant "power structures" (capitalism, Christianity, patriarchy and all the rest).

No longer were these forms to be criticized on their ability to inspire, awe, shock, fascinate, illustrate, or depict: all that mattered was how well (or how poorly) they critiqued the boogeymen of gender studies departments.

Like overzealous Freudian psychologists who manage to link virtually every human experience back to childhood sexual trauma, progressive cultural critics find a way to interpret every artistic expression through their own particular lens of victimhood.

Lisa Ruddick, an English professor at the University of Chicago (an institution in the running for the smartest and most forward-looking university of modern times) is one of a growing number of dissidents challenging this orthodoxy. In her influential essay, "When Nothing Is Cool," she describes how one scholar used critical studies to turn Buffalo Bill, the sadistic antagonist of *Silence of the Lambs,* into a gender-defying feminist hero.[206]

By removing and wearing women's skin, Bill apparently refutes the idea that maleness and femaleness are carried within us. "Gender," Judith Halberstam explains, is "always posthuman, always a sewing job which stitches identity into a body bag." The corpse, once flayed, "has been degendered, it is postgender."

Halberstam blends her perspective uncritically with the hero-villain's posthuman sensibility, which she sees as registering "a historical shift" to an era marked by the destruction of gender binaries and "of the boundary between inside and outside."

202

MILO

The lunacy here isn't just that a serial killer who targets only women could in any way be a feminist hero, it's that the scholar who wrote it actually thought her interpretation was believable. To most people, *Silence of the Lambs* is simply a masterful psychological thriller, full of compelling characters, emotionally powerful moments, and no deeper meaning beyond the protagonist's terrifying and engrossing journey through a world of cannibals and serial killers.

To a left-wing culture critic like Halberstam, it's unacceptable that a movie could simply be intended to entertain, shock, or amuse. It *must* say something deeper, even if its creator didn't intend it to. And if a piece of art or entertainment *really* seems designed with no hidden political message? Well then, that means its creator and those who enjoy it must be just fine with the status quo—this makes them either blind, or the enemy (depending on how far gone the libtard is).

To a culture critic, everything is political, even when it's not trying to be. *The Los Angeles Times* interviewed Jordan Peele, the creator of *Get Out*, one of few politically motivated movies that still manages to entertain, and asked him about the significance of one of the white actresses in his film drinking milk. "Milk," *The Los Angeles Times* offers, "is the new symbol of white supremacy in America, owing to its hue and the notion that lactose intolerance in certain ethnicities means that milk-absorbing Caucasian genetics are superior."

Get Out is about a white family that kidnaps black people so they can brain swap with their younger, "cooler," and physically superior bodies. The theme could not possibly be more racially motivated, and still, the *The Los Angeles Times* has felt the need to find racism wherever it looks. Peele did not back up this milk drinking as racism thesis in any way, and yet, *Los Angeles Time's* headline still read,

"Jordan Peele explains 'Get Out's' creepy milk scene, and ponders the recent link between dairy and hate."[207]

Little wonder that culture warriors hate video games, many of which are clearly designed for no purpose other than wild abandon. Imagine the fury of Anita Sarkeesian and her dour erstwhile male assistant Jonathan McIntosh, as they scoured games like *Team Fortress 2* and *Pong* for hidden political messages. Imagine it dawning on them that the millions of people who log into *World of Warcraft* every day are doing so primarily to have fun with their friends, and not to consider how well Illidan Stormrage symbolizes inexorable patriarchal forces.

To a leftist, where everything is political and nothing is fun, gamers are a nightmare. Gamers feel the same about their critics.

Gaming culture is naturally resistant to political correctness. Online video games were the original social networks: gamers were chatting on games like *Everquest* and *Runescape* years before Facebook and Twitter came into their own. And, crucially, communication in these games tended to be anonymous. Like 4chan and Reddit, the furthest most people would come to identifying another player was via their pseudonym—and there's not much you can do to track someone down when the only lead you have is a username.

Anonymity, mixed with the competitive nature of many online games, led to a culture of "trash talk" amongst gamers.

Keemstar, a popular YouTuber, explains how alien and shocking gamer culture must seem to polite society:

> I've received many death threats. I've been told that I'm going to be raped. People have said they were going to

do sexual things to me while I was playing these games, because it's part of gaming culture. I'm not saying it's right, but any real gamer has experienced this, and they know it to be somewhat normal. This is what people say online to each other while they are gaming.[208]

If you're not familiar with gaming culture, the whole idea that this kind of talk is normal must seem very strange. But this is merely the kind of joshing that goes on between best friends, especially in young male communities. Nobody feels threatened because everyone knows the rules of the game.

For example: "Hey filthy fucking dickwaffle," might be used as a friendly greeting. Some of the most common topics for casual jokes include rape, necrophilia, and Nazism. If someone thinks you're behaving stupidly or disagrees with you, "go kill yourself" will be a common, almost automatic, offhand remark. The biggest mistake you can make is to take any of this language at face value. Sure, it may be jarring for someone who's not used to the conventions of this speech community, but that is no excuse for condemning it as bigoted or misogynist, when it clearly is not.

And if you don't like it, online games afford multiple opportunities to set up your own gaming servers with stricter rules.

Mainstream society finds it impossible to reconcile this language with the reality that most gamers are actually left-wing, not to mention completely comfortable with diverse, tolerant societies. To leftists, rejecting their language codes is the same as being racist, sexist, or homophobic. Gamers know it isn't. And that made them the perfect enemies for an increasingly progressive movement hell-bent on shaming ordinary people for violations of their dreary, stultifying language codes.

SHAMERS

In the years preceding GamerGate, left-wing SJWs had turned social media into their personal playground. With the aid of outlets like *BuzzFeed*, *Gawker* and *The Guardian,* they engaged in relentless public shaming campaigns to socially ostracize individuals, businesses and organizations that failed to abide by their increasingly restrictive set of politically-correct norms. Justine Sacco, a communications executive whose life was upended by *Gawker* after she tweeted a joke about white people not being able to catch AIDS, is a well-known example. Ironically, Sacco's tweet was an attempt to make a point about the injustices of white privilege. For that crime, she became the most hated woman in America, and lost her job. The point of public shaming isn't merely to offend or annoy, but to cause total social ostracism—the ultimate punishment for violating society's taboos.

Video games did not escape the rise of public shaming. In May 2014, a small-time video games developer, Russ Roegner, discovered his career was in jeopardy.

"Be careful with me," warned *Gamasutra's* Leigh Alexander. "I am a megaphone... I wouldn't mind making an example out of you."

"This has been an amazing look at someone just starting out burning every bridge possible," remarked games journalist Ben Kuchera.

"Really. Just. Stop," said Ian Miles Cheong, editor-in-chief of *Gameranx*. "You're not helping your case."

What had Roegner said to attract such warnings?

"There's no issue with gender equality in the game industry. I wish people would stop saying there is."

Expressing such a view was career endangering in the video game industry of 2014.

Another infamous case of media-led public shaming in the gaming industry was the campaign against Brad Wardell, CEO of software and games development company Stardock. In 2010, Wardell was falsely accused of sexual harassment by a former employee.

Ben Kuchera wrote an article initially claiming that the case against Wardell had "damning evidence," and included some of the most disgusting accusations from Wardell's accuser (including the claim that he asked her if she "enjoyed tasting semen.") Wardell was not contacted for comment before the article ran.[209]

Kotaku ran the same story, covering the accuser's allegations in similarly lurid detail. The article contained the full allegations of Wardell's accuser, but, deplorably, no counter-arguments from Wardell or his legal representation. That was because *Kotaku* had only given Wardell an hour to respond with his side of the story.[210]

As a result of this sloppy, *Rolling Stone*-tier journalism, Wardell faced years of smears and attacks, and even told me that his kids were being shamed at school because the first Google result for his name was the *Kotaku* article. It is worth noting that Wardell is one of the few open political conservatives with a position of prominence in the gaming industry, which might explain why the campaign against him was so relentless.

The case was dismissed in 2013, and the former employee apologized for her claims.[211] *GamePolitics*, one of the outlets that reported on the unsubstantiated allegations against him, apologized for its sloppy reporting. Others followed suit, but it was too little too late. There's no way to unstab someone once your pitchfork has pierced their flesh.

Public shaming relies on isolating its victims, who are made to believe that they are alone against an overwhelming tide of majority opinion. It's a feeling that was shared by Donald Trump supporters—until they started winning. In reality, the shamers are usually part of a vocal minority, allowed to dominate the conversation by terrifying others into silence.

But gamers are hard to frighten. During GamerGate, they came out in droves to show the world how small and hysterical the purveyors of social ostracism really were. KotakuInAction, the leading Reddit community for GamerGate supporters, has more than 70,000 subscribers. GamerGhazi, the hub for feminists and social justice warriors in gaming, has a mere 11,000.

Gawker, one of the worst public shaming organizations to ever exist, was even kowtowed by GamerGate. Editor Sam Biddle, who had been personally responsible for destroying Justine Sacco's life, was forced to apologize for anti-GamerGate tweets he said were jokes. It was a rare apology from one of the most unscrupulous sites on the internet. Soon, *Gawker*'s disgusting lack of journalistic integrity would kill the site. If it weren't for GamerGate, *Gawker* would still be here.

Through numbers and tenacity, gamers broke through their fear of social justice warriors. The months following the birth of GamerGate saw a full-scale backlash against SJWs. Sites like *Kotaku* and *Polygon*, bastions of SJWs, created new disclosure policies in response to GamerGate demands.[212]

MILO

Before GamerGate, victims of public shaming like Justine Sacco had virtually no allies in the press. Many disagreed, but did not want to get on the wrong side of the social justice mobs. After GamerGate, victims like Dr. Matt Taylor, the British astrophysicist who was driven to tears after he was attacked for wearing a shirt featuring allegedly "sexualized" drawings of sci-fi women, could rely on an increasingly confident community of moderate liberals and conservatives who loudly and sternly condemned their persecutors. The silence had been broken. And we had gamers to thank for it.

Unlikely Heroes

GamerGate was hugely significant. It was the first time consumers of a major entertainment medium staged a mass resistance to the influence of the political left. Gamers showed frightened, isolated dissidents that it was possible to fight the cultural left, and win.

No one was more amazed than I was. I once described gamers as dorky weirdoes in yellowing underpants. And, let's be fair, some of them are. Probably perfectly nice people. Yet here were these dorky weirdoes, taking on the fury of the leftist media-activist complex without flinching. Unpaid, undisciplined, and in some cases, yes, unhygienic—but they were winning cultural victories that eluded even million-dollar conservative PACs.

After GamerGate, never again can gamers be mocked as awkward losers. They might be awkward, but they're definitely not losers. In a *Breitbart* column on the movement's one-year anniversary, I compared them to Hobbits; unlikely heroes who just wanted to be left alone, but ended up saving the world. In retrospect, it's perhaps not so surprising that a bunch of people who spend all their spare time conquering kingdoms, killing dragons, and racking up high scores knew how to win.

The Left didn't know what they were getting themselves into when they went after video games. This was the hobby of the millennial generation, enjoyed by millions around the world—often together. What chance did the Left have, with their usual allegations of bigotry, against such a naturally diverse hobby? The sight of the Left attacking innocent gamers as a menacing force of intolerance was laughable. Perhaps the fears of the Left weren't so hysterical. Gamers were the first group of people to beat them in the millennial culture wars. Their tactics helped inspire a new movement of cultural libertarians, setting off a chain of events that put Trump in the White House. When *The Washington Post* called Donald Trump the "GamerGate of American Politics," they weren't entirely wrong.[213]

While most of the hard work was conducted by tireless, relentless, and often anonymous gamers who received no thanks for it beyond smears from the mainstream media, I was proud to be a part of the movement as well.

Gamers taught me that with humor, memes, and a little bit of autistic single-mindedness, no battle is unwinnable.

11

WHY MY COLLEGE TOURS ARE SO AWESOME

"The aim of totalitarian education has never been to instill
convictions but to destroy the capacity to form any."
—*Hannah Arendt*

I was in the middle of a speech at Rutgers University in New Jersey, when three hysterical young ladies in the audience stood up and smeared what looked like blood on their faces, hysterically shrieking "BLACK LIVES MATTER" over and over.

None of the students, incidentally, were black.

I later discovered that the blood was fake, but that didn't make it any less absurd, or any less troublesome for the janitors, who had to deal with the trail of red paint left by the protesters after their two minutes of fame were up. Peaceful attendees who had come to hear a speech instead found themselves splashed with fake blood, while at least one attendee was assaulted by a protester who deliberately smeared him with the stuff.

More surprising to me than the protests at Rutgers, par for the course on college campuses, was what happened the following morning. Students at Rutgers University were so traumatized by my presence that the administration held a group therapy session.

Those who attended the therapy reported that students described "feeling scared, hurt, and discriminated against," because of my innocent lecture about the importance of free speech on campuses.

If a few comments from me about the free and open exchange of ideas are enough to put college students into therapy, what's going to happen when they encounter someone who's *actually* intolerant and bigoted?

When my tour started, I'd been in the spotlight for about a year, as a rising star of the online right, fighting battles against the whiny, spoiled social justice warriors of the internet. Having grappled with some of their more absurd web-based campaigns, like the fight against "online harassment" (which, like "hate speech," means anything they disagree with), I was now prepared to break out of tech journalism and take the fight to them in the real world. It sure was fun triggering them on the internet, but as I'd discovered during my protest of the 2015 Los Angeles Slut Walk, it was a lot *more* fun to hear their banshee-like shrieks of distress in real life.

I knew my opponents were prone to emotional hysterics. I called my jaunt across college campuses the "Dangerous Faggot" tour for that very reason: to mock students who seriously believed that a flouncing queer from across the pond posed some kind of "threat" to students.

MILO

Soon after Rutgers, I arrived at Bucknell University, a small liberal arts college located in the sleepy rural town of Lewisburg, Pennsylvania. The chaos at my previous stop brought me to the attention of the administrators there, who booted me from the on-campus guest residence over concerns that I presented a safety threat to the community. As if I might corrupt the basketball team, or something. Some generous fraternity brothers took pity on me and put me up in their house.

By Thursday evening, Bucknell administrators had decided that students wouldn't be permitted to speak to me directly during my speech, but rather that they'd have to write their questions down on index cards, with my host Tom Ciccotta, now a *Breitbart* reporter, reading them aloud to me. Furthermore, the Bucknell University Conservatives Club wouldn't be permitted to film the event. Instead, the administration would film the lecture and then release the footage to Tom if the proceedings didn't reflect poorly upon the university.

Shortly after I left Bucknell, Tom was removed from his position as class president. They said it was because he missed a few meetings, and who knows, maybe he had. But everyone on campus knew the real reason the rules were suddenly being applied so rigidly. Social justice leftists are running modern American universities, and they're so very, very petty.

Did Bucknell's administrators really believe I was such a corrupting influence on young minds that I couldn't be allowed to speak to students directly? Did they believe I *really* was dangerous? Nah. At best it was another pointless restriction designed to make conservatives on campus suffer. At worst, it was outright censorship.

DANGEROUS

Rutgers and Bucknell weren't outliers. As my tour progressed, it became apparent that lunacy was the norm, not the exception, on American college campuses. At the University of Pittsburgh, protesters were in the crowd, although they were less rowdy than the ones at Rutgers. Even their placards were quiet! They used tiny signs printed on ink jet printers. I had to have them read aloud because I couldn't see them. Really, Pittsburgh protesters, you were a disappointment.

Afterward, their Student Government Board held a meeting to discuss my appearance on campus. The student government president told college reporters that he "teared up" when he heard the stories of traumatized students. Another board member argued that my words constituted "real violence" and that left-wingers at the event felt they were in "literal physical danger."

"Free speech should not trump safety," she said. These students truly believe that open discourse is a form of violence.

The tour as a whole was anything but a disappointment. Videos of my talks, filmed on a shoestring, attracted millions of views on YouTube. Stories on *Breitbart* about the chaos and hysterics at my events received tens of thousands of comments and shares. I was exposing the angry, poorly dressed underbelly of American campus politics, and the world was rapt.

By the time I reached Pittsburgh, it was only February 2016. I was not a month into my tour, and had performed at fewer than six colleges—yet it was already clear that I'd tapped into something massive. And so, after a brief series of meetings at *Breitbart*'s Los Angeles offices and in Cannes during the film festival, I was told to go out, double down, and be more outrageous than ever.

By then, word had spread to other colleges that there was a dangerous faggot on the loose. This caused protesters to up the ante. At DePaul University in Chicago, I stood transfixed as Edward Ward, a Black Lives Matter activist, local minister and alumnus, stormed the stage with an angry look in his eyes. Once I calmed my raging boner, I realized he had grabbed the microphone from my student host and had essentially taken over the event. Meanwhile, a shrieking female accomplice had jumped on stage too and began to swing her fists an inch from my face.

The police did nothing, something I later found out was a result of administrators ordering them to stand down.[214] I ended up cancelling my talk and leading my supporters outside for a protest march in defense of free speech. Despite groveling to the left-wing protesters who wreaked havoc at the event, the University President, Dennis H. Holtschneider tendered his resignation just two weeks later after pressure from left-wing students and faculty members who were angry that he hadn't banned me from campus altogether.[215] Although the response of the university was pathetic, no one had been seriously hurt, and I was glad to see that my words were so vexing to the campus left. Rage was building.

I find it difficult to understand how anyone could hate me. But such was the anger I confronted at every event that I came up with some theories. And those theories all boil down to one simple fact: I'm tremendous.

I have single-handedly flummoxed the campus censors. In the years before my arrival, they had been on a roll, stopping even mild-mannered conservative columnists like George Will from speaking on their campuses.[216] Yet here I was, a magnificent blond bastard who told edgy jokes and—horror of horrors—occasionally said celebrities were ugly. I was freely romping into their cherished safe spaces and there was nothing they could do to stop me. I had resources, I had the backing of *Breitbart*, the most fearless news organization in America, and I was riding a wave I had helped to create: a new movement of young, politically dissident troublemakers.

Just as I was attracting fanatical hatred, I was also attracting a devoted fan base. The shouts and shrieks of my protesters were loud, yes, but not as loud as the chants of "MILO! MILO!" and "USA! USA!" from eager audiences. At UC Santa Barbara, my fans even started the tradition of carrying me into lecture halls on a golden throne. It felt…right.

As my college tour progressed, it was clear that conservatives, libertarians, non-totalitarian liberals, and other political dissidents on campus were becoming bolder and more mischievous. The old order of political correctness was crumbling around us—we could all sense it. This was, after all, the glorious summer of Donald Trump's presidential campaign. At the University of Michigan, college crybabies went so far as to call the police after spotting pro-Trump chalk drawings on campus.[217] Other students went further with their triggering pranks, even constructing mock "Trump walls" on campus.[218] If George Will were to arrive on a campus that summer, leftists would have been too busy protesting a dozen other outrages to notice.

Sometimes people don't understand just how loopy college campuses are. So let me tell you about one of the things campus crybabies get most upset about.

"Cultural appropriation" is the buzzword the Left currently uses to torment people it accuses of disrespecting other cultures. White girls wearing dreadlocks or hoop earrings are a particularly popular target, as are Halloween parties, where ponchos mean peril and you can be scalped for wearing a headdress. Wearing the garb, or dancing the dances, or even writing from the perspective of another culture is a grave act of neo-colonial oppression, we are told.

But compare that fantasy complaint with the reality of art. The *Final Fantasy* series borrows from George Lucas, who borrowed from Akira Kurosawa, who borrowed from Dostoyevsky and Shakespeare. Without appropriation, culture as we know it would not exist. Civilization would resemble a Nickelback album.

Cultural appropriation only applies to white people using/wearing/ enjoying things created by non-white people. Black people can wear jeans, drink Guinness, eat spaghetti, and use electricity with no concern for the cultural ramifications of their actions. Why, if I didn't know better, I might conclude that cultural appropriation was just an excuse to paint white men as history's eternal villains.

One particularly amusing example of cultural appropriation panic occurred in July 2015, when Boston's Museum of Fine Arts announced "Kimono Wednesdays," in which visitors were encouraged to pose in kimonos next to Claude Monet's painting *La Japonaise*, which depicts the artist's wife in a similar outfit. Local leftists found the prospect of whiteys dressing up in oriental outfits outrageous, and promptly conducted a sit-in at the museum.

But, hilariously, the (mostly white, college-age) protesters soon found themselves joined by counter-protesters who, by contrast, were actually Japanese. According to *The Boston Globe*, the counter-protesters carried signs welcoming others to share in Japanese culture. Among the counter-protesters was Etsuko Yashiro, a 53-year old Japanese immigrant who helps organize Boston's Japan Festival. Yashiro told *The Globe* that she was "disappointed by the other side," and reportedly blamed the incident on the protester's youth. Other local Japanese residents were similarly befuddled. The Deputy Consul General of Japan in Boston, Jiro Usui, told *The Globe,* "We actually do not quite understand what their point of protest is. "[219] You and me both, Jiro.

Few things betray the short-sighted, joyless, anti-human stupidity of the Left as much as cutural appropriation. Virtually every book, film, play, video game, and work of art is the result of a long history of cultural appropriation.

It's how art works. But, to the campus Left, it's just another form of racism.

One of reasons college students get so upset about everything is the poor quality of teaching they receive. Well-educated people are generally unshockable. The reason progressive students—and most of the media—get so riled up about me is that *they don't know anything.* They have no intellectual hinterland and no curiosity about the world around them or about anything that has preceded their own lives. Centuries of history, culture and wisdom are dismissed as the products of "dead white men."

The smuggest, supposedly smartest people in America are actually among the most hilariously stupid and poorly schooled.

RISE OF THE DANGEROUS FAGGOT

Like most power-mad cowards, leftists made desperate attempts to reassert control from the group's inviting me to their campuses. Their primary hope was that university administrations, which were often bursting with leftists themselves, would stop me from appearing.

MILO

At UC Irvine, administrators allowed our event to proceed. I, a gay guy, who loves black men, wore police fetish gear while scolding Black Lives Matter for not giving a shit about black lives. No one else in pop culture is making subversive statements like that anymore.

After I left UC Irvine, the College Republicans group was slapped with a one-year ban by the university for having the temerity to invite me back. Their justification for the ban was that the College Republicans had failed to provide a certificate of insurance for the security hired for my initial event. Although, given that the college administrators issued their ban just one hour after a meeting with College Republican president Ariana Rowlands, during which she revealed her intention to invite me to UC Irvine a second time, the excuse was suspect from the start.

After heavy coverage in *Breithart* and the conservative media, as well as a terrific show of force by Rowlands, who refused to compromise with the administration, UC Irvine eventually engaged in a humiliating u-turn, lifting the suspension on the College Republicans and allowing me to return.

As my tour gathered steam, the tactics used by frightened administrators to stop me became more underhanded and slippery. At the University of Alabama, administrators hit my student hosts with a $7,000 security fee at the last minute. Again, after negative coverage in the conservative media and some stern lawyering, the university said that the College Republicans would not face any expense for security, and that they had been "trying all along" to help them host a successful event.

Other universities tried similarly slimy methods. The University of Miami cancelled over "security concerns," which mysteriously arose mere days before my event was scheduled to take place. The University of Maryland unwisely decided to copy the University of Alabama, slapping student organizers with a $6,500 security fee a few days before my event. Their defiance won't last. I'm coming for them, and they know it. We will hold an event at the University of Maryland, come hell or high water, because they are a public institution and they are prohibited by law from denying their students the right to hear differing opinions. The student hosts brave enough to invite me, and earn the enmity of their administrations, deserve large amounts of praise.

Despite the road bumps, by fall 2016 I could tell we were making a difference. This is a movement, and it's going to take back American college campuses. And it's already so much fun.

THE FAG BUS ROLLS IN

Picture a tour bus. You know, like the ones rock stars and rappers have. A beautiful, sleek steel beast, coated in black. Only, the picture on the side isn't of a singer or a supermodel; it's a giant picture of my face, staring directly at you, beside bold text that reads "DANGEROUS FAGGOT." I don't think the word FAGGOT has ever been printed so large before.

By the time the second leg of my tour rolled around in September 2016, I was a superstar. So naturally, I got my own bus. I decided to call it "Anita," because I knew the bus would end up more famous than GamerGate antagonist Anita Sarkeesian. (I was right.)

I used to think I was so hot that nothing could make it easier for me to pick up dates. It turns out I was wrong. Having a tour bus with your face on it helps tremendously. So does leaking a tour rider to the press that includes two-dozen de-thorned white roses, fifty doves, four topless Abercrombie and Fitch models, a snow-cone machine and horse-oil hand lotion.[220]

Anita the Fag Bus was soon spotted on dozens of college campuses, until she was eventually retired after being vandalized by Californian anarchists.

After my early successes in triggering America's college crybabies, the invitations came pouring in, so we staged a 38-date tour of the entire country. We began in Texas, wound our way through Louisiana's coastline down into Florida, and then drove up through Georgia, Alabama, and the Carolinas, leaving a trail of furious college lefties and jubilant college conservatives in our wake.

This time, we were doing it properly. I had a full camera crew, a creative director, a speechwriter, a personal trainer, and a small Mexican dude I kept around to carry my bags and manage my vast wardrobe. We were prepared for anything.

At first, protests were surprisingly disappointing. Then again, we were travelling across the south, which is Milo country. Many was the time in Texas we were stopped by a burly, aviator-clad biker or a cowboy-hat wearing pickup truck driver for autographs, even when I toppled out of the bus into a truck stop wearing a silk robe or a dress. Exactly the sort of people that Democrats call bigots and homophobes were stopping by the Dangerous Faggot's bus to get his autograph.

Contrary to the progressive stereotype of bigoted, backwater hicks, my audience is far more open-minded than a leftist safe-space dweller. When I sold out Louisiana State and tried to troll my own audience by appearing as my drag queen alter-ego, Ivana Wall, they gave me a standing ovation.

DANGEROUS

The groundswell of attention that the Rutgers incident brought to my tour forced organizers to move my lectures to bigger venues. The 400-seat venue at Bucknell University filled to capacity in just 15 minutes and more students were turned away at the door. At Louisiana State, we sold out a 1,200-seater in just 48 hours. Everywhere I go there are lines around the block.

Are these students simply seduced by the controversy and mystery surrounding me and my lectures, or have I actually kick-started a full-scale revolt populated by disenfranchised young people who are fed up with political correctness, safe spaces, trigger warnings, and social justice?

This leg of the tour offered up magical moments beyond count. At the first new stop, in Houston, Texas, an Army Sergeant First Class gifted me his dog-tags. It was the closest I've ever come to shedding a tear. The Fort Sam Houston soldier told me, "You give a voice to us who have to be silent, who have to deal with having the political correctness shit pushed down our throats." (He may have been referring to my politically incorrect report on the horror of women in combat.[221])

By the end of the tour I'd gone all-out on the theatrics. I submitted myself to a college "hazing" live on stage at Dartmouth.

Sometimes, and even I must admit it, audience members stole the show. At the University of South Florida, a girl named Sarah Torrent, who fled a Muslim marriage in her home country, called on leftists and feminists to meet her outside "for an ass-kicking" if they still insisted on bringing her persecutors into the West.[222]

In Clemson, South Carolina, where the school banned references to the deceased gorilla Harambe and the internet meme Pepe the Frog

222

over racism concerns (no, really), we discovered a budding James O'Keefe. Conservative student Caleb Ecarma spent months infiltrating an anti-Milo group on campus ahead of my visit, mapping out their connections to faculty members and monitoring their attempts to block my visit. I was amazed by the passion and devotion that my tour was inspiring.

As Anita the Fag Bus headed up the east coast, we began to encounter more protests. At West Virginia University, masked "anti-fascists" (they call themselves that, yet they seem awfully keen on political violence) appeared in ski-masks carrying placards. One of these said "MILO SUCKS." Given that the statement was, frankly, perfectly true, I decided that I must possess the placard, and a helpful fan was able to obtain it for me during the grapple going on between protesters, attendees, and campus security in the hallway.

During a particularly bitter winter stop at Michigan State University, members of my crew and I thought it would be good fun to don our own ski-masks and join the protesters ourselves. It was a daring operation, which we made more exciting by the deliberate misspelling we put on our placards. Would anyone notice? Would our cover be blown? Thankfully, our tactic worked—the placards were so badly spelled that they must have assumed we were on their level of intelligence.

Berkeley In Flames

The protests on the east coast were tumultuous, but nothing compared to what lay ahead on west coast campuses. After their campus cry-ins, leftists moved on to throwing tantrums... extremely destructive tantrums.

Dangerous

The first signs of trouble were at UC Davis in January 2017, where I was due to hold a discussion with entrepreneur and Wu Tang Clan fan Martin Shkreli. The discussion never happened. Protesters rushed the venue around thirty minutes before my event was due to begin, overturning barricades and throwing them at campus police officers. Reports of protesters wielding hammers and smashing windows to gain access to the venue quickly spread. Meanwhile, outside the venue, an ABC10 reporter was attacked with hot coffee, while my own cameraman Matt Perdie was shoved and spat on.[223] It was pandemonium.

Within minutes of the barricades being overturned, campus officials were on the phone to my team and the College Republicans, urging them to cancel the event. The Republican group later said they were intimidated by the UC Davis administration, who they said told them that they would be held "personally liable for property damage and injury to people and even death."[224]

I was determined not to let UC Davis's cowardly response, their intimidation of the College Republicans, and the thuggery of left-wing protesters result in a victory for censorship. So, the next morning, I led a protest march across campus in defense of free speech. The protesters returned, but didn't dare attack anyone in broad daylight. I even took a few selfies with them. All was as it should be; violence and intimidation had not won the day.

But the tumult at UC Davis was just a warning, a sign of the far greater violence and destruction that was to come. The far Left had responded to Donald Trump's victory with panic and fury, making dangerous analogies to 1930s fascism, Nazi Germany, and something they called "The Resistance."[225] A host of militant grassroots organizations sprang up, with threatening names like "Disrupt J20" (January 20th was the date of Trump's inauguration) and "By Any Means Necessary" (BAMN)[226] James O'Keefe, a legendary conservative journalist who specializes in infiltration and exposure, caught activists on tape threatening to "fight the police" and burn houses a few days before the inauguration.[227]

Inauguration Day saw protesters in D.C. torching trash cans, engaging in running battles with the police, and burning a limousine (ironically, it belonged to a chauffeur service owned by a Muslim immigrant). Elsewhere in the city, white nationalist leader Richard Spencer took a punch to the face while he was giving an interview, to the joy of left-wing commentators, who quickly set about turning "punch a Nazi" into a meme. "Do Punch Nazis," wrote a columnist for *Observer* who argued that the "violent nature" of white supremacy made the punch an act of self-defense.[228] Spencer actually rejected political violence in the very interview during which he was punched, proof that liberal journalists are a step beneath even white nationalists like Spencer.

Newsweek reported that many liberals had, through watching the video of the punch, rediscovered "the joy in life."[229] *The Independent* published a "supercut" of Nazis being punched in the face, with the Spencer punch featured alongside clips from *Indiana Jones* and *Inglorious Basterds*.

Punching Nazis sounds almost reasonable—but only almost—until you recall that the Left considers anyone to the right of Jane Fonda to be racist, fascist, neo-Nazi, or some combination of the three. If that sounds like an exaggeration, remember what prompted their violence: the election and inauguration of Donald Trump, a social liberal from New York who took Ted Cruz to task because the Texas Senator was opposed to Caitlyn Jenner using women's bathrooms. I also face the same ludicrous allegation that I'm a jackbooted white supremacist. If this is what counts as a Nazi in 2017, we're *all* going to get punched—the act of reading this book is enough to label you a Nazi, apparently.

Extreme political violence from the Left became more and more apparent as I travelled up and down the west coast, where the temper tantrums and physical attacks escalated. When I arrived at the University of Washington in Seattle, on Inauguration Day, I was greeted by a banner that urged onlookers to "STAB MILO." University officials took it down, but it was a portent of the violence that would take place later that night. I was, after all, in the city that hosted the "Battle in Seattle," an outbreak of left-wing violence in 1999 in which 40,000 protesters and more than 200 thugs from the "black bloc"— black-masked left-wing anarchists known for their love of political violence—caused massive damage. (Ironically, the 1999 rioters were there to protest globalism, the very ideology that Donald Trump is busily fighting in Washington, DC.)

Rehearsals for my Seattle show had barely begun before a huge mass of protesters arrived on campus, throwing buckets of paint and burning things in front of rows of riot police. The police helicopters buzzing in the sky—a first for me—testified to the seriousness of the situation. Outside the venue, my cameraman was assaulted yet again, taking a punch to the face and having his equipment broken.[230]

Soon we heard an even more sinister report from outside the venue. Someone had been shot. I was in the middle of my talk and decided to carry on with it, refusing to be canceled by violence.

After the show, police evacuated attendees through an underground car park, telling them to remove their Make America Great Again hats. By now, the anti-Milo protesters had been joined by anti-inauguration protesters from elsewhere in the city, and the crowd swelled to over a thousand. As the critically injured man was rushed to hospital, reports emerged that the police had confiscated wooden poles, heavy pipes and other weaponry from the black-clad protesters.[231]

The precise circumstances of the shooting were (and remain) murky, but it was clear that things were getting out of hand. I continued to preach more speech as the only appropriate response to ideological disagreement.

The final stop on the Dangerous Faggot tour was UC Berkeley, perhaps the most famous left-wing college in America. In the 1960s, Berkeley was host to Mario Savio's Free Speech Movement, which fought against the administration's restrictions on political activities on campus. Savio was an ardent left-winger, yet he operated at a time when the Left fought against censorship rather than in favor of it.

A shy, chronic stutterer, Savio understood the importance of speech. It was no accident that he founded a movement that stressed the value of free speech as inherent to human dignity.

I wrote earlier in this book that conservatism is the new counter-culture. The inversion of beliefs that has taken place on American college campuses makes my point for me. Once again, Berkeley would be the site of free-speech protests, only this time, it was the *protestors* calling for censorship.

As at UC Davis, protesters showed up around 30 minutes before I was due to speak. As at the University of Washington, they were well-organized, obviously privately funded, armed, clad in black masks, and determined to cause mayhem. They seized barricades and used them as battering rams to smash windows of the Martin Luther King Student Union, showing ironic contempt and disrespect for King's revered teachings on civil disobedience.

These weren't sporadic, disorganized outbreaks of violence. The black-masked protesters arrived in a single group and attacked as a single group, storming the building as a unit before melting back into the crowd of "peaceful" protesters, who happily concealed them. Attendees of the event caught outside were treated mercilessly: one man appeared on camera with a bloody face. A girl wearing a "MAKE BITCOIN GREAT AGAIN" cap was pepper-sprayed in the middle of her interview with a local news channel. Later in the evening, video footage emerged of a man lying unconscious on the ground while protesters surrounded him.

The rioters—let's dispense with "protesters"—were not satisfied with the cancellation of my event. After word spread that my speech would not happen, the thugs marched into the town of Berkeley itself, where they proceeded to vandalize businesses, including four local banks and a Starbucks (irony level 1,000). The final estimated crowd size was 1,500 and the total damage was estimated at $100,000 on campus and $500,000 in Berkeley itself.[232]

The response of city and campus officials was depressingly predictable. The police did not lift a finger to stop the ongoing riot. They did not even form a shield-wall as they had done at the University of Washington. John Bakhit, a lawyer for the union representing the UC system's police force, later complained that the police officers "weren't allowed to do their jobs."[233]

"UC Berkeley's attitude amounts to this," wrote *The San Francisco Chronicle*. "We'd rather deal with broken windows than broken heads."[234] The article recalled the lawsuit that had emerged from the Occupy protest at UC Davis in 2011, in which the University of California had to pay out $1 million in a legal settlement after a university police officer pepper-sprayed a passive protester. The fires and smashed windows, by contrast, cost UC Berkeley around $100,000. It's not hard to do the math, although it remains unclear who issued the order for police to stand down.

The Mayor of Berkeley, Jesse Arreguin, was similarly feeble in his response. Arreguin started the evening by condemning me, tweeting that, "Using speech to silence marginalized communities and promote bigotry is unacceptable," and that "hate speech isn't welcome in our community." The idea that speech can somehow "silence" others is an insidious progressive meme used to justify censorship.

As violence broke out, Arreguin returned to Twitter to half-heartedly proclaim, "Violence and destruction is not the answer."[235] The following morning he put out a statement condemning the violence, while also condemning me as a white nationalist. My lawyers forced him to retract and apologize.[236] Turns out, Arreguin is Facebook friends with Yvette Felarca, that wonderful little Asian teacher who is the face of the "resistance" movement, BAMN (By Any Means Necessary).

Leftist attempts to shut me down backfired. President Trump himself intervened, tweeting that if UC Berkeley could not defend free speech, he might consider withdrawing federal funding. I was invited on both *The Today Show* and *Tucker Carlson Tonight* (I went with Tucker, obviously), and my media profile soared. Once again, the Left had tried to strike me down, and once again, they had made me more powerful—and more fabulous—than they could possibly have imagined.

But that does not mean we should celebrate the Left's dark turn. Under the banner of "anti-fascism," the Left is bringing the actual tactics of fascists—armed political violence—to America's streets. Some on the Left have realized how much this hurts their cause, which is why former Labor Secretary and current Berkeley professor Robert Reich pushed the ludicrous conspiracy that the riots were part of a plot by Steve Bannon, *Breitbart* and me to discredit the Left. With BAMN's Yvette Felarca boasting to the media about the riot's "stunning success" in shutting me down,[237] this was a difficult argument to maintain, and even *The Washington Post* scorned the theory.[238]

It was bad enough when the radical Left was clowning itself by running to safe spaces and therapy sessions whenever a conservative speaker arrived on campus. Now it was shocking America in another way, by bringing armed political thuggery to the nation's streets in response to respectable, mainstream conservative and libertarian opinion.

My visit to Berkeley sent a clear signal to conservatives, libertarians, and other free-speech defenders: it was in this California college town where the Left's rabid, violent contempt for freedom of thought and expression could be exposed. At the time of this writing, I am planning a week-long rally at Berkeley. Myself, Ann Coulter, and other heroes of the Right will be in attendance, defending free speech. I'll also be handing out the first ever Mario Savio Award, in honor of Berkeley's famous free speech defender.

For free speech to have any true meaning, it must be practiced where it is most unwanted. One day, perhaps, the Left will realize that the only way to claw back toward credibility is to meet their opponents with calm, reasoned debate. But if Berkeley, Seattle, and UC Davis were any guide, that day is still a few generations off.

Happy Warriors

Despite the hellraising, my campus tour was about more than just causing a ruckus. There was method to my madness. For too long, the American campus has been the preserve of leftists, who channel funding into crackpot gender studies courses and radicalize students against political tolerance, openness to opposing ideas, and ultimately against reason itself. For too long, they've gone unchallenged.

So how do we fight back against an American educational system that provides coloring books, warm cookies and emotional support puppies to students who can't handle the kind of classy, unthreatening feminism of Christina Hoff Sommers?

Three things separate my brand of conservatism from the tired "suit and tie conservatives" American college students are so familiar with: humor, mischief, and sex appeal. Conservatives typically don't have fun. When I think of an American conservative, I think of stuffy bores like Ted Cruz, who, while brilliant, puts me to sleep. I've injected these three things into right-wing politics, and thus during my tour I've developed a new and growing coalition of young conservatives and libertarians.

The Dangerous Faggot Tour made great strides in the battle being waged on American college campuses. Despite the setbacks and punishments laid out by regressive administrators, we earned several significant victories. After my visit to Rutgers, university president Robert Bachi released a statement in which he reaffirmed the institution's commitment to free speech and academic freedom:

> Both academic freedom and our First Amendment rights are at the core of what we do. Our University policy on speech is clear. All members of our community enjoy the rights of free expression guaranteed by the First Amendment. Faculty members, as private citizens, enjoy the same freedoms of speech and expression as any private citizen and shall be free from institutional discipline in the exercise of these rights. In addition, they also enjoy academic freedom of expression when functioning in their roles as faculty members...While I will not defend the content of every opinion expressed by every member of our academic community, or of speakers who we invite to our campus, I will defend their right to speak freely. That freedom is fundamental to our University, our society, and our nation.[239]

At Emory University in Atlanta, Georgia, students protested and rallied outside the office of the president after campus sidewalks were chalked with pro-Trump sentiments. The special snowflakes at Emory told reporters they felt threatened by the pro-Trump students, and the campus was no longer a safe space for them.

I knew immediately I had to make a trip to Atlanta. When I finally made it to Emory, there was anxiety from students concerned over my impending arrival. Although they spent time preparing signs and chants, their protest efforts were largely ignored. The event was so well attended that students filled the hall around the venue, listening to the event and hoping to get a chance to peek in. At the end of my lecture, I led the Emory students out onto a center quad, and encouraged them all to express themselves on the sidewalk.

With students surrounding me, I took a piece of chalk and wrote "Dangerous Faggot" in the middle of the quad. After I finished, I took the bucket of chalk and passed it around to the students in attendance. Students wrote everything from "Fuck Milo" to "Build the Wall." It was a glorious example of what an American university should be.

Shortly after my visit, Emory's president James W. Wagner took a piece of chalk himself to the sidewalk right next to where I had laid down my own message, and wrote in big letters "EMORY STANDS FOR FREE EXPRESSION."

It turns out Wagner attended Emory for his undergraduate studies. "It was always [a] great, friendly, challenging discussion that really taught you to critically think," Wagner said, noting these discussions helped to hone his political opinions and prepare him for his career as an attorney. "I took that with me to law school where I was challenged more on my viewpoints. It's really important to understand the opposing side and their arguments, where they're coming from, and to form your own opinions. It's formative. And it's absolutely required, in my opinion, at the university level."

So there you have it. With a few pieces of chalk, what started off as a light-hearted prank to trigger leftists on campus gradually morphed into a symbol of political free speech. We started off having fun, and we ended up winning a major ideological victory. That's the beauty of being a happy warrior: you achieve victories without even realizing you've been fighting.

DANGEROUS

At a high school in Des Moines, Iowa in September 2015, a soon-to-be-unemployed man addressed a room full of students.

"I don't agree that you, when you become students at colleges, have to be coddled and protected from different points of view," he said. "Anybody who comes to speak to you and you disagree with, you should have an argument with 'em. But you shouldn't silence them by saying, 'You can't come because I'm too sensitive to hear what you have to say.' That's not the way we learn either."

The man in question was Barack Obama, then still president of the United States.

It says a lot that even Obama, well to the Left and far more supportive of identity politics than many moderate Democrats, thinks there's a problem on America's college campuses. But he's not alone. Many of the voices now joining conservatives in their critique of coddled students are moderate liberal ones: Jonathan Chait, Judith Shulevitz, and Jonathan Haidt to name a few.[240]

In May 2016, Nicholas Kristof, a *New York Times* columnist, who once published an article titled, "When Whites Just Don't Get It," and, more recently, "Trump Embarrasses Himself And Our Country," released a rare admission that progressive intolerance had gone too far on college campuses.

> We progressives believe in diversity, and we want women, blacks, Latinos, gays and Muslims at the table—er, so long as they aren't conservatives.
>
> Universities are the bedrock of progressive values, but the one kind of diversity that universities disregard

is ideological and religious. We're fine with people who don't look like us, as long as they think like us.[241]

Although he moderated his opening by saying that it might be a "little harsh," Kristof went on to conclude that:

> Universities should be a hubbub of the full range of political perspectives from A to Z, not just from V to Z. So maybe we progressives could take a brief break from attacking the other side and more broadly incorporate values that we supposedly cherish—like diversity—in our own dominions.

If Nicholas Kristof and Donald Trump (who called student protesters at the University of Missouri "babies" and criticized the college's "weak, ineffective leadership" for caving in to their demands) agree that there's a problem with out-of-control lefties on college campuses, then we truly have a broad consensus. The question is, what next?

Putting pressure on colleges to follow the University of Chicago's lead would be a good start. Chicago told its 2016 intake of students point-blank not to expect any trigger warnings or safe spaces at their educational establishment.

"Fostering a free exchange of ideas reinforces a related University priority—building a campus that welcomes people of all backgrounds," wrote the Dean of Students, Jay Ellison, in a letter to freshmen. "Diversity of opinion and background is a fundamental strength of our community. The members of our community must have the freedom to espouse and explore a wide range of ideas."

DANGEROUS

The University of Chicago is distinguishing itself as a home of free expression, with feisty professors like medievalist Rachel Fulton Brown, who writes the popular blog *Fencing Bear*.

When colleges start to take intellectual and political diversity as seriously as they take the more superficial forms of diversity, then there will no longer be a need for Milo. Until then, look for the Dangerous Faggot at a campus near you. In America and beyond, I will continue to fight for my vision of campus life; one of constant intellectual and political simulation, where dangerous ideas are welcomed rather than shunned. Where violating some great taboo will lead to spirited debate, not a trip to the office of an Orwellian "Bias Task Force." I will fight for the sound of laughter in the hallways and quads.

Colleges should be aware that there's a price for quashing free speech and caving in to the radical, hateful activists of the regressive Left. If you let things get as bad as Berkeley, you might see your campus set on fire, be denounced by the President, and have to cooperate with an FBI investigation. You might see a MILO Bill show up in your state legislature.

In some cases the government won't even need to get involved. Just look at the University of Missouri, which became the poster child for left-wing radicalism in 2015 after activists forced the resignation of the college president and demanded the administration submit all students in all departments to a "racial awareness and inclusion curriculum," created and overseen by a board composed of "students, staff, and faculty of color."[242] In the wake of protests, and the university's decision to cave in to them, Missouri suffered a massive shortfall in enrolments and alumni donations. Its lack of enrollments forced it

MILO

to shutter two residence halls, which were ironically called "Respect" and "Excellence."[243] The lesson? Stand up to political bullies, or lose Respect and Excellence.

There are already signs that UC Berkeley might become afflicted by the Mizzou disease. Soon after the riots on campus, and the woeful response from campus police, Scott Adams, the creator of the syndicated comic strip *Dilbert*, himself a Berkeley alumnus, announced he would no longer donate to the college.[244] Here's another lesson colleges need to learn: if you lose your balls, your money will follow.

During my college tour, I learned that not all millennial students are pampered, sheltered snowflakes. There are thousands upon thousands of students up and down the country ready to fight back against the intellectually stifling environment that surrounds them. Students who are no longer willing to sit back and be bullied by administrators, faculty members, and leftist activists who want to shut their views down.

We can't assume that the entire millennial generation is made up of snowflakes. Remember, some of the social justice Left's greatest foes are millennials themselves. Just look at Lauren Southern: she was still a college student when she almost single-handedly destroyed the feminist "slut walk" movement with a series of viral counter-protests. Not satisfied, she went on to cause the resignations of a number of social justice warriors in the Libertarian Party of Canada, stalling its descent into hand-wringing leftism. Now she's a rising star of the Right, producing powerful journalism on the Islamic takeover of Europe. If the millennial generation can produce women like Southern, it's hardly fair to call them all "snowflakes."

Dangerous

Perhaps millennials are thin-skinned because the culture they grew up with was so soft around the edges. I was in the last few years of teens who grew up with Marilyn Manson, Guns 'n' Roses, Nine Inch Nails, Madonna, *The Dark Crystal*, *Time Bandits* and the *Never-Ending Story*. If you're reading this and you're 22 or 23, by comparison your culture has been remarkably fluffy and peril-free. When I was growing up, not every story had a happy ending and it wasn't always obvious who the bad guys where. I idolized Mariah Carey, Paris Hilton, Skeletor, Darth Vader and Margaret Thatcher.

My generation and all generations before me were exposed at a young age to the reality that life can be cruel and being "a good person" isn't going to change that. Your generation, not so much. Partly because you grew up on Justin Bieber instead of Rage Against The Machine, but also because your teachers and professors have insulated you from any and all forms of trauma.

Professors who want to follow the example of the University of Chicago should suffer in silence no longer; now is the perfect time to start a resistance movement. There will be pushbacks and reprisals in the beginning, sure, but in the long run it will pay off. The defenders of the status quo are too few and unpopular to cling on to power for very long.

Dissident faculty members, I've given you an army: use it!

There is no better time to achieve a revolution on college campuses. Potential allies are starting to multiply. Everywhere you look, there are moderate liberals conceding defeat to conservatives and admitting that political correctness has gone too far. A new coalition is waiting to be built.

I can live with that.

MILO

Fighting the good fight isn't all bad. I've become ever more notorious—the most disinvited campus speaker of 2016.[245] But that's just a bonus! There's a revolution brewing on college campuses. My tour is one important component. Two million dollars later, we've forced colossal change in American higher education, achieving more than two generations of conservatives and libertarians before us. And we're just getting started. My next tour, which might be underway already by the time you read this, will be called TROLL ACADEMY.

Every time they try to ban me, I get more powerful—because I don't back down. You could say I'm only theatrical because they force me to be. Would there be a market for Milo if conservative and libertarian opinions were treated just as fairly as everyone else's? If Batman is the yin to Joker's yang, perhaps Milo had to exist to balance out Lena Dunham.

You'll know I've won when no one comes to my shows any more. In the meantime, as everyone knows, there are lines out the door everywhere I show up. That tells you all you need to know about the state of free thought on college campuses.

Administrators should have learned the lesson by now. If you think I'm crass and boorish and a cancer on your school's intellectual life, how about you start hiring more conservative academics? Because if you leave it just to the students, you're going to end up with a lot more people like me.

MILO'S COLLEGE RANKINGS: HEROES AND ZEROES

Want to know what college you should send your kids to, donate to, or apply to? Look no further. These are the colleges that have distinguished themselves – for better or worse.

ZEROES:

The University of Missouri: 2015's poster child for spinelessness saw its president resign over largely made-up racism complaints from privileged student activists. Do not enroll. Do not donate.

U.C. Berkeley: 2017's poster child for spinelessness. University police stood back and watched rioters set fires, loot buildings, and beat up anyone who looked vaguely pro-Trump.

U.C. Davis: Bullied college Republicans into cancelling my event minutes before it was scheduled to begin after violent protesters stormed the venue.

DePaul University: Administrators instructed campus police not to intervene when belligerent activists stormed the stage and swung their fists in my face.

The University of Maryland: Forced college organizers to cancel my event by hiking security fees at the last minute.

The University of Miami, Florida: Cancelled my event for vague, undefined "security concerns."

New York University: Ordered a professor, Michael Rectenwald, to go on leave after he publicly criticized political correctness and declared himself a "deplorable" on social media.

Villanova University: Caved in to activists who demanded the cancellation of my event.

Iowa State University: Forced the cancellation of my event by – you guessed it – levying a last-minute security fee hike on student organizers.

HEROES:

The University of Chicago: The Chicago Principles on Free Expression, outlining the college's absolute commitment to free inquiry and free expression, are widely considered to be the gold standard in the fight against campus censorship. In 2016, the university greeted freshmen by warning them not to expect any "safe spaces" during their time at college.

California Polytechnic State University: Its president, Jeffrey Armstrong, refused to compromise with activist attempts to cancel my event, despite calls for his resignation.

The University of Minnesota: Minnesota's law faculty quickly moved to strengthen free speech protections on campus after protesters attempted to disrupt my lecture on campus.

Oklahoma Wesleyan University: Its president, Dr. Everett Piper, issued a letter to supporters of safe spaces in 2015, informing them that his college is not a "day care."

Emory University: When activists demanded action against students chalking pro-Trump slogans on campus grounds, Emory's president, James W. Wagner, responded by chalking his own message: "Emory Stands for Free Expression."

Ohio State University: Administrators ended a Missouri-style sit-in protest in 2016 with quiet efficiency, by threatening protesters with expulsion and arrest if they did not disperse.

Michigan State University: In contrast to the feeble response of campus security at U.C. Berkeley, police at Michigan State arrested no fewer than six unruly protesters and sent the rest running.

HOW TO BE A
DANGEROUS FAGGOT
(EVEN IF YOU'RE NOT GAY)

Over the next decade, social justice warriors and busybodies are going to be beaten into submission by the forces of freedom and fun. We are going to win, and it's not thanks to a ferocious conservative press, or killer political candidates or great Republican authors and thinkers. It's you, buying this book, laughing at the crybabies on Twitter and Facebook, finally throwing your hands up in disgust and saying, "Enough."

From college students sick of attending mandatory consent workshops and learning 42 new gender pronouns, to video game fans who just want to be left alone, the past couple of years have shown the power of ordinary people to defy elites and radically alter the cultural consensus. We're nowhere near sick of winning yet, and I am filled with excitement when I imagine what brilliant conquests our gang of deplorables will achieve next.

MILO

The moon landing? Pfft. There is no more exciting time to be alive than now. We are living in an age of heroes, villains and revolution, and no one quite knows where the next uprising will come from.

The attempt to stifle cultural expression has gotten so bad that even leftists are getting sick of it. Lionel Shriver, author of *We Need To Talk About Kevin*, is one of the most accomplished leftist authors in the world. In 2010, she authored *So Much For That*, a book about a man who has to sell his business and give up his dreams to pay for his sick wife's healthcare costs. It is essentially a critique of the pre-Obamacare American model of private healthcare.

Yet even Shriver has figured out that something has gone terribly, disastrously wrong with identity politics. Her keynote speech at the Brisbane Writers' Festival in September 2016, which she delivered wearing a sombrero, was an evisceration of the Left's new obsessions: identity, cultural appropriation, and feelings. She went as far as to call the identitarian Left the "culture police" and announced a sincere desire for them to go away soon.

> I am hopeful that the concept of "cultural appropriation" is a passing fad: people with different backgrounds rubbing up against each other and exchanging ideas and practices is self-evidently one of the most productive, fascinating aspects of modern urban life.

Shriver also committed what is, for a leftist, an unforgivable sin: she explained the actual reason for the rise of Donald Trump.

DANGEROUS

> The Left's embrace of gotcha hypersensitivity inevitably
> invites backlash. Donald Trump appeals to people who
> have had it up to their eyeballs with being told what they
> can and cannot say. Pushing back against a mainstream
> culture of speak-no-evil suppression, they lash out in
> defiance, and then what they say is pretty appalling.[246]

Shriver's speech was an important moment, due to her stature in the world of left-wing literature. But she was just one of many liberal-leaning creators who have begun to speak out against the regressive Left. Other renowned authors, like my literary hero Bret Easton Ellis, have also spoken up.

The imagination cannot help but rebel against the shackles that the regressive Left would seek to put on it. The cultural libertarian revolution is only just beginning.

Like you, I'm sick of the odious blue-haired fucks on college campuses. I'd rather be at home watching Netflix, sucking off my boyfriend, or spending thousands of dollars in Louis Vuitton. I do what I do because I have to, because no one else can or will right now. Until, perhaps, this book gets out there and inspires the next generation of culture warriors.

I have to go through the motions, day after day, absorbing the vitriol from the media and idiotic protesters, because every other conservative and libertarian figurehead has utterly failed you. I'm like Cincinnatus, the Roman general who dropped his plough to lead an army to victory and secure the safety of his homeland, before immediately returning to the farm and his slave girls. In my case it would be a harem of Nubian catamites, but otherwise the picture is the same. In my heart of hearts I want to declare victory, or at least to pass the baton on, so I can go back to the chaise longue and indulge myself in silk and champagne.

But I know that will never happen in my lifetime, so I am resigned to the fight. I will wage war as long as there are dykes in gender studies departments telling lies about innocent young boys, as long as Black Lives Matter activists are attacking people for their skin color and as long as Britney has to withhold music videos because her managers are worried they aren't feminist enough. I will fight so long as free expression and creativity are at risk from thick-as-pigshit New York bloggers and social-justice activists.

I've always felt an acute sense of personal ordainment—as though my life was meant for something greater. It's why I always related to *Buffy the Vampire Slayer*. I'm the chosen one. I was chosen to fight the dark forces that pervade our world. As long as America needs me, I am yours.

At least for now, I am rejoicing. Because together, we have struck a savage blow in what will be a decades-long fight to reclaim creative freedom and freedom of speech from the political Left. I'm talking, of course, about Daddy.

It was 1:40 AM on November 9, 2016, and I was in New York, giggling uncontrollably. I was giggling because *The Associated Press* had just called Pennsylvania for Donald Trump. I could imagine the looks of bewilderment, despair and outrage on the faces of mainstream reporters covering the results just a few hallways away from me and it made me laugh uncontrollably. The West was not doomed to die an ignominious death at the hands of open border-obsessed globalists. I was giggling because we had won.

The earthquake heralded by the election of Donald J. Trump had been a long time coming. It was the culmination of nearly thirty years of hectoring from both the mainstream Left and the mainstream Right; about how we should shut up if we knew what's good for us, about how we need to make up for a history of racism, sexism, and every "phobia" under the sun, about how entertaining this dangerous thought or making that dangerous joke would be the end of our careers.

Well, it turns out that the real danger lies in *not* daring to be dangerous. I dare to be dangerous every day, and I can't *stop* winning.

My ascendancy has marked the overturning of an old order. GamerGate bloodied the leftist vigilante squads on social media and their friends in the press. Brexit put a stake through the heart of the bureaucratic, globalist European Union. And then Donald Trump came, to annihilate thirty years of politically correct consensus in the United States.

Leftists think 2016 was The Worst Year Ever, and not just because so many of their favorite celebrities died. Given the scale of their political defeats, they have some justification, but they are also pessimistic by nature. These are the people who believe racism is worse than it's ever been, that rates of sexual assault on college campuses approximate the Congo, and that Brexit will herald World War III.

Steven Pinker, a sensible liberal, reminds us that this is not the case. The world is getting better, and has been for some time. As he ceaselessly reminds a pessimistic public, "Extreme poverty, child mortality, illiteracy, and global inequality are at historic lows; vaccinations, basic education, including girls, and democracy are at all-time highs." Rates of murder, violence, sexual assault and other crimes in the West also continue, by and large, to fall.[247] Socially, the millennial generation is the most tolerant ever and the incoming president is also likely to be the most gay-friendly man ever elected to the presidency.

MILO

Now that leftists are out of power, America is on track to be less divided, safer, and more stable than ever before. By the time the next election rolls around, I predict Democrats will struggle to downplay the nation's success.

NEVER APOLOGIZE

The Left delights in extracting apologies from the victims of public shaming. From Jack "The Southern Avenger" Hunter to Justine Sacco, one of the first signs of leftist victory is the sight of someone verbally flogging themselves in public. Like prisoners emerging from Big Brother's torture chamber in room 101, you can expect to see the phrases that mark a broken spirit: "I'm sorry." "I'll try to do better." "I'm learning to be a better person every day." "Thank you, mob of faceless Internet vigilantes, for educating me."

If you want to win, the first step is not to admit defeat. The only exception to this rule is if you say something you didn't intend to, and people are left thinking you mean something you don't.

But in general, never apologize.

WORK HARDER THAN EVERYONE ELSE

I'm not the best because I'm the funniest or the smartest or the most attractive person among conservative and libertarian celebrities. I'm the best because I work harder than everyone else and I surround myself with people who are smarter than I am.

I love to bang on about Mariah Carey but my real idol is Madonna. Madonna isn't the best singer or dancer in the world. But she's the hardest working person in the business and has been for decades. Like me, she's merely above average at everything.

DANGEROUS

Like me, she is a great talent scout and has terrific instincts for what's coming next.

The same goes for Paris Hilton and Kim Kardashian. I'm obsessed with both of them.

You don't have to be born with preternatural talents like Billie Holiday or Dusty Springfield. You just have to show up to work and resolve every day to crush the competition.

You can be number one through sheer force of will. I'm living proof.

STAY HUMBLE

I'm the best at being humble. No one can touch my modesty. Be like me, and stay grounded!

BE TWICE AS FUNNY AS YOU ARE OUTRAGEOUS

Does anyone remember how the alt-right died? An idiot named Richard Spencer took control of the movement. Spencer is offensive and hateful without being funny. He does his best to emulate the wittier elements of the movement, cringingly referencing Pepe and "meme magic" in his speeches, but it doesn't convince anyone. In the early days of the alt-right, tweeters were having fun with forbidden ideas. Spencer was having forbidden (and bad) ideas about things and trying to transplant the fun in afterwards.

I want people to be allowed to make jokes about, and discuss, *anything they want*. I don't think people should be ostracized for doing so. I don't fear the ideas of people like Spencer, nor do I feel a need to hide them from view. I have enough trust in ordinary people to examine and reject bad ideas on their own. Bill Maher is right, "Sunlight is the best disinfectant."

MILO

I will always defend the right of people to make jokes about whatever they choose, and mercilessly attack people who want to destroy the lives of 20-somethings over alt-right memes and 4chan trolling campaigns.

Be twice as funny as you are outrageous, because no one can resist the truth wrapped in a good joke.

"Not an Argument"

This one doesn't come from me, but from Canadian philosopher Stefan Molyneux. Molyneux, who frequently dabbles in dangerous topics like race, intelligence, anarchism and religion, has said this so often on his YouTube channel that it has become a meme.

Simply put, when someone calls you names, as the Left is so fond of doing, there is no need to be upset, ruffled, or apologetic. These are just outbursts of moral rage, full of sound and fury, signifying nothing. If you make a point, or reveal a fact, and someone responds with cries of "Racist!" "Sexist!" "Homophobe!" or any other ways that the Left now spells "heretic," just coolly respond with that now-immortal phrase:

"Not an argument!"

Facts Over Feelings

In this book, you will have encountered several excellent examples of what the internet calls "hate facts." You now know, for instance, that black gang violence eclipses police violence as a threat to black lives. You will now know that the fabled "rape culture" on college campuses doesn't exist, and the "gender pay gap" is a myth. You will know that being fat isn't healthy, although quite frankly, I think most of you are smart enough to have figured that last one out on your own.

Dangerous

You should never miss an opportunity to spread these facts around, especially if you're at college. Your peers are currently living in one of the most brainwashed eras of our history. The media, academia, and pop culture are all working overtime to get them to believe things that simply are not true. They are offended when this fragile worldview is confronted with reality, which is one of the reasons why so many of the younger generation today retreats into safe spaces. However, you cannot spare their feelings.

The only way to beat propaganda is to spread the truth faster than the machine spreads lies.

Facts over feelings.

And that brings me to my favorite rule of all …

Seek Attention

People often accuse me of being an attention-seeker. They're right, of course.

Or at least mostly right.

I may be a flamboyant egotistical attention-whoring diva faggot, but all my flouncing, Valley-girl craving for attention also serves a noble purpose: it draws attention to my arguments, my principles, and the causes I champion *as well as* my impeccable sense of style and Adonis-like good looks.

One of the mistakes libertarians make endlessly is that they assume people actually *read* their brilliant essays on why roads should be privatized. I mean, they're probably flawless, but that doesn't mean anything if *no one's paying attention.*

I've galvanized a movement because I know how to put on a good show. I don't turn up on stage and reel off a list of staid talking points. I turn up on stage dressed as Marilyn Monroe, have my deputy slap me in the face with whipped cream, throw up a slideshow of the hottest and spiciest memes of the moment… and *then* I reel off a list of talking points, after I've ensured no one at the back is falling asleep.

We live in an age where the competition for attention is getting tougher and tougher. Half a century ago, everyone watched the same channels on TV because, well, there wasn't much else. Now there are thousands of channels, YouTube feeds, books, games, and websites competing for the public's eyeballs. If what you have to say is important, you have to know how to get people listening.

BE HOT

This sounds difficult, but it's very important. You have *got* to be hotter than your opponents. We live in an age of "fat acceptance" and the celebration of the mediocre. A high school sports day where everyone gets a prize. No.

Don't settle for second-best. Hit the gym, go on a diet, go to a tanning salon. Don't waste money on McDonald's, spend it at Louis Vuitton.

Advocate for tax exemptions for anyone under 12% body fat!

Keep in mind that it's not hard to be hotter than many of your opponents, so you don't even have a good excuse. Be Tomi Lahren, not Lena Dunham.

Always keep women worried you might steal their boyfriends when they're not looking. Always keep men worried your dicking skills far surpass their own.

Be hot.

Dangerous

Have Fun

This is one of the most important requirements of being a Dangerous Faggot, and probably the most important reason I win.

What do leftists do when they get together? Sit in a circle and share their feelings with each other. They'll talk about how unsafe they feel, and gently pat each other on the shoulders. In public, they'll get angry, yell slogans, and whine about how offended they are by our side's words.

They don't look like they're having much fun, do they?

Establishment conservatives do a little better on the "sense of humor" scale, but you can never escape the feeling that they'd rather be at a Heritage Foundation speaker event. Like the leftists, they can be dreadfully serious sometimes.

My followers win because they know politics isn't everything. That's why they mistrust overly serious establishment conservatives, and that's why they're so at odds with the Left, who wish to politicize everything from video games to pop songs.

My whole career so far has been an experiment in identity politics designed to reduce the Left to tears and incoherence. Who knows, maybe one day I'll come out as straight and we can all laugh at how I pulled the wool over their eyes?

No one wants to hang out with squares. They want to go to the party with blackjack and hookers, not the one with Scrabble and Diet Coke.

And right now, I'm throwing the best party in town.

Have fun.

Be Dangerous

We live in an age where one side of the political spectrum would like all debate, all challenge to their viewpoints, all diversity of thought to be snuffed out. Why? Because they're scared. Scared that their political, social and cultural consensus, carefully constructed and nurtured over the past few years, with its secular religions of feminism, enforced diversity, multiculturalism, and casual hatred for straight white men, is built on a foundation of sand.

They have watched as the threats to their order, and the worldview it represents, multiply. They have watched the dream of multiculturalism die at the hands of Islam, despite all their attempts to downplay and cover up the atrocities.

They have watched as the idea of "socially constructed" genders and races, once dogma in the academy, slowly fades into irrelevance, swept away by a new wave of research on the innate roots of our identities, despite all attempts to suppress it.

They have seen their stranglehold on culture, once so steely and strong, slip away. Comedians have grown tired of new language codes. Movie directors and video game designers are fed up with demands for diversity quotas. Artists, ever longing to provoke and challenge, are slowly waking up and realizing that to be left-wing today is to be the establishment.

It's a scary time to be a leftist. So it's little wonder that I'm considered to be dangerous, with my mild demands for free speech on campuses, my fact-based objections to feminism and Black Lives Matter, and my wariness of the sexism and homophobia that drifts slowly westward from the swamp of modern Islam.

Those who are frightened of free speech, whether it's ideas and facts that challenge their side, or jokes that prod at their carefully constructed social taboos, are almost always frightened of something else. It's not the speech, or even the so-called "hurt feelings" that bother them. It's that nagging concern which plagues all defenders of fact-free dogma: they might be wrong or they might be unpersuasive. And they just can't handle that.

Well, no matter. You don't need to convince them. You're responsible for your own mind, not theirs.

So use your mind. Be dangerous. Read all the books that your college is too afraid to stock in their library. Find the thinkers and the writers and the artists who have been shamed out of the mainstream, and find out why. You won't have to look far, I'll be bringing them to you with my new publishing imprint, Dangerous Books. Get together with your friends and pledge to be as dangerous as possible.

You might not ever be a gay Rosa Parks or Jewish Martin Luther King, Jr., like me. But you can make a dent.

You're already reading a book you're not supposed to. Go watch a movie you're not supposed to.

Or better yet, go *make* a movie you're not supposed to.

Write a song you're not supposed to.

Design a video game you're not supposed to.

Start a blog you're not supposed to.

Discuss ideas you're not supposed to.

Get on social media and tell a joke you're not supposed to.

Share a meme you're not supposed to.

State some facts you're not supposed to.

Be dangerous.

Like that hot guy on the cover.

ACKNOWLEDGMENTS

I f you're looking for someone to blame for the Milo phenomenon, here are a few people who ought to be in your crosshairs. Troll them! They will love it. My former editor at *Breitbart*, Alex Marlow, has the best judgment of any journalist working today and saved me from plenty of near-misses in early drafts of this manuscript. I wouldn't be where I am without him.

My deputy, Allum Bokhari, without whom this book would never have got off the ground, is a major journalistic talent and will eclipse me when I finally collapse unconscious onto a pile of Nigerian rent boys. Colin Madine flawlessly executed the most difficult job in media throughout 2016 -- keeping Milo Yiannopoulos on the straight and narrow.

Thank you to my dark angel Lexica for helping me to produce the best pop album of 2017. You shaped my thinking and I am forever grateful. One day we will be free at a Snctm party in the Hills.

James Cook: wise counsel. Scott Walter and Rachel Fulton Brown provided constant intellectual nourishment. Based Mom, Christina Hoff Sommers, kept me kind. Drake Bell kept a smile on my face.

DANGEROUS

Azealia Banks for being the big sis I never had. Ann Coulter has been both a friend and a professional inspiration. Lee Habib taught me how to be a star. David Horowitz saw my genius before almost anyone else and gave me the Annie Taylor award for journalistic bravery, which I keep on my desk as a reminder of his good taste and judgment.

My assistants Marc and Marc make sure I show up within an hour or two of the advertised time. My legal team does a lot of heavy lifting and they never so much as raise an eyebrow at my ludicrous demands. Thanks to the squad for keeping the travelling Dangerous Faggot circus fed, watered and looking fabulous -- Mike, Hayden, Hunter, Seabass, Blake and of course Will Magner Fitness and my Dangerous Faggot tour manager Andrew Greider. Matt Perdie is the most remarkable colleague I have ever had. Thanks Gabe, for keeping the lights on last year. Alexander Macris, thank you for captaining the ship with a steady hand. Will Ross -- we miss you.

Thanks to my partner in crime Pizza Party Ben for keeping the meme tank full. I could have been a better friend while on tour and while writing this book to Alicia, Colette and Sascha for the past three years. But I know they will forgive me eventually. My new friend David Suarez threw me a bone without which this book could not have been published.

And of course I couldn't have done it without Thomas Flannery.

THANK YOU TO ALL THE HATERS -- WITHOUT YOU I'D BE NOWHERE. TO ALL THE HUNGRY TIGERS WHO TRIED IT - STAY MAD! TO EVERYONE WHO SAID I COULDN'T MAKE IT, LOOK AT ME NOW! IN PARTICULAR: Anita Sarkeesian! Couldn't have done it without you, babe. Leslie Jones, for making me even more famous. And Jack Dorsey, who did so much to get Daddy elected.

Finally: thanks to Steve Bannon and to God -- jointly, for everything else.

ENDNOTES

1   Milo Yiannopoulos, "GamerGate Critic Sarah Nyberg Claimed To Be A Pedophile," Breitbart, Sep. 11, 2015 (http://www.breitbart.com/big-journalism/2015/09/11/leading-gamergate-critic-sarah-nyberg-claimed-to-be-a-pedophile-apologised-for-white-nationalism/).

2   James Meikle and Josh Halliday, "Louise Mensch's former business partner Luke Bozier accepts caution," The Guardian, May 20, 2013 (https://www.theguardian.com/uk/2013/may/20/louise-mensch-luke-bozier-caution).

3   Milo Yiannopoulos, "Tech City Darling Chris Leydon Guilty of Making Indecent Images of Children," Breitbart, April 27, 2015 (http://www.breitbart.com/london/2015/04/27/tech-city-darling-chris-leydon-guilty-of-making-indecent-images-of-children/).

4   According to the London tech editor of Business Insider, his trial is scheduled for 2018.

5   Milo Yiannopoulos, "Meet the Progressives Defending Gamergate Critic Sarah Nyberg," Breitbart, Sep. 12, 2015 (http://www.breitbart.com/big-journalism/2015/09/12/meet-the-progressives-defending-gamergate-critic-sarah-nyberg/).

6   Janet Upadhye, "'I'm not a monster': A pedophile on attraction, love and a life of loneliness," Salon, May 17, 2016 (https://archive.is/0XGRX).

7   Manisha Krishnan, "A Paedophile Opens Up About Being Targeted by Vigilantes," VICE, Jan. 6, 2017 (https://www.vice.com/en_uk/article/a-pedophile-opens-up-about-being-targeted-by-vigilantes).

8   Milo Yiannopoulos, "Here's Why The Progressive Left Keeps Sticking Up For Pedophiles," Breitbart, Sep. 21, 2015 (http://www.breitbart.com/big-

government/2015/09/21/heres-why-the-progressive-left-keeps-sticking-up-for-pedophiles/).

9   Charles C. W. Cooke, "On Salon's Much-Maligned Pedophile Piece," National Review, Sep. 21, 2015 (http://www.nationalreview.com/corner/424373/salons-much-maligned-pedophilia-piece-charles-c-w-cooke).

10 Start with Taylor Swift, Justin Bieber and Nicki Minaj

11 Milo Yiannopoulos, "How to Stop Mass Shootings," Breitbart, Oct. 2, 2015 (http://www.breitbart.com/big-government/2015/10/02/how-to-stop-mass-shootings/).

12 Milo Yiannopoulos, "The Milo Show Teaser: Lesbian Shooters," The Milo Yiannopoulos Show, June 23, 2016 (https://www.youtube.com/watch?v=C6zo1CqDIrM).

13 Andrew Anglin, "Stormer Book Club Crusader: The Final Solution to the Milo Problem," Daily Stormer, Sep. 27, 2016 (http://www.dailystormer.com/stormer-book-club-crusade-the-final-solution-to-the-milo-problem/).

14 Tom Whitehead, "Labour wanted mass immigration to make UK more multicultural , says former adviser," The Telegraph, Oct. 23, 2009 (http://www.telegraph.co.uk/news/uknews/law-and-order/6418456/Labour-wanted-mass-immigration-to-make-UK-more-multicultural-says-former-adviser.html).

15 Mayhill Fowler, "Obama: No Surprise That Hard-Pressed Pennsylvanians Turn Bitter," The Huffington Post, Nov. 17, 2008 (http://www.huffingtonpost.com/mayhill-fowler/obama-no-surprise-that-ha_b_96188.html).

16 Publius Decius Mus, "The Flight 93 Election," The Claremont Institute, Sep. 5, 2016 (http://www.claremont.org/crb/basicpage/the-flight-93-election/).

17 Tucker Carlson, "Donald Trump Is Shocking, Vulgar and Right," Politico, Jan. 28, 2016 (http://www.politico.com/magazine/story/2016/01/donald-trump-is-shocking-vulgar-and-right-213572?o=0).

18 Intersecting Axes of Privilege, Domination, and Opression, https://archive.is/VWMLg (April 22, 2017).

19 Andrew Anglin, "Disease-Ridden Jew Acronym MILO Threatens to Buy 4chan," Daily Stormer, Oct. 9, 2016 (http://www.dailystormer.com/disease-ridden-jew-acronym-milo-threatens-to-buy-4chan/).

20 Tom Ciccotta, "FAKE NEWS: NBC News Issues Correction After Falsely Branding MILO as 'White Nationalist,'" Breitbart, Jan. 7, 2017 (http://www.breitbart.com/milo/2017/01/07/fake-news-nbc-news-issues-correction-falsely-branding-milo-white-nationalist/).

Charlie Nash, "FAKE NEWS: USA Today Issues Correction After Falsely Branding MILO as 'White Nationalist,' 'Alt-Right,'" Breitbart, Jan. 4, 2017 (http://www.breitbart.com/milo/2017/01/04/fake-news-usa-today-issues-correction-after-falsely-branding-milo-as-white-nationalist-alt-right/).

21 Joshua Seidel, "I'm a Jew, and I'm a Member of the Alt-Right," Forward, Aug. 25, 2016 (http://forward.com/scribe/348466/im-a-jew-and-im-a-member-of-the-alt-right/).

22 Rosie Gray, "How 2015 Fueled The Rise Of The Freewheeling, White Nationalist Alt Right Movement," BuzzFeed, Dec. 27, 2015 (https://www.buzzfeed.com/rosiegray/how-2015-fueled-the-rise-of-the-freewheeling-white-nationali?utm_term=.rejRmEWWD#.na5RYMDD0).

23 John Sexton, "Ayers and Obama: What the Media Hid," Breitbart, June 4, 2012 (http://www.breitbart.com/big-journalism/2012/06/04/obama-ayers/).

24 Andrew Anglin, "Stormer Book Club Crusade: The Final Solution to the Milo Problem," Daily Stormer, Sep. 27, 2016 (http://www.dailystormer.com/stormer-book-club-crusade-the-final-solution-to-the-milo-problem/).

25 Kimberly A. Strassel, "Steve Bannon on Politic as War," The Wall Street Journal, Nov. 18, 2016 (https://www.wsj.com/articles/steve-bannon-on-politics-as-war-1479513161).

26 "Alt Right – RIP," Nov. 23, 2016 (https://www.youtube.com/watch?v=n8HBLX_khwQ).

27 Michael Nunez, "Former Facebook Workers: We Routinely Suppressed Conservative News," Gizmodo, May 9, 2016 (http://gizmodo.com/former-facebook-workers-we-routinely-suppressed-conser-1775461006).

28 Michael Nunez, "Want to Know What Facebook Really Thinks of Journalists? Here's What Happened When It Hired Some," Gizmodo, May 3, 2016 (http://gizmodo.com/want-to-know-what-facebook-really-thinks-of-journalists-1773916117?rev=1462295407082).

29 Sam Thielman, "Facebook news selection is in hands of editors not algorithms, documents show," The Guardian, May 12, 2016 (https://www.theguardian.com/technology/2016/may/12/facebook-trending-news-leaked-documents-editor-guidelines).

30 Deepa Seetharaman, "Facebook Employees Pushed to Remove Trump's Posts as Hate Speech," The Wall Street Journal, Oct. 21, 2016 (https://www.wsj.com/articles/facebook-employees-pushed-to-remove-trump-posts-as-hate-speech-1477075392).

31 Pamela Geller, "Pamela Geller: Why I Am Suing Facebook," Breitbart, July 13, 2016 (http://www.breitbart.com/tech/2016/07/13/pamela-geller-suing-facebook/).

32 Ben Kew, "Report: Facebook Employees Wanted to Censor 'Hate Speech' from Trump, 'Threatened to Quit,'" Breitbart, Oct. 21, 2016 (http://www.breitbart.com/tech/2016/10/21/report-facebook-employees-wanted-to-censor-hate-speech-from-trump-threatened-to-quit/).

33 Joel B. Pollak, "Facebook's Zuckerberg Defends Trump Supporter Peter Thiel," Breitbart, Oct. 20, 2016 (http://www.breitbart.com/california/2016/10/20/facebook-zuckerberg-defends-trump-supporter-peter-thiel/).

34 Jefferson Graham, "Twitter's Dorsey describes time in Ferguson, Mo., as wake-up call," USA Today, June 1, 2016 (http://www.usatoday.com/story/tech/news/2016/06/01/twitters-dorsey-describes-time-ferguson-mo-wake-up-call/85270192/).

35 Milo Yiannopoulos, "MILO At University Of Colorado Boulder: Why Ugly People Hate Me," Jan. 25, 2017 (https://www.youtube.com/watch?v=UTBaflj-ay0).

36 Jessie Thompson, "Thank You Twitter – By Unverifying Milo Yiannopoulos, You Are Standing Up for Women Online," The Huffington Post, Jan. 9, 2017 (http://www.huffingtonpost.co.uk/jessie-thompson/milo-yiannopoulos-unverified-twitter-blue-tick_b_8944126.html).

37 Patrick Frater, "Sony's movie division is taking $1 billion loss after recent box-office failures," Business Insider UK, Jan. 30, 2017 (http://uk.businessinsider.com/sonys-movie-division-1-billion-loss-2017-1?r=US&IR=T).

38 Ezra Dulis, "Leslie Jones Was Punching Down on Twitter for Hours Before Milo Ever Mentioned Her," Breitbart, July 20, 2016 (http://www.breitbart.com/big-hollywood/2016/07/20/leslie-jones-twitter-trolls-milo-yiannopoulos/).

39 Milo Yiannopoulos, Twitter, July 18, 2016 (http://media.breitbart.com/media/2016/07/CntB-7vUEAA-Nn1.jpg).

40 Milo Yiannopoulos, Twitter, July 18, 2016 (http://media.breitbart.com/media/2016/07/CntCAM3VIAAR7T-.jpg).

41 Ben Kew, "#SCREWNERO Written On Boardroom Wall At Twitter HQ," Breitbart, Sep. 29, 2016 (http://www.breitbart.com/milo/2016/09/29/screwnero-written-blackboard-twitter-hq/).

42 Leslie Jones, Twitter, July 18, 2016 (https://archive.is/hHzf6).

43 Leslie Jones, Twitter, July 18, 2016 (https://archive.is/9Qsz8).

44 Twitter won't say how many.

45 Breitbart News, "No Action Taken by Twitter After Rapper Calls Black Breitbart Reporter 'Coon,'" Breitbart, July 20, 2016 (http://www.breitbart.com/big-hollywood/2016/07/20/rapper-talib-kweli-attacks-breitbarts-jerome-hudson-calls-coon-twitter-not-banned-platform/).

46 Dailymail.com Reporter, "More than 12,000 tweets have called for Trump's assassination since the inauguration," Daily Mail, Feb. 3, 2017 (http://www.dailymail.co.uk/news/article-4189124/More-12-000-tweets-call-Trump-s-assassination.html).

47 Ed Ho, "An Update on Safety," Twitter, Feb. 7, 2017 (https://blog.twitter.com/2017/an-update-on-safety).

48 Therese Poletti, "Twitter tanks and becomes fodder for M&A chatter again," Market Watch, Feb. 12, 2017 (http://www.marketwatch.com/story/twitter-tanks-and-becomes-fodder-for-ma-chatter-again-2017-02-09).

49 Robert Epstein, "SPUTNIK EXCLUSIVE: Research Proves Google Manipulates Millions to Favor Hillary Clinton," Sputnik News, September 12, 2016 (https://sputniknews.com/us/201609121045214398-google-clinton-manipulation-election/).

50 Wikileaks, Status Memo.pdf, (https://wikileaks.org/podesta-emails/emailid/12403)

51 Wikileaks, Fwd: 2016 thoughts, (https://wikileaks.org/podesta-emails/emailid/37262)

52 David Dayen, "Google's Remarkably Close Relationship With the Obama White House, in Two Charts," The Intercept, April 22, 2016 (https://theintercept.

com/2016/04/22/googles-remarkably-close-relationship-with-the-obama-white-house-in-two-charts/).

53   Robert Epstein and Ronald E. Robertson, "The search engine manipulation effect (SEME) and its possible impact on the outcomes of elections," Proceedings of the National Academy of Sciences of the United States of America, July 8, 2015 (http://www.pnas.org/content/112/33/E4512.full.pdf?with-ds=yes).

54   Joel Snape, "Manspreading arrests: the long arm of the law just invaded our personal space," The Telegraph, June 1, 2015 (http://www.telegraph.co.uk/men/thinking-man/11643052/Manspreading-arrests-the-long-arm-of-the-law-just-invaded-our-personal-space.html).

55   Annemarie Dooling with Leigh Cuen, "The Eggplant Emoji Is The Next Frontline Of Online Harassment," Vocativ, June 10, 2015 (http://www.vocativ.com/culture/society/the-eggplant-emoji-is-the-next-frontline-of-online-harassment/).

56   Radhika Sanghani, "Air conditioning in your office is sexist. True story," The Telegraph, July 24, 2015 (http://www.telegraph.co.uk/women/womens-life/11760417/Air-conditioning-in-your-office-is-sexist.-True-story.html).

57   Radhika Sanghani, "Only 7 per cent of Britons consider themselves feminists," The Telegraph, Jan. 15, 2016 (http://www.telegraph.co.uk/women/life/only-7-per-cent-of-britons-consider-themselves-feminists/).

58   Sarah Kliff, "Only 18 percent of Americans consider themselves feminists," Vox, April 8, 2015 (http://www.vox.com/2015/4/8/8372417/feminist-gender-equality-poll).

59   Emily Swanson, "Poll: Few Identify As Feminists, But Most Believe In Equality of the Sexes," The Huffington Post, April 16, 2013 (http://www.huffingtonpost.com/2013/04/16/feminism-poll_n_3094917.html).

60   Anna Maria Barry-Jester, "Attitudes Toward Racism And Inequality Are Shifting," FiveThirtyEight, June 23, 2015 (http://fivethirtyeight.com/datalab/attitudes-toward-racism-and-inequality-are-shifting/).

61   Christian Jarrett, "Activists have an image problem, say social psychologists," BPS Research Digest, Jan. 2, 2014 (http://bps-research-digest.blogspot.co.uk/2014/01/activists-have-image-problem-say-social.html).

62   Public Policy Polling, "Democrats and Republicans differ on conspiracy theory beliefs," April 2, 2013 (http://www.publicpolicypolling.com/pdf/2011/PPP_Release_National_ConspiracyTheories_040213.pdf).

63   American Society of Clinical Oncology, Breast Cancer: Statistics, http://www.cancer.net/cancer-types/breast-cancer/statistics (April 22, 2017).
American Society of Clinical Oncology, Prostate Cancer: Statistics, http://www.cancer.net/cancer-types/prostate-cancer/statistics (April 22, 2017).

64   National Cancer Institute, Funding for Research Areas, https://www.cancer.gov/about-nci/budget/fact-book/data/research-funding (April 22, 2017).

65   Larry Copeland, "Life expectancy in the USA hits a record high," USA Today, Oct. 8, 2014 (http://www.usatoday.com/story/news/nation/2014/10/08/us-life-expectancy-hits-record-high/16874039/).

66   Jack Hadfield, "Male Suicide Rates Massively Increase," Breitbart, April 28, 2016 (http://www.breitbart.com/tech/2016/04/28/male-suicide-rates-massively-increase/).

67   Denis Campbell, "More than 40% of domestic violence victims are male, report reveals," The Guardian, Sep. 4, 2010 (https://www.theguardian.com/society/2010/sep/05/men-victims-domestic-violence).

68   "Men Sentenced To Longer Prison Terms Than Women For Same Crimes, Study Says," The Huffington Post, Sep. 11, 2012 (http://www.huffingtonpost.com/2012/09/11/men-women-prison-sentence-length-gender-gap_n_1874742.html).

69   Ellie Flynn, "Female office manager who went on £38k luxury shopping spree with company card is spared jail by judge because he 'hates sending women to prison,'" The Sun, Jan. 10, 2017 (https://www.thesun.co.uk/news/2579876/female-office-manager-who-went-on-38k-luxury-shopping-spree-with-company-card-is-spared-jail-by-judge-because-he-hates-sending-women-to-prison/).

70   Caroline Cordell, "Shocking Statistics Show the Bleak Reality of Joint Custody in Nebraska," Men's Rights, n.d. (http://mensrights.com/shocking-statistics-show-the-bleak-reality-of-joint-custody-in-nebraska/).

71   National Organization for Women – New York State, "NOW-New York State Oppose Legislation," March, 2005 (http://www.nownys.org/archives/leg_memos/oppose_a00330.html).

72   Milo Yiannopoulos, "'The Red Pill' Filmmaker Started to Doubt Her Feminist Beliefs…Now Her Movie Is At Risk," Breitbart, Oct. 26, 2015 (http://www.breitbart.com/big-hollywood/2015/10/26/the-red-pill-filmmaker-started-to-doubt-her-feminist-beliefs-now-her-movie-is-at-risk/).

73   94 David Futrelle, "'Red Pill' director Cassie Jaye hits a new low with her appearance on a white supremacist podcast," We Hunted the Mammoth, Oct. 24, 2016 (http://www.wehuntedthemammoth.com/2016/10/24/red-pill-director-cassie-jaye-hits-a-new-low-with-her-appearance-on-a-white-supremacist-podcast/).

74   Elle Hunt, "The Red Pill: Melbourne cinema drops men's rights film after feminist backlash," The Guardian, Oct. 26, 2016 (https://www.theguardian.com/film/2016/oct/26/the-red-pill-melbourne-cinema-drops-mens-rights-film-after-feminist-backlash).

75   Riaz Sayani-Mulji, "Open Letter: Why I don't participate in Movember," Rabble, Nov. 27, 2013 (http://rabble.ca/news/2013/11/open-letter-why-i-dont-participate-movember).

76   Amelia Abraham, "Why the 'Cock in a Sock' Thing Is Vain Bullshit," VICE, March 27, 2014 (https://www.vice.com/en_au/article/the-cockinasock-thing-cancer-charity-vanity).

77   Nora Crotty, "On #CockInaSock and Pubic Hair Double Standards," Fashionista, March 26, 2014 (http://fashionista.com/2014/03/cockinasock).

78   Milo Yiannopoulos, "Male University of York Student Commits Suicide on Day His University Ditches International Men's Day After Pressure from Feminists,"

Breitbart, Nov. 18, 2015 (http://www.breitbart.com/big-journalism/2015/11/18/male-university-of-york-student-commits-suicide-on-day-his-university-ditches-international-mens-day-after-pressure-from-feminists/).

79 "cisgendered" is left-speak for normal

80 Sheila Coronel, Steve Coll, and Derek Kravitz, "'A Rape on Campus' What Went Wrong," Rolling Stone, April 5, 2015 (http://www.rollingstone.com/culture/features/a-rape-on-campus-what-went-wrong-20150405).

81 Lizzie Crockner, "Why the New 'One in Four' Campus Rape Statistic is Misleading," The Daily Beast, Sep. 21, 2015 (http://www.thedailybeast.com/articles/2015/09/21/how-misleading-is-the-new-one-in-four-campus-rape-statistic.html).

82 Sofi Sinozich, Lynn Langton, Ph.D., "Rape and Sexual Assault Among College-Age Females, 1995-2013," Bureau of Justice Statistics, Dec. 11, 2014 (https://www.bjs.gov/index.cfm?ty=pbdetail&iid=5176).

83 Patrick deHahn, "Study: 89% of colleges reported zero campus rapes in 2015," USA Today, May 11, 2017 (http://college.usatoday.com/2017/05/11/study-89-of-colleges-reported-zero-campus-rapes-in-2015/)

84 Steven Pinker and Andrew Mack, "The World Is Not Falling Apart," Slate, Dec. 22, 2014 (http://www.slate.com/articles/news_and_politics/foreigners/2014/12/the_world_is_not_falling_apart_the_trend_lines_reveal_an_increasingly_peaceful.html).

85 NP Mota, M. Burnett, and J. Sareen, "Associations between abortions, mental disorders, and suicidal behavior in a nationally representative sample," National Center for Biotechnology Information, April, 2010 (https://www.ncbi.nlm.nih.gov/pubmed/20416147).

86 University of Texas Medical Branch at Galveston, "Study finds injectable birth control causes significant weight gain and changes in body mass," EurekAlert!, March 4, 2009 (https://www.eurekalert.org/pub_releases/2009-03/uotm-sfi030409.php).

87 Ailesbury Media, "Dr. Patrick Treacy discusses 'The History of Cellulite,'"PRLog, Oct. 29, 2009 (https://www.prlog.org/10392821-dr-patrick-treacy-discusses-the-history-of-cellulite.html).

88 Stephanie Pappas, "Fertile Gals Have All the Right Dance Moves," Live Science, Aug. 15, 2012 (http://www.livescience.com/22402-women-dances-ovulation-fertility.html).

89 112 Daniel DeNoon, "Pill Users Choose 'Wrong' Sex Partners," CBS News, Aug. 13, 2008 (http://www.cbsnews.com/news/pill-users-choose-wrong-sex-partners/).

90 Marianne Bertrand, Claudia Goldin, and Lawrence F. Katz, "Dynamics of the Gender Gap for Young Professionals in the Financial and Corporate Sectors," American Economic Journal: Applied Economics 2, July, 2010 (http://scholar.harvard.edu/files/goldin/files/dynamics_of_the_gender_gap_for_young_professionals_in_the_financial_and_corporate_sectors.pdf).

US Department of Labor, "An Analysis of Reasons for the Disparity in Wages Between Men and Women: A Forward," CONSAD Research Corp, n.d. (http://www.hawaii.edu/religion/courses/Gender_Wage_Gap_Report.pdf).

91   Bureau of Labor Statistics, "National Census of Fatal Occupational Injuries in 2015," U.S. Department of Labor, Dec. 16, 2016 (https://www.bls.gov/news.release/pdf/cfoi.pdf).

92   John Tierney, "The Real War on Science," City Journal, Autumn, 2016 (http://www.city-journal.org/html/real-war-science-14782.html).

93   Synapse, "Why Do More Boys Have Autism," n.d. (http://www.autism-help.org/points-gender-imbalance.htm).

94   R.A. Lippa, "Abstracts for BBC Internet Survey Papers," Archives of Sexual Behavior, n.d. (http://psych.fullerton.edu/rlippa/abstracts_2009.htm).

95   Christopher Drew, "Where the Women Are: Biology," The New York Times, Nov. 4, 2011 (http://www.nytimes.com/2011/11/06/education/edlife/where-the-women-are-biology.html).

96   WebMD, "Why Men and Women Handle Stress Differently," WebMD, June 6, 2005 (http://www.webmd.com/women/features/stress-women-men-cope).

97   Health Editor, "How Jealousy is Different for Men and Women," Health, Jan. 14, 2015 (http://news.health.com/2015/01/14/straight-men-more-prone-to-jealousy-over-sexual-infidelity-study/).

98   Tony Grew, "Celebs Split over trans protest at Stonewall Awards," Pink News, Nov. 7, 2008 (http://www.pinknews.co.uk/2008/11/07/celebs-split-over-trans-protests-at-stonewall-awards/).

99   LU Staff, "Liberal parents on Twitter distraught that their children are normal and healthy," Liberty Unyielding, Sep. 2, 2016 (http://libertyunyielding.com/2016/09/02/liberal-parents-twitter-distraught-children-normal-healthy/).

100 Douglas Main, "Seven in 10 American Adults are Overweight or Obese," Newsweek, June 22, 2015 (http://europe.newsweek.com/7-10-american-adults-are-overweight-or-obese-329130?rm=eu).

101 Trust for America's Health and Robert Wood Johnson Foundation, "The Healthcare Costs of Obesity," The State of Obesity, n.d. (http://stateofobesity.org/healthcare-costs-obesity/).

102 Lindsay Abrams, "A Case for Shaming Obese People, Tastefully," The Atlantic, Jan. 23, 2013 (http://www.theatlantic.com/health/archive/2013/01/a-case-for-shaming-obese-people-tastefully/267446/   ).

103 The Affirmative Consent Project, "Affirmative Laws (Yes Means Yes) State by State," Affirmative Consent, http://affirmativeconsent.com/affirmative-consent-laws-state-by-state/ (April 23, 2017).

104 Milo Yiannopoulos, "Did Black Lives Matter Organizer Shaun King Mislead Oprah Winfrey by Pretending to be Biracial?" Breitbart, Aug. 19, 2015 (http://www.breitbart.com/big-government/2015/08/19/did-black-lives-matter-organiser-shaun-king-mislead-oprah-winfrey-by-pretending-to-be-biracial/).

105 Shaun King, "Race, love, hate, and me: A distinctly American story," Daily Kos, Aug. 20, 2015 (http://www.dailykos.com/story/2015/8/20/1413881/-Race-love-hate-and-me-A-distinctly-American-story).

106 Chuck Ross, "Leading Ferguson Activist's Hate Crime Claim Disputed By Police Report, Detective," The Daily Caller, July 21, 2015 (http://dailycaller.com/2015/07/21/leading-ferguson-activists-hate-crime-claim-disputed-by-police-report-detective/).

107 Chuck Ross, "Shaun King's Charity Fundraising Comes Under More Scrutiny," The Daily Caller, Dec. 16, 2015 (http://dailycaller.com/2015/12/16/shaun-kings-charity-fundraising-comes-under-more-scrutiny/).

108 Heather Mac Donald, "Black and Unarmed: Behind the Numbers," The Marshall Project, Feb. 8, 2016 (https://www.themarshallproject.org/2016/02/08/black-and-unarmed-behind-the-numbers#.t7yfHNI5z).

109 Heather Mac Donald, "The Nationwide Crime Wave Is Building," The Wall Street Journal, May 23, 2016 (http://www.wsj.com/articles/the-nationwide-crime-wave-is-building-1464045462).

110 Dara Lind, "The 'Ferguson effect,' a theory that's warping the American crime debate, explained," Vox, May 18, 2016 (http://www.vox.com/2016/5/18/11683594/ferguson-effect-crime-police).

111 Heather Mac Donald, "The Myths of Black Lives Matter," The Wall Street Journal, July 9, 2016 (http://www.wsj.com/articles/the-myths-of-black-lives-matter-1468087453).

112 Troy Hayden, "Activist critical of police undergoes use of force scenarios," FOX 10 Phoenix, Jan. 8, 2015 (http://www.fox10phoenix.com/news/1382363-story).

113 Janie Boschma and Ronald Brownstein, "The Concentration of Poverty in American Schools," The Atlantic, Feb. 29, 2016 (http://www.theatlantic.com/education/archive/2016/02/concentration-poverty-american-schools/471414/).

114 Brad E. Hamilton, Ph.D., Joyce A. Martin, M.P.H., Michelle J.K. Osterman, M.H.S., Sally C. Curtin, M.A., and T.J. Mathews, M. S., "Births: Final Data for 2014," Centers for Disease Control and Prevention, Dec. 23, 2015 (https://www.cdc.gov/nchs/data/nvsr/nvsr64/nvsr64_12.pdf).

115 Matt Naham, "Rand Paul is getting more black support than almost any other Republican," Rare, May 19, 2014 (http://rare.us/story/rand-paul-is-getting-more-black-support-than-almost-any-other-republican/).

116 Paul Cassell, "Why Michael Brown's best friend's story isn't credible," The Washington Post, Dec. 2, 2014 (https://www.washingtonpost.com/news/volokh-conspiracy/wp/2014/12/02/why-michael-browns-best-friends-story-is-incredible/?utm_term=.85d6c391b992).

117 Anthony Furey, "Black Lives Matter co-founder appears to label white people 'defects,'" Toronto Sun, Feb. 11, 2017 (http://www.torontosun.com/2017/02/11/black-lives-matter-co-founder-appears-to-label-white-people-defects).

118 CBC News, "Black Lives Matter Toronto co-founder under fire for controversial tweet," CBC News, June 15, 2016 (http://www.cbc.ca/news/canada/toronto/black-lives-matter-controversial-tweet-1.3523055).

119 Jasper Hamill, "Google promotes controversial claim it's NOT possible for ethnic minorities to be racist against white people," The Sun, Oct. 3, 2016 (https://www.thesun.co.uk/news/1901544/google-promotes-controversial-claim-its-not-possible-for-ethnic-minorities-to-be-racist-against-white-people/).

120 Gene Demby, "A Discomforting Question: Was The Chicago Torture Case Racism?" National Public Radio, Jan. 9, 2017 (http://www.npr.org/sections/codeswitch/2017/01/09/508607762/a-dscomfitting-question-was-the-chicago-torture-case-racism).

121 Japanese Government, "National Diet Live Broadcast, 4th Meeting of the House of Counselors Committee on Financial Affairs: On the Subject of Postponing an Increase of the Consumption Tax," November 17, 2016 (http://www.webtv.sangiin.go.jp/webtv/detail.php?ssp=27153&type=recorded).

122 Michael Tracey, "The Mainstream Media Has a Donald J. Trump-Sized Blind Spot," The Daily Beast, Sep. 6, 2016 (http://www.thedailybeast.com/articles/2016/09/06/the-mainstream-media-has-a-donald-j-trump-sized-blind-spot.html).

123 Kyle Foley, "Vice Reporter Fired: Story On Lena Dunham's Primary Vote Included Home Address," Heat Street, Nov. 11, 2016 (http://heatst.com/world/vice-reporter-fired-after-story-questioning-whether-lena-dunham-voted-in-primary/).

124 Jim Hoft, "BREAKING: Liberals Create List of 'Fake' News Websites Including: Breitbart, Infowars, Zerohedge, Twitchy, The Blaze," Gateway Pundit, Nov. 16, 2016 (http://www.thegatewaypundit.com/2016/11/breaking-media-list-fake-news-websites-includes-breitbart-infowars-zerohedge-twitchy-blaze/).

125 Doug Elfman, "Joe Rogan's three-hour podcast show tops 11 million monthly downloads," Las Vegas Review Journal, Dec. 31, 2014 (https://www.reviewjournal.com/entertainment/joe-rogans-three-hour-podcast-show-tops-11-million-monthly-downloads/).

126 Larry O'Connor, "Newsweek Calls Drudge's Lewinsky Bombshell 'Epic Newsweek Scoop,'" Breitbart, Dec. 26, 2012 (http://www.breitbart.com/big-journalism/2012/12/26/newsweek-claims-credit-for-drudge-scoop-lewinsky/).

127 David Remnick, "Obama Reckons with a Trump Presidency," The New Yorker, Nov. 28, 2016 (http://www.newyorker.com/magazine/2016/11/28/obama-reckons-with-a-trump-presidency?mbid=social_twitter).

128 The New Yorker, Nov. 28, 2016.

129 Tom Ciccotta, "FAKE NEWS: NBC News Issues Correction After Falsely Branding MILO as 'White Nationalist,'" Breitbart, Jan. 7, 2017 (http://www.breitbart.com/milo/2017/01/07/fake-news-nbc-news-issues-correction-falsely-branding-milo-white-nationalist/).

130 John Carroll, "Why would Martin Shkreli hike an old drug price by 5000%? Only a 'moron' would ask," Sep. 20, 2015 (http://www.fiercebiotech.com/biotech/why-would-martin-shkreli-hike-an-old-drug-price-by-5000-only-a-moron-would-ask).

131 Zoe Thomas and Tim Swift, "Who is Martin Shkreli – 'the most hated man in America'?" BBC News, Sep. 23, 2015 (http://www.bbc.co.uk/news/world-us-canada-34331761).

132 Margaret Sullivan, "It's time to retire the tainted term 'fake news,'" The Washington Post, Jan. 8, 2017 (https://www.washingtonpost.com/lifestyle/style/its-time-to-retire-the-tainted-term-fake-news/2017/01/06/a5a7516c-d375-11e6-945a-76f69a399dd5_story.html?utm_term=.308ff1d9821b).

133 Emily Smith and Daniel Halper, "Donald Trump's media summit was a 'f---ing firing squad,'" New York Post, Nov. 21, 2016 (http://nypost.com/2016/11/21/donald-trumps-media-summit-was-a-f-ing-firing-squad/).

134 Zack Ford, "LGBT media condemns Out Magazine for Milo Yiannopoulos puff piece," Think Progress, Sep. 22, 2016 (https://thinkprogress.org/out-magazine-milo-open-letter-e0d3db3fe7ac#.byw95ncrs).

135 Chadwick Moore, "I'm a gay New Yorker – and I'm coming out as a conservative," New York Post, Feb. 11, 2017 (http://nypost.com/2017/02/11/im-a-gay-new-yorker-and-im-coming-out-as-a-conservative/).

136 Dave Rubin, "Why I Left the Left," PragerU, Feb. 6, 2017 (https://www.prageru.com/courses/political-science/why-i-left-left).

137 Ben Kew, "'Twinks for Trump' Photographer Fired After Being Praised by Milo," Breitbart, Aug. 29, 2016 (http://www.breitbart.com/tech/2016/08/29/twinks-for-trump-photographer-fired-after-being-praised-by-milo/).

138 Charlie Nash, "Pierogi Art Gallery Realtor Threatens To Sue Lucian Wintrich Over Pro-Trump Art Exhibit," Breitbart, Oct. 7, 2016 (http://www.breitbart.com/milo/2016/10/07/pierogi-art-gallery-lucian-wintrich-sue-trump/).

139 Jim Downs, "Peter Thiel Shows Us There's a Difference Between Gay Sex and Gay," Advocate, Oct. 14, 2016 (http://www.advocate.com/commentary/2016/10/14/peter-thiel-shows-us-theres-difference-between-gay-sex-and-gay).

140 T.W.H., "Unmanly Manhood," Classroom Electric, http://www.classroomelectric.org/volume2/price/remembered/womans_journal.htm (April 23, 2017).

141 Peter Tatchell, "Peter Tatchell: Quentin Crisp was no gay hero," Independent, Dec. 29, 2009 (http://www.independent.co.uk/voices/commentators/peter-tatchell-quentin-crisp-was-no-gay-hero-1852122.html).

142 Florence King, "The Battle of Little Big Clit," in Lump It or Leave It (New York: St. Martin's, 1990), 164, 166.

143 Camille Paglia, Vamps and Tramps (Vintage Books, New York, 1994), 70, 86.

144 ABC News, "Why RuPaul Doesn't Think He or 'RuPaul's Drag Race' Can Go Mainstream," May 13, 2016 (https://www.youtube.com/watch?v=hnHEWU-WhGE&app=desktop).

145 Chadwick Moore, "I'm a gay New Yorker – and I'm coming out as a conservative," New York Post, Feb. 11, 2017 (http://nypost.com/2017/02/11/im-a-gay-new-yorker-and-im-coming-out-as-a-conservative/).

146 Richard Lawson, "Gay Men Are Skinnier Than Straight Men, Duh," Gawker, June 8, 2010 (http://gawker.com/5558318/gay-men-are-skinnier-than-straight-men-duh).

147 King, "The Battle of Little Big Clit," 168-9.

148 Ana Marie Cox, "Glenn Beck Is Sorry About All That," The New York Times Magazine, Nov. 21, 2016 (http://www.nytimes.com/2016/11/27/magazine/glenn-beck-is-sorry-about-all-that.html?_r=0).

149 Naomi Lim, "Glenn Beck: Opposing Trump is 'moral' choice – even if Clinton is elected," CNN, Oct. 11, 2016 (http://edition.cnn.com/2016/10/11/politics/glenn-beck-hillary-clinton-moral-ethical-choice/).

150 Perez Hilton, "Kanye West's 'Psychotic Break' Reportedly Fueled By Rifts With Kim Kardashian, Sleep Deprivation, & MORE," Perez Hilton, Nov. 22, 2016 (http://perezhilton.com/2016-11-22-kanye-west-psychiatric-evaluation-breakdown-report#.WKMfnVWLTIU).

151 Joseph Curl, "Joy Villa's Album Sales Rise 54,300,100%!" The Daily Wire, Feb. 13, 2017 (http://www.dailywire.com/news/13420/joy-villas-album-sales-rise-54350100-joseph-curl#).

152 PragerU, "Why I Left the Left," Feb. 6, 2017 (https://www.youtube.com/watch?v=hiVQ8vrGA_8).

153 Milo Yiannopoulos, "Star Wars 'Reeks of Misogyny': SJW Satirist Punks BBC World Service," Breitbart, April 17, 2015 (http://www.breitbart.com/london/2015/04/17/star-wars-reeks-of-misogyny-sjw-satirist-punks-bbc-world-service/).

154 Grantmakers in the Arts, http://www.giarts.org/ (April 23, 2017).

155 Tricia Tongco, "Your Radical Guide To Fighting Discrimination In The Arts," Grantmakers in the Arts, March 7, 2016 (http://www.giarts.org/blog/steve/your-radical-guide-fighting-discrimination-arts).

156 Christopher Brennan, "Trump's 'America First' policy echoes group that opposed fighting the Nazis," Daily News, Jan. 20, 2017 (http://www.nydailynews.com/news/national/america-policy-echoes-group-opposed-fighting-nazis-article-1.2951883).

157 Jim Hoft, "Bill Kristol: White Working Class Should be Replaced by Immigrants (VIDEO)," Gateway Pundit, Feb. 9, 2017 (http://www.thegatewaypundit.com/2017/02/bill-kristol-white-working-class-replaced-immigrants-video/).

158 Parker Lee, "Fox News Hoped Tucker Carlson Could Live Up to Megyn Kelly's Popularity. Now the Ratings Are In…," Independent Journal Review, January, 2017 (http://ijr.com/2017/01/778808-fox-hoped-tucker-carlson-could-live-up-to-megyn-kellys-popularity-now-the-ratings-are-in/).

159 Dan Duray, "Donald Trump's 'Hit Man' Hones His Dark Arts," Vanity Fair, July 20, 2016 (http://www.vanityfair.com/news/2016/07/roger-stone-donald-trumps-hit-man).

MILO

160 Daniel Henninger, "McCarthyism at Middlebury," The Wall Street Journal, March 8, 2017 (https://www.wsj.com/articles/mccarthyism-at-middlebury-1489016328).

161 Ian Drury, "Four out of five migrants are NOT from Syria: EU figures expose the 'lie' that the majority of refugees are fleeing war zone," Daily Mail, Sep. 18, 2015 (http://www.dailymail.co.uk/news/article-3240010/Number-refugees-arriving-Europe-soars-85-year-just-one-five-war-torn-Syria.html).

162 Rick Noack, "Leaked document says 2,000 men allegedly assaulted 1,200 German women on New Year's Eve," The Washington Post, July 11, 2016 (https://www.washingtonpost.com/news/worldviews/wp/2016/07/10/leaked-document-says-2000-men-allegedly-assaulted-1200-german-women-on-new-years-eve/?utm_term=.e4a508573a0a).

163 Ingrid Carlqvist, "Sweden: Summer Inferno of Sexual Assaults," Gatestone Institute, Aug. 13, 2016 (https://www.gatestoneinstitute.org/8579/sweden-sexual-assaults).

164 Frank Furedi, "Why is Europe giving Muslim migrants sex-ed lessons?" Spiked, Jan. 19, 2016 (http://www.spiked-online.com/newsite/article/why-is-europe-giving-muslim-migrants-sex-ed-lessons/17939#.WDMUy9WLTIU).

165 Reuters, "No evidence Paris attack mastermind was ever in Greece – Greek official," Daily Mail, Nov. 19, 2015 (http://www.dailymail.co.uk/wires/reuters/article-3325789/No-evidence-Paris-attack-mastermind-Greece-Greek-official.html).

166 Milo Yiannopoulos, "Milo at Orlando Shooting Site," June 15, 2016 (https://www.youtube.com/watch?v=xLqkizGtFo0K).

167 Walter Berns, "Flag-Burning & Other Modes of Expression," Commentary, Oct. 1, 1989 (https://www.commentarymagazine.com/articles/flag-burning-other-modes-of-expression/).

168 Sean Illing, "Sam Harris talks Islam, ISIS, atheism, GOP madness: 'We are confronting people, in dozens of countries, who despise more or less everything that we value,'" Salon, Nov. 25, 2015 (http://www.salon.com/2015/11/25/harris_and_illing_correspondence/).

169 Teju Cole, "Unmournable Bodies," The New Yorker, Jan. 9, 2015 (http://www.newyorker.com/culture/cultural-comment/unmournable-bodies).

170 Jenny Sterne, "80 per cent of UK Universities restrict free speech," Mancunion, March 5, 2015 (http://mancunion.com/2015/03/05/80-per-cent-of-uk-universities-restrict-free-speech/).

171 Glenn Greenwald, "204 PEN Writers (Thus Far) Have Objected to the Charlie Hebdo Award - Not Just 6," The Intercept, April 30, 2015 (https://theintercept.com/2015/04/30/145-pen-writers-thus-far-objected-charlie-hedbo-award-6/).

172 Scroll Staff, "Salman Rushdie slams fellow writers for boycotting ceremony to honour 'Charlie Hebdo,'" Scroll, April 27, 2015 (http://scroll.in/article/723627/salman-rushdie-slams-fellow-writers-for-boycotting-ceremony-to-honour-charlie-hebdo).

173 Alison Flood, "Neil Gaiman leads authors stepping in to back Charlie Hebdo PEN award," The Guardian, May 5, 2015 (https://www.theguardian.com/books/2015/may/05/neil-gaiman-pen-award-charlie-hebdo).

174 Patrick L. Smith, "We brought this on ourselves: After Paris, it is time to square our 'values' with our history," Salon, Nov. 15, 2015 (http://www.salon.com/2015/11/15/we_brought_this_on_ourselves_after_paris_it_is_time_to_square_our_values_with_our_history/).

175 Patrick L. Smith, "We brought this on ourselves, and we are the terrorists, too," Salon, March 27, 2016 (http://www.salon.com/2016/03/27/we_brought_this_on_ourselves_and_we_are_the_terrorists_too/).

176 David A. Graham, "How Did Maajid Nawaz End Up on a List of 'Anti-Muslim Extremists'?" The Atlantic, Oct. 29, 2016 (http://www.theatlantic.com/international/archive/2016/10/maajid-nawaz-splc-anti-muslim-extremist/505685/).

177 Kira Cochrane, "The fourth wave of feminism: meet the rebel women," The Guardian, Dec. 10, 2013 (https://www.theguardian.com/world/2013/dec/10/fourth-wave-feminism-rebel-women).

178 Alice Marwick, "Donglegate: Why the Tech Community Hates Women," Wired, March 29, 2013 (https://www.wired.com/2013/03/richards-affair-and-misogyny-in-tech/).

179 Sara Malm, "'Twitter gave me PTSD': Woman claims mean comments and 'cyberstalking' gave her an illness usually suffered by WAR VETERANS," Daily Mail, April 17, 2014 (http://www.dailymail.co.uk/news/article-2605888/Woman-claims-PTSD-Twitter-cyberstalking-says-bit-war-veterans.html).

180 Amanda Wallace, "Depression Quest Dev Faces Extreme Harassment Because She's a Woman," Game Skinny, Dec. 15, 2013 (http://www.gameskinny.com/o3t09/depression-quest-dev-faces-extreme-harassment-because-shes-a-woman).

181 Rebecca Savransky, "'Gamergate' critic Brianna Wu running for Congress in 2018: report," The Hill, Dec. 21, 2016 (http://thehill.com/homenews/news/311302-game-developer-brianna-wu-eyeing-run-for-congress-in-2018).

182 "The Zoe Post," https://thezoepost.wordpress.com/ (April 24, 2017).

183 "Critical Distance," Deep Freeze, http://www.deepfreeze.it/outlet.php?o=critical_distance (April 24, 2017).

184 "Leigh Alexander, the Guardian," Deep Freeze, http://www.deepfreeze.it/journo.php?j=leigh_alexander (April 24, 2017).

185 Leigh Alexander, "'Gamers' don't have to be your audience. 'Gamers' are over," Gamasutra, Aug. 28, 2014 (http://www.gamasutra.com/view/news/224400/Gamers_dont_have_to_be_your_audience_Gamers_are_over.php).

186 Arthur Chu, "It's Dangerous to Go Alone: Why Are Gamers So Angry?" The Daily Beast, Aug. 28, 2014 (https://archive.is/9NxHy#selection-615.147-615.184).

187 Luke Plunkett, "We Might Be Witnessing The 'Death of An Identity,'" Kotaku, n.d. (https://archive.is/YlBhH#selection-2977.81-2977.156).

188 Mike Pearl, "This Guy's Embarrassing Relationship Drama Is Killing the 'Gamer' Identity," VICE, Aug. 29, 2014 (https://archive.is/L4n6p).

189 Aja Romano, "The sexist crusade to destroy game developer Zoe Quinn," The Daily Dot, Aug. 20, 2014 (https://archive.is/ILNXC).

190 "TotalBiscuit discusses the state of games journalism, Steam Greenlight, ethics, DMCA abuse and Depression Quest," Reddit, n.d. (https://www.reddit.com/r/gaming/comments/2dz0gs/totalbiscuit_discusses_the_state_of_games/).

191 "Boogie banned from NeoGAF, threats against him were put into effect," Reddit, n.d. (https://www.reddit.com/r/KotakuInAction/comments/2j5s1k/boogie_banned_from_neogaf_threats_against_him/).

192 "GamerGate," Know Your Meme, 2014 (http://knowyourmeme.com/memes/events/gamergate#CensorOn4chan).

193 Dante D'Orazio, "Gamergate scandal convinced 4chan founder Moot to leave the site," The Verge, March 14, 2015 (http://www.theverge.com/2015/3/14/8214713/gamergate-scandal-convinced-4chan-founder-moot-to-leave-the-site).

194 "From the time of posting the 'Hell hath no fury' to the dmca the video only had 4599 views … It really wasn't rising that much." - Matt "MundaneMatt" Jarbo, Aug. 12, 2015.

195 Nate Anderson, "Scientology fights critics with 4,000 DMCA takedown notices," Ars Technica, Sep. 8, 2008 (https://arstechnica.com/uncategorized/2008/09/scientology-fights-critics-with-4000-dmca-takedown-notices/).

196 "Tweets per day: @TheQuinnspiracy, @Vahn16, and #GamerGate," https://unsubject.files.wordpress.com/2014/09/topsy_gamergatehashtag.png (April 24, 2017).

197 Wil Wheaton. "Anonymous trolls are destroying online games. Here's how to stop them," The Washington Post, Nov. 11, 2014 (https://www.washingtonpost.com/posteverything/wp/2014/11/11/anonymous-trolls-are-destroying-online-games-heres-how-to-stop-them/).

198 "#NotYourShield – BURRRRNED!!" Know Your Meme, http://knowyourmeme.com/photos/829804-notyourshield (April 24, 2017).

199 Arthur Chu, Twitter, Oct. 18, 2014 (https://twitter.com/arthur_affect/status/523554495276806144).

200 Casey Johnston, "Chat logs show how 4chan users created #GamerGate controversy," Ars Technica, Sep. 9, 2014 (https://arstechnica.com/gaming/2014/09/new-chat-logs-show-how-4chan-users-pushed-gamergate-into-the-national-spotlight/).

201 CJ Ferguson and J. Killburn, "Much ado about nothing: the misestimation and overinterpretation of violent video game effects in eastern and western nations: comment on Anderson et al. (2010)," National Center for Biotechnology Information, March, 2010 (http://www.ncbi.nlm.nih.gov/pubmed/20192554).

202 276 Jonathan McIntosh, Twitter, March 1, 2014 (https://webcache.googleusercontent.com/search?q=cache:1o0GlYr4qBEJ:https://twitter.com/

radicalbytes/status/439947821999857665%3Flang%3Den+&cd=1&hl=en&ct
=clnk&gl=uk).

203 Milo Yiannopoulos, "Killer virgin was a Madman, not a Misogynist,"
Breitbart, May 27, 2014 (http://www.breitbart.com/london/2014/05/27/
virgin-killer-was-not-a-misogynist-but-a-madman/).

204 AlterNet Staff, "8 Things You May Not Know About Elliot Rodger's Killing Spree,"
AlterNet, May 28, 2014 (http://www.alternet.org/culture/8-things-you-may-not-
know-about-elliot-rodgers-killing-spree).

205 Factual Feminist, "Are video games sexist?" American Enterprise Institute, Sep. 16,
2014 (https://www.youtube.com/watch?time_continue=3&v=9MxqSwzFy5w).

206 Lisa Ruddick, "When Nothing Is Cool," The Point, 2015 (https://thepointmag.
com/2015/criticism/when-nothing-is-cool).

207 Jen Yamato, "Jordan Peele explains 'Get Out's' creepy milk scene, ponders the
recent link between dairy and hate." LA Times, March 1, 2017 (http://www.
latimes.com/entertainment/movies/la-et-mn-get-out-milk-horror-jordan-peele-
allison-williams-20170301-story.html)

208 "Anita Sarkeesian: #GamerGate A call to Boycott Sponsors of News Media,"
Youtube video posted by FaZe Keemstar, January 20, 2015. https://www.
youtube.com/watch?v=KcMBr8yHeEw (accessed January 25, 2015)

209 Milo Yiannopoulos, "How Sloppy, Biased Video Games Reporting Almost Destroyed
a CEO," Breitbart, Sep. 23, 2014 (http://www.breitbart.com/london/2014/09/23/
how-sloppy-biased-video-games-reporting-almost-destroyed-a-ceo/).

210 Jason Schreler, "Stardock Lawsuits Dropped, Ex-Employee Apologizes,"
Kotaku, Sep. 24, 2013 (http://kotaku.com/stardock-lawsuits-dropped-ex-
employee-apologizes-1377925759).

211 James Fudge, "A Long Overdue Correction and an Apology to Brad Wardell,"
Game Politics, Nov. 11, 2014 (https://archive.is/yl34h).

212 William Usher, "Polygon, Kotaku Revise Their Policies Amidst Controversy,"
Cinema Blend, n.d. (http://www.cinemablend.com/games/Polygon-Kotaku-
Revise-Their-Policies-Amidst-Controversy-66962.html).

213 Alyssa Rosenberg, "Donald Trump is the Gamergate of Republican politics," The
Washington Post, Dec. 7, 2015 (https://www.washingtonpost.com/news/act-four/
wp/2015/12/07/donald-trump-is-the-gamergate-of-republican-politics/).

214 Michael Sitver, "University Admins Surrender to Violent Protesters, Shutter
Event," Huffington Post, May 25, 2016 (http://www.huffingtonpost.
com/entry/university-admins-surrender-to-violent-protesters-shutter_
us_57454738e4b00853ae7b5ae3).

215 Tom Ciccotta, "DePaul President Capitulates to Outraged Anti-Milo Students,
Tenders Resignation," Breitbart, June 13, 2016 (http://www.breitbart.com/
milo/2016/06/13/depaul-president-step-facing-backlash-milo-event/).

216 Brad Richardson, "George Will Uninvited from Scripps College," The
Claremont Independent, Oct. 6, 2014 (http://claremontindependent.com/
george-will-uninvited-from-scripps-college/).

217 Mark Tapson, "U of Michigan Students Call Police Over 'Trump 2016,' 'Stop Islam,' Chalk Markings," Truth Revolt, April 1, 2016 (https://www.truthrevolt.org/news/u-michigan-students-call-police-over-trump-2016-stop-islam-chalk-markings).

218 Chad Sokol, "WSU students plan to raise a controversial 'Trump wall' on campus," The Spokesman-Review, Sep. 9, 2016 (http://www.spokesman.com/stories/2016/sep/09/wsu-students-plan-to-raise-a-controversial-trump-w/).

219 Stephanie McFeeters, "Counter-protesters join kimono fray at MFA," The Boston Globe, July 19, 2015 (https://www.bostonglobe.com/arts/2015/07/18/counter-protesters-join-kimono-fray-mfa/ZgVWiT3yIZSlQgxCghAOFM/story.html).

220 Paul Bond, "Milo Yiannopoulos Documentary in the Works as Outrageous Tour Demands Revealed (Exclusive)," The Hollywood Reporter, Aug. 30, 2016 (http://www.hollywoodreporter.com/news/milo-yiannopoulos-outrageous-tour-demands-924248).

221 Milo Yiannopoulos, "The Left's Bloody War on Women: Sending Chicks into Combat Betrays Men, Women and Civilization," Breitbart, July 7, 2016 (http://www.breitbart.com/milo/2016/07/07/real-war-on-women-chicks-in-combat/).

222 Ben Kew, "Watch: Arab Girl Destroys Muslim Apologists at Milo's USF Event," Breitbart, Dep. 26, 2016 (http://www.breitbart.com/milo/2016/09/26/watch-arab-girl-destroys-arab-apologists-milos-usf-event/).

223 Ben Kew, "ABC10 Photographer Attacked With Hot Coffee Outside Milo UC Davis Event," Breitbart, Jan. 13, 2017 (http://www.breitbart.com/milo/2017/01/13/milo-abc-uc-davis-hot-coffee/).

224 Ben Kew, "WATCH: MILO Video Producer Pushed, Spat On By UC Davis Protesters," Breitbart, Jan. 13, 2017 (http://www.breitbart.com/milo/2017/01/13/watch-uc-davis-protestors-assault-spit-milos-cameraman/).

225 Molly Ball, "Is the Anti-Trump 'Resistance' the New Tea Party," The Atlantic, Feb. 9, 2017 (https://www.theatlantic.com/politics/archive/2017/02/resistance-tea-party/516105/).

226 Lee Stranahan, "Radical Berkeley Anti-Milo Protest Leader: 'No Regrets,'" Breitbart, Feb. 6, 2017 (http://www.breitbart.com/big-government/2017/02/06/radical-berkeley-anti-milo-protest-leader-no-regrets/).

227 Joel B. Pollak, "New O'Keefe Video: Leftists Planning Stink Bombs at 'Deploraball'" Breitbart, Jan. 16, 2017 (http://www.breitbart.com/big-government/2017/01/16/new-james-okeefe-video-leftists-planning-stink-bombs-deploraball/).

228 Ari Paul, "Do Punch Nazis: Richard Spencer Attack Was Self-Defense," Observer, Jan. 24, 2017 (http://observer.com/2017/01/do-punch-nazis-anti-semite-white-supremacist-richard-spencer/).

229 Zach Schonfeld, "Is It OK to Punch a Nazi in the Face? Leading Ethicists Weigh In: 'No,'" Newsweek, Jan. 24, 2017 (http://europe.newsweek.com/richard-spencer-punch-nazi-ethicists-547277?rm=eu).

230 Lucas Nolan, "MILO Cameraman Assaulted, Equipment Broken," Breitbart, Jan. 20, 2017 (http://www.breitbart.com/milo/2017/01/20/milo-cameraman-assaulted-equipment-broken/).

231 Tom Ciccotta, "Seattle Protesters Armed with Wooden Poles, Heavy Pipes, Shields," Breitbart, Jan. 20, 2017 (http://www.breitbart.com/milo/2017/01/20/seattle-police-recover-wooden-poles-metal-pipes-shields-milo-protesters/).

232 Bea Karnes, "Rioters Damage Property At UC Berkeley, Downtown Berkeley, Paint 'Kill Trump' Graffiti," Berkeley Patch, Feb. 2, 2017 (http://patch.com/california/berkeley/violent-demonstration-uc-berkeley).

233 Breitbart Tech, "Questions Arise Over 'Hands-Off' Police Response to Berkeley Riot," Breitbart, Feb. 7, 2017 (http://www.breitbart.com/milo/2017/02/07/questions-arise-hands-off-police-response-berkeley-riot/).

234 Matier & Ross, "Why UC police let anarchists run wild in Berkeley," San Francisco Chronicle, Feb. 5, 2017 (http://www.sfchronicle.com/bayarea/matier-ross/article/Why-UC-police-let-anarchists-run-wild-in-Berkeley-10908034.php).

235 Sam J., "CLUELESS Mayor of Berkeley Jesse Arreguin tweets BS about hate speech, regret-tweets 3 hours," Twitchy, Feb. 2, 2017 (http://twitchy.com/samj-3930/2017/02/02/clueless-mayor-of-berkeley-jesse-arreguin-tweets-bs-about-hate-speech-regret-tweets-3-hours-later/).

236 Tom Ciccotta, "Berkeley Mayor Apologizes, Retracts Claim that MILO is a 'White Nationalist'...And Replaces It With A New Lie," Breitbart, Feb. 2, 2017 (http://www.breitbart.com/milo/2017/02/02/mayor-berkeley-apologizes-retracts-claim-milo-white-nationalist/).

237 Charlie Nash, "Organizer Calls Berkeley Riot 'Stunningly Successful,' Warns Repeat if MILO Returns," Breitbart, Feb. 8, 2017 (http://www.breitbart.com/milo/2017/02/08/organizer-calls-berkeley-riot-stunningly-successful-warns-repeat-if-milo-returns/).

238 Paul Cassell, "Did Yiannopoulos secretly send more than 100 thugs to Berkeley to break up his own speech?" The Washington Post, Feb. 6, 2017 (https://www.washingtonpost.com/news/volokh-conspiracy/wp/2017/02/06/did-yiannopoulos-secretly-send-more-than-one-hundred-thugs-to-berkeley-to-break-up-his-own-speech/).

239 Office of the President, "Rutgers President on Free Speech and Academic Freedom," Rutgers, n.d. (http://president.rutgers.edu/public-remarks/speeches-and-writings/rutgers-president-free-speech-and-academic-freedom).

240 Jonathan Chait, "Not a Very P.C. Thing to Say," New York, Jan. 27, 2015 (http://nymag.com/daily/intelligencer/2015/01/not-a-very-pc-thing-to-say.html).

Judith Shulevitz, "In College and Hiding From Scary Ideas," The New York Times, March 21, 2015 (https://www.nytimes.com/2015/03/22/opinion/sunday/judith-shulevitz-hiding-from-scary-ideas.html).

Greg Lukianoff and Jonathan Haidt, "The Coddling of the American Mind," The Atlantic, September, 2015 (http://www.theatlantic.com/magazine/archive/2015/09/the-coddling-of-the-american-mind/399356/).

241 Nicholas Kristof, "A Confession of Liberal Intolerance," The New York Times, May 7, 2016 (https://www.nytimes.com/2016/05/08/opinion/sunday/a-confession-of-liberal-intolerance.html).

242 Andre Vergara, "Missouri protest: List of demands issued to university," FOX Sports, Nov. 8, 2015 (http://www.foxsports.com/college-football/story/missouri-protesters-issue-list-of-demands-to-university-110815).

243 Stephen Ganey, "Mizzou closes two dorms due to lack of students applying for housing," FOX4, News, April 10, 2016 (http://fox4kc.com/2016/04/10/mizzou-closes-two-dorms-due-to-lack-of-students-applying-for-housing/).

244 Martha Ross, "'Dilbert' creator Scott Adams ends UC Berkeley support over Milo Yiannopoulos protests," The Mercury News, Feb. 8, 2017 (http://www.mercurynews.com/2017/02/08/dilbert-creator-scott-adams-ends-uc-berkeley-support-over-milo-yiannopoulos-protests/).

245 Maureen Sullivan, "Provocateur Milo Yiannopoulos Was The Speaker Most Likely To Be Disinvited To Colleges In 2016," Forbes, Dec. 30, 2016 (http://www.forbes.com/sites/maureensullivan/2016/12/30/provocateur-milo-yiannopoulos-was-the-speaker-most-likely-to-be-disinvited-to-colleges-in-2016/).

246 Lionel Shriver, "Lionel Shriver's full speech: 'I hope the concept of cultural appropriation is a passing fad,'" The Guardian, Sep. 13, 2016 (https://www.theguardian.com/commentisfree/2016/sep/13/lionel-shrivers-full-speech-i-hope-the-concept-of-cultural-appropriation-is-a-passing-fad).

247 Julia Belluz, "It may have seemed like the world fell apart in 2016. Steven Pinker is here to tell you it didn't," Vox, Dec. 22, 2016 (http://www.vox.com/science-and-health/2016/12/22/14042506/steven-pinker-optimistic-future-2016).

INDEX